THE IDEA OF
THE UNIVERSITY

———

A REEXAMINATION

THE IDEA OF
THE UNIVERSITY

A REEXAMINATION

Jaroslav Pelikan

Yale University Press

New Haven and London

Set in Sabon type by The Composing Room of Michigan,
Inc., Grand Rapids, Michigan.
Printed in the United States of America by Vail-Ballou Press,
Binghamton, New York.

The paper in this book meets the guidelines for permanence
and durability of the Committee on Production Guidelines for
Book Longevity of the Council on Library Resources.

10 9 8 7 6 5 4 3

Library of Congress Cataloging-in-Publication Data
Pelikan, Jaroslav Jan, 1923–
The idea of the university—a reexamination /
Jaroslav Pelikan.
p. cm.
A commentary on John Henry Newman's The Idea
of a university.
Includes bibliographical references and index.
ISBN 0-300-05725-3
1. Newman, John Henry, 1801–1890. Idea of a university.
2. Education, Higher. 3. Universities and colleges.
I. Newman, John Henry, 1801–1890. Idea of a university.
II. Title.
LB2321.P383 1992
378—dc20   92-2928

For the Centennial of the University of Chicago
1892–1992
Crescat scientia, vita excolatur

CONTENTS

PREFACE

Although this book bears the Newmanesque title *The Idea of the University—A Reexamination,* it could almost as well have taken another of his books as a model and called itself *Apologia pro Vita Sua,* for it is in some ways a personal essay about how I define my vocation as well as a book about how I define the university. It is, moreover, in some sense an essay about the university as I have experienced it, in the German university through my family heritage and then personally at the University of Chicago and at Yale, just as Newman's is about the university as he had experienced it at Oxford and at Dublin. But as my notes and bibliographical materials suggest, I have amplified, deepened, and corrected my experience (and his) by reference to that of a cloud of witnesses, past and present.

The book owes its origin to an invitation from the president of Yale University, Benno C. Schmidt, Jr., to deliver a set of public lectures together with a seminar during the academic year 1990–91 on "The Future of the University," as the first in a series of events in preparation for the observance of Yale's tricentennial. As a result, I was able to invite a series of colleagues to respond to individual lectures and have been able to make extensive revisions on the basis of their reactions. They are: Millicent D. Abell, Guido Calabresi, Donald Kagan, Jerome J. Pollitt, John G. Ryden, Benno C. Schmidt, Jr., Eustace D. Theodore, Sheila W. Wellington, and H. Edward Woodsum, Jr. I am very grateful for the editorial suggestions of John G. Ryden, of Laura Jones Dooley, and of Timothy S. Healy. I have also benefited greatly from the criticisms, comments, and questions of the international audiences to whom I have delivered one or more of these discourses over a period of years. Some of these are: the University of Alabama, the Association of American University Presses, the Association of Research Libraries, Brown University, the University of Chicago, Comenius University of Bratislava, Czechoslovakia, Emory University, Georgetown University, the Institute for Advanced Study, the Library of Congress, the Massachusetts Institute of Technology, Southern Methodist University, Stanford University, Tulane University, the Woodrow Wilson Center of the

Smithsonian Institution, and the University of York, England. A research grant from the Chairman of the National Endowment for the Humanities, Lynne V. Cheney, and an appointment as Senior Fellow of the Carnegie Foundation for the Advancement of Teaching by its President, Ernest L. Boyer, enabled me to read myself into the literature about the university. As some readers will know, I have considered some of these same issues as they pertain specifically to "the idea of graduate education" in *Scholarship and Its Survival,* written during my previous tenure as Senior Fellow of the Carnegie Foundation for the Advancement of Teaching and published by the foundation in 1983, as well as in other pieces composed for various occasions before and since. Having changed my mind about some questions and reinforced my earlier convictions about others, I have felt free both to diverge from those discussions and to cannibalize them without making specific reference to them each time.

Throughout this volume I am engaged in an ongoing dialogue with one book: John Henry Newman, *The Idea of a University Defined and Illustrated*: I. In Nine Discourses Delivered to the Catholics of Dublin [1852]; II. In Occasional Lectures and Essays Addressed to the Members of the Catholic University [1858] (edited with Introduction and Notes by I. T. Ker, Oxford: Clarendon, 1976). This work is available in several other editions, and to facilitate my references for readers who are using one of these I cite it in parentheses within the body of the text by part (I or II), discourse (in lowercase Roman numerals), and section (in Arabic numerals). In quoting this work and all of Newman's other works, I have retained their (inconsistent) punctuation and capitalization.

The dedication is the expression of my filial piety toward my Alma Mater, for having taught me the idea of the university and for having, on two occasions separated by exactly forty-five years, conferred upon me the title of Doctor.

I

I

IN DIALOGUE WITH
JOHN HENRY NEWMAN

At least two books by "eminent Victorians" (borrowing Lytton Strachey's celebrated title from 1918) probably ought to be part of the canon for anyone concerned about the reexamination of the idea of the university or in general about the reexamination of scholarship, whether inside or outside the university. As it happens, the first book is by a woman, and the second by a man: George Eliot's *Middlemarch* and John Henry Newman's *Idea of a University*. A recent study has described the process by which "in the 1970s, references to *Middlemarch* abounded," references that pointed "both to a fantasy world of salvation through romantic love and to a public world of salvation through social commitment." As a result of this complicated process, that study declares, "the most central and compelling novel in the Eliot canon was *Middlemarch*" during this entire period. It is no less central and compelling as a story about scholars, although it may not have been used that way quite as often in the recent past. For in her description of Edward Casaubon, "scholarly and uninspired, ambitious and timid, scrupulous and dim-sighted," George Eliot has given us, as Richard Ellmann once put it, a "pedant of such Saharan aridity that the temptation to identify him has not often been resisted," despite the absence of agreement among scholars about who the historical prototype (or prototypes) for the character in the novel may have been. Eliot's portrait of Casaubon is assuredly one of the most chilling depictions of a pedant in all of literature, just as Richard Wagner's caricature of his critic Eduard Hanslick as Sixtus Beckmesser in *Die Meistersinger von Nürnberg* (composed about a decade earlier than *Middlemarch*) is at once one of the most comical and one of the most pathetic. "Such capacity of thought and feeling as had ever been stimulated in him by the general life of mankind," George Eliot observes about Casaubon, "had long shrunk to a sort of dried preparation, a lifeless embalmment of knowledge." Or, as another character in the novel says of him, "he dreams footnotes, and they run away with all his brains"; and again, his "learning is a kind of damp," a species of intellectual mildew. That makes it even more of a shock than it would otherwise be to discover that this bookworm, who throughout his adult life has been piling up research notes for an enormous but utterly unpublishable *Key to All Mythologies*—a kind of proleptic caricature of Sir James George Frazer's *Golden Bough*—is unencumbered by any ability to read German. Yet German was the very language in which most of the important scholarship on those subjects had been written throughout the eighteenth and nineteenth centuries, as George Eliot had good reason to know, having skillfully but anonymously translated into English the massive and iconoclastic *Life of Jesus* by David Friedrich Strauss. *Middlemarch* is certain to go on serving as a cautionary tale for many generations of scholars in all fields.

When George Eliot first read John Henry Newman's autobiographical *Apologia pro Vita Sua* in 1864, she called it "the revelation of a life—how different in form from one's own, yet with how close a fellowship in its needs and burthens—I mean spiritual needs and burthens." Almost as if he were describing Edward Casaubon—although it must be granted that the university of his day, and of ours, certainly provided other no less impressive examples in abundance—Newman had pungent comments to make about such a "lifeless embalmment of knowledge." Citing a character not from a novel by George Eliot but from one by Sir Walter Scott (whom in a youthful letter he had once hailed with somewhat excessive enthusiasm as "a second Shakespeare"), Newman spoke in a lecture of 1854 about the "scientific pedantry" of one who was "imprisoned or fossilized in his erudition" (II.iii.2.2). "There are," he wrote even more acerbically earlier in *The Idea of a University,* "authors who are as pointless as they are inexhaustible in their literary resources. They measure knowledge by bulk, as it lies in the rude block, without symmetry, without design. . . . Such readers are only possessed *by* their knowledge, not possessed *of* it." In opposition to various kinds of bluenoses, he warned that it was not only the imagination, with its "barren fancies," that could be overstimulated; so, he reminded them, could the memory, with its "barren facts." When that happened to the learned, Newman wryly commented, "Reason acts almost as feebly and as impotently as in the madman; once fairly started on any subject whatever, they have no power of self-control; they passively endure the succession of impulses which are evolved out of the original exciting cause; they are passed on from one idea to another and go steadily forward, plodding along one line of thought in spite of the amplest concessions of the hearer, or wandering from it in endless digression in spite of his remonstrances" (I.vi.7). Had he known a present-day American metaphor that comes from petroleum exploration, he could well have added: "After a while, if you don't strike oil, stop boring!"

John Henry Newman was born on 21 February 1801 and died on 11 August 1890, his life thus spanning practically the entire century. With his importance for the history of the development of Christian doctrine I shall not be dealing here, having devoted other publications to that question. What is most important about Newman for present purposes is that, as he wrote in his journal for 1863, "from first to last, education . . . has been my line." He arrived at Oxford University in June 1817, when he was barely sixteen years old, and remained there for almost twenty-nine years, first as an undergraduate at Trinity College, then as Fellow of Oriel College, subsequently as vice-principal of Alban Hall, and eventually as vicar of Saint Mary's. On 9 October 1845 John Henry Newman became a Roman Catholic, which compelled his taking painful leave, on 23 February 1846, of a place where he had expected to know, as he would say in the *Apologia pro Vita Sua,* "perpetual residence even unto death." He went to Rome to prepare for ordination (that is, re-ordination), and then established an English chapter of the Oratory of Saint Philip Neri.

The historical backgrounds for Newman's composition of *The Idea of a University* have been described in every biography of Newman, in the introductions to the several modern editions of the work, and in at least two monographs. As one of his biographers has put it, "what happened in regard to the setting up of the proposed Catholic University in Dublin constitutes probably the most astonishing episode in Newman's career. It was certainly one of the most exasperating." The suggestion that there should be an Irish Roman Catholic university came in response to the predicament of Roman Catholic laymen from Ireland who enrolled as students at Oxford and Cambridge. By 1851, when Archbishop Paul Cullen of Armagh undertook to establish a "Catholic University of Ireland" in Dublin, the obvious advice about getting it started was, he was told, "First get Newman"; and on 18 July 1851 the archbishop visited Newman to offer him the rectorship, which Newman accepted. He resigned the position on 12 November 1858, when the burdens of the office and his relations to the Irish hierarchy, particularly to Archbishop Cullen, had become unbearable. "He has never done any thing," Newman complained, "but take my letters, crumple them up, put them in the fire, and write me no answer."

It is, however, fair to say that at least one important positive result came out of Newman's frustrating experience as a university administrator. To inaugurate the Catholic University of Ireland, the new rector delivered, beginning on 10 May 1852, a series of discourses that, with various revisions and additions, became the book we now know as *The Idea of a University*. An appropriate way to introduce the present reexamination of the idea of the university, then, is with the words Newman himself used to introduce his first discourse on the subject: "In addressing myself, Gentlemen, to the consideration of a question which has excited so much interest, and elicited so much discussion at the present day, as that of university education, I feel some explanation is due from me for supposing, after such high ability and wide experience have been brought to bear upon it, that any field remains for the additional labours either of a disputant or of an inquirer" (I.i.1).

Since those words were spoken in 1852, almost a century and a half ago, much more "discussion" about the university has been "elicited," and much though by no means all of it has been characterized by what Newman calls "high ability and wide experience" (or, in some instances perhaps, by at least one of those two qualities). Therefore it is, if anything, more the case at the end of the twentieth century than it was at the middle of the nineteenth that "some explanation is due" from anyone who seems to presume that even now "any field remains for the additional labours either of a disputant or of an inquirer," even if such "labours" are indeed, as is this book, far more those of an inquirer than of a disputant.

Yet even today there is probably no need for anyone, inquirer or disputant, to provide an explanation or defense (or, as Newman might have preferred to call it, an apologia) for undertaking such a discussion of the university by entering into dialogue with Newman's *Idea of a University*. The testimonials to the author, and to the abiding importance of the book, sound like answers to a publisher's prayer for jacket blurbs. "The perfect handling of a theory" is what Walter Pater, another eminent Victorian, called it. "Of all the books written in these hundred years," said Sir Arthur Quiller-Couch (best known as editor of *The Oxford Book of English Verse*, first published in 1900), "there is perhaps none that you can more profitably thumb and ponder." According to J. M. Cameron, "modern thinking on university education is a series of footnotes to Newman's lectures and essays." Recent books on the subject of the university in the English-speaking world and beyond it have paid Newman the compliment of echoing his title in theirs. Jacques Barzun, who cannot be accused of excessive sympathy for Newman's theology, nevertheless speaks of "the greatest theorist of university life, Cardinal Newman," but then does not refer to him again. Page Smith's recent polemic about the university selects the epigraph for one of its chapters from Newman (as well as another from

John Amos Comenius), but likewise never again refers to him. Newman's book has even qualified for inclusion in the bibliography of Francis X. Dealy's exposé, *Win at Any Cost: The Sell Out of College Athletics,* which is, however, based almost exclusively on interviews rather than on such essays as Newman's.

George N. Shuster, in his introduction to an edition of 1959, felt able to assert with confidence: "No doubt the book has done more than any other to stimulate reflection on the character and aims of higher education." The Newman scholar Martin J. Svaglic, in his introduction to an edition that appeared a year after Shuster's, called it "that eloquent defense of a liberal education which is perhaps the most timeless of all his books and certainly one of the most intellectually accessible to readers of every religious faith and of none." Or, in the words of G. M. Young, quoted by Martin Svaglic and then more amply by Ian T. Kerr,

> He employs all his magic to enlarge and refine and exalt this concep-
> tion of intellectual cultivation as a good in itself, worth while for
> itself, to be prized and esteemed for itself beyond all knowledge and
> all professional skill; while, all the time, so earnestly does he affirm its
> inadequacy, its shortcomings on the moral side, its need to be stead-
> ied and purified by religion, that at the end we feel that what we have
> heard is the final utterance, never to be repeated or needing to be
> supplemented, of Christian Humanism: as if the spirit evoked by
> Erasmus had found its voice at last.

A toast to Oxford near the beginning of what is probably the most beautifully crafted of all academic mystery stories blends Newman with Matthew Arnold: "Oxford has been called the home of lost causes: if the love of
learning for its own sake is a lost cause everywhere else in the world, let us
see to it that here at least, it finds its abiding home." My late friend and
colleague A. Bartlett Giamatti spoke of him in 1980 as "one of the subtlest
and most powerful minds of the nineteenth century, [an] Englishman who
thought profoundly about the nature of education"; and he devoted an
entire address in 1983, under the title "The Earthly Use of a Liberal Education," to a defense of Newman's definition of the university.

This reexamination of the idea of the university is of approximately the
same length as Newman's original nine discourses, although it says something about the difference between Victorian and present-day audiences—
or between Victorian and present-day lecturers—that it consists of exactly
twice as many discourses; it has also drawn the titles of its chapters from
phrases in Newman (italicized on first being quoted). It is in a real sense the

outcome of a scholarly and theological dialogue with John Henry Newman
that has been going on for my entire lifetime. For one thing, I can claim to
have shared the experience of also having participated for a few years, as
did Newman (and at almost exactly the same age as he, in my early fifties),
in the joys and frustrations of university governance, although I, too,
would acknowledge, as he did at the end of his treatise, that I am not "fitted
for the task of authority, or of rule, or of initiation" (I.ix.10). But in addition I do feel able to claim a deep-seated scholarly affinity with him on at
least two other counts. Like Newman, I have devoted much of my research,
teaching, and publishing (to invoke the categories I discuss in part II) over
several decades to that crucial period of history during which the classical
and Christian understandings of life and reality collided and yet came
together—the period of the church fathers, East and West, which was the
intellectual cradle both of medieval Western and of Byzantine Eastern
culture. Among the church fathers, moreover, it was the Greek Christian
theologians of the fourth century who engaged Newman's attention (as
they continue to engage mine), already in his first book, *The Arians of the
Fourth Century* (1833), and then in his four successive editions and translations of the writings of the fourth-century defender of trinitarian orthodoxy, Athanasius of Alexandria. Nor is it only in the subject matter of
Newman's scholarship that I have been following a parallel course of study.
The very subtitle of my five-volume lifework, *The Christian Tradition: A
History of the Development of Doctrine,* is an indication of the central
position that the concept of the development of doctrine has come to
assume in my thinking and authorship, as a heuristic instrument for making some sense of the complex relations between continuity and change in
the history of the teachings of Christianity. My use of this concept of
development of doctrine is as well a tribute to John Henry Newman, because the most important examination of it has been Newman's work of
1845 (the year of his conversion to Roman Catholicism), *An Essay on the
Development of Christian Doctrine,* which he revised significantly in
1878.

When he undertook to define the idea of a university, therefore, Newman was coming out of the university as he knew it best on the basis of that
study, and so am I. As a student and then a fellow in the University of
Oxford he had read himself far more deeply into patristic literature and
history than into any other academic discipline. He makes that background evident in major themes of *The Idea of a University,* for example in
the five discourses out of nine in which the word *theology* or *religious* or
church is part of the title. Sometimes it is manifested in small asides, such as

a reference (without seeming to require any further identification for his readers, beyond his earlier quotations from these authorities) to "our Lord, St. Paul, St. Chrysostom, and all Saints" (I.iv.12). That must not be taken to mean that he was writing only for the tiny (and, alas, still shrinking) coterie of scholars who could read the ancient Christian writers in Greek and Latin. His stance throughout the book made it clear that the object of the university as he was discussing it was, as he said in his preface, "intellectual, not moral"; for, he continued, if its object were "religious training, I do not see how it can be the seat of literature and science" (I.pr.). That is what has made his work, in Martin Svaglic's words, "intellectually accessible to readers of every religious faith *and of none.*" The fact remains, nevertheless, that the most important treatise on the idea of the university ever written in any language was conceived and born within what Etienne Gilson calls Newman's "patristic intellectual formation," and also that it interpreted the problems of university education, including the achievement of intellectual and personal maturity through university education, in the light of the principle of development.

Unlike many (though not all) of those that have preceded it, therefore, this dialogue with Newman about the idea of the university does consciously locate itself within the circle of discourse in which he thought and wrote. Newman strove, though perhaps not always with complete success, to disengage his educational arguments from his own specific theological stance. "I am not discussing theological questions at all," he frequently disclaimed (I.viii.3); or more fully, he said he was "treating [the university] as a philosophical and practical, rather than as a theological question, with an appeal to common sense, not to ecclesiastical rules" (I.ix.1). Therefore it is of course not mandatory to share his theological stance if one wants to engage him in dialogue about the idea of the university; yet such a stance is not, I would suppose, automatically to be counted a disadvantage, even though he was, as he maintained, "insisting simply on Natural Theology." Natural, rather than supernatural, theology did set the boundaries within which he found it possible to make the points he was making, although at the same time he had to admit to being "confident that no one can really set himself to master and to teach the doctrine of an intelligent Creator in its fulness [as natural and philosophical theology] without going on a great deal farther [to revealed and orthodox theology]" (I.iii.10).

In some important respects, therefore, the real question here in this reexamination of the idea of the university is not whether the fundamental metaphysical assumptions of Newman's *Idea of a University* are philosophically tenable or theologically defensible (crucial though I believe those questions to be, in ultimate terms), but whether these assumptions can still contribute to conclusions about the idea of the university that are educationally justifiable for those who do not accept the assumptions philosophically and theologically as well as for those who do. To test that question, this book takes its stand where Newman's does, and it carries on its dialogue with him there.

2

THE STORM BREAKING
UPON THE UNIVERSITY:
THE UNIVERSITY
IN CRISIS

What Newman identified as "the turning point of his life" was his election to a fellowship at Oriel College in 1822, which was "at that time the object of ambition of all rising men in Oxford." It was therefore with an abiding sense of devotion to Oriel that thirty years later he would describe its role in the crisis of Oxford: "As their collegiate reform synchronized with that reform of the Academical body, in which they bore a principal part, it was not unnatural that, *when the storm broke upon the University* from the North, their Alma Mater, whom they loved, should have found her first defenders within the walls of that small College, which had first put itself into a condition to be her champion" (I.vii.3.). The "storm breaking upon the University from the North" was the utilitarian attack on the traditional Oxford curriculum, to which Newman responded with his insistence that knowledge is an end in itself.

But there is a storm breaking upon the university again, and this time from north, south, east, and west. A critical reexamination of the idea of the university—not simply of John Henry Newman's idea of it, or of someone else's idea of it, but of the idea itself—has become an urgent necessity. When Newman entitled the ninth and last of his discourses "Duties of the Church towards Knowledge" (I.ix), he was acknowledging, also on the basis of his own often bitter experiences as a man with a foot in each camp, the long record of hostility and mutual recrimination between church and university. It is a record of hostility to which, during the century or so since Newman, extremists in both institutions have somehow managed to go on making ever-new contributions. But in one respect at least, the two institutions have much in common: despite dismissals of "the hysterical hyperbole of crisis," both are caught today in the throes of a situation that it is difficult to describe as anything but a crisis, a crisis of confidence that is at the same time a crisis of self-confidence. Each in its own way, both the university and the church (though the latter even more than the former) are often dismissed by those who claim to speak on behalf of "the real world" as museum pieces from another, simpler era, still good places perhaps for the young to learn something about the past but definitely not the places to look for guidance about the real world and its future—which is why there is more than a touch of irony in A. Bartlett Giamatti's use of the phrase "The Real World of the University" as the subtitle for his book.

University-bashing seems to have become a favorite indoor sport, the modern academic equivalent of the anticlericalism of the eighteenth century. It has also become a cottage industry, with books bearing such titles as *Profscam: Professors and the Demise of Higher Education, Tenured Radicals: How Politics Has Corrupted Our Higher Education, Killing the Spirit, Illiberal Education,* and *The Moral Collapse of the University* appearing one after another. In the periodical press, too, articles entitled "Gripes of Academe" and "Higher Education Feels the Heat" echo the refrain. All have been voicing, often from mutually contradictory intellectual and ideological presuppositions, the widely felt sense of disappointment or downright betrayal among those who have come to feel, as Newman once said about the critics of the church within the university, "sore, suspicious, and resentful" (I.ix.3), but this time against the university itself (though not infrequently against the church as well). Nor is this criticism confined to family quarrels within the academy or to discussions that deal primarily with the university. For example, a widely read recent essay in political economy devotes an early chapter to what the author calls "capitalist theologians" at universities past and present who provided much of the rationale for what he regards as the inequities in recent economic changes. Although he acknowledges that "the importance of academicians can easily be overstated," the author does conclude that these "conservative thinkers helped build the foundation for a decade of re-emergent enterprise, wealth and inequality." He also observes, with evident disapproval, that "the number of U.S. universities offering entrepreneurship programs climbed from 163 in 1981 to 250 in 1985."

Like the usual reactions of the church to its critics, the response from within the university to such attacks has frequently been less than constructive. Through a deadly combination of internal confusion and external pressure, the university has all too often maneuvered itself into a defense of the status quo, a carping posture in relation to the cultural and political mainstream, and a bunker mentality that can attribute the widespread support for an attack, not of course to any basic flaw in the university, but to "the strength of Americans' recoil from the disturbing effects of the contemporary academy." Everyone would agree that the almost daily headlines about the university—controversy over affirmative action, debates about "publish or perish," athletic scandals, "the university-industrial complex" in such areas as biotechnology, and the relation between the university and the community—do raise serious and troubling questions. A modern society is unthinkable without the university. But it does seem fair to say that as Western societies move toward the twenty-first century (and the third millennium) of the Common Era, the university is in a state of crisis and is in danger of losing credibility. In Sweden, for example, one observer could hail the reforms in curriculum and governance at the University of Uppsala that followed the Second World War as "the greatest improvement in this field since the days of Gustavus Adolphus," but at the same time can declare that "the old university structure was creaking at the joints" and much more was needed. To the extent that the university is unaware of this, its crisis is all the more grave, and its future all the more problematical.

The subtitle of this chapter, "The University in Crisis," is intentionally ambiguous, referring simultaneously to this crisis within university walls and to the position of the university in relation to the crises of the age beyond its walls. Obviously the two crises are related, but just as obviously they are by no means identical. As Hannah Arendt once observed in a trenchant comment that would seem to be more accurate today than it was when it was written in 1958, "It is somewhat difficult to take a crisis in education as seriously as it deserves. It is tempting indeed to regard it as a local phenomenon, unconnected with the larger issues of the century." Historically, the larger issues of at least some centuries have in fact been directly brought on by a crisis in the university, and have in turn gone on to precipitate such a crisis. The Reformation of the sixteenth century, for example, began in the university, and its chief protagonist was a university professor. Martin Luther was neither speaking as a political figure nor acting chiefly as an ecclesiastical figure, but exercising his responsibilities as an academic figure, when on 31 October 1517 he issued his Ninety-five Theses inviting (or challenging) his colleagues and all others to an academic disputation "about the power of indulgences." For years before that, he had been working out the main lines of Reformation teaching in the process of preparing and delivering his academic lectures at the University of Wittenberg. "I have never wanted to do this and do not want to do it now," he said in 1530, explaining how he had become a reformer. "I was forced and driven into this position in the first place when I had to become a Doctor of Holy Scripture against my will [in 1512]. Then, *as a doctor in a general free university*, I began, at the command of pope and emperor, to do what such a doctor is sworn to do, expounding the Scriptures for all the world and teaching everybody. Once in this position, I have had to stay in it, and I cannot give it up or leave it yet with a good conscience."

Once the Reformation had been set in motion as a consequence of this professorial crisis, moreover, the venue of the Reformation continued in great measure to be the university. The roster of foreign students at Wittenberg during the sixteenth century—115 students from Poland alone studied there during the crucial decade between 1554 and 1565—reads like a list of reformers-in-the-making from all over Catholic Europe. According to Shakespeare's anachronism, even Hamlet, prince of Denmark in the Middle Ages, had studied there (at a university not founded until 1502). As Claudius the king says to him,

> For your intent
> In going back to school in Wittenberg,
> It is most retrograde to our desire.

The introduction of the Reformation into a new country likewise often began with that country's universities, where the reformation of the church became the basis for fundamental programs of academic reorganization, and vice versa. In Hamlet's own Copenhagen, for example, the university had been allowed to fall into desuetude during the decades immediately preceding the Reformation. As a modern history of the University of Copenhagen puts it, after "the University's activities came to a complete stop" in the upheavals of the Reformation, it was "to Wittenberg [that they turned] for assistance in re-establishing the Danish University." For those developments in the sixteenth century, and for many others in many other centuries, for example in the People's Republic of China and then in Central and Eastern Europe during the final two decades of the twentieth century, what Hannah Arendt calls "the crisis in education" and what she calls "the larger issues of the century" were locked together in an intimate, problematical connection.

In any age, it is that connection that makes a reexamination of the idea of the university so essential and yet so complicated. At the risk of superficiality, it may be useful here to outline a few of those larger issues of the century, as prolegomena to the next several chapters examining the first principles involved in the idea of the university. Such an outline is, of course, not how these issues chiefly deserve to be studied, in their own right and in depth. Each has become the subject of an entire bibliography of studies and is part of the agenda of several university departments, schools, and fields. But we do need to glimpse at the ambiguous relation of (staying with Hannah Arendt's helpful formulations) these larger issues to the crisis in education and to the idea of the university. One critic of the critics of the university has observed that "their rhetoric is consistently apocalyptic," while another has likewise noted that "the genre is quasi-apocalyptic." Yet in a consideration of the larger issues of the century (if not also in a consideration of the crisis in education), it does remain, lamentably, as appropriate as it was when William Blake memorialized them in his art and poetry, to visualize them by looking at the Four Horsemen of the Apocalypse, who "were given power to kill [1] with sword and [2] with famine and [3] with pestilence and [4] by wild beasts of the earth."

The life of the university throughout the twentieth century has been dominated by the threat and the reality of War, the First Horseman of the Apocalypse. In one way or another this is true of every institution in every society, but the experience of the university with the realities of war has been marked by special tragedy. Describing this as "a position which few today are ready to put forward publicly or with conviction" because it seems to be "stating an élitist canon," George Steiner has put the issue with his characteristically provocative acuity: "Where it is absolutely honest, the doctrine of a high culture will hold the burning of a great library, the destruction of Galois at twenty-one, or the disappearance of an important [musical] score, to be losses paradoxically but none the less decidedly out of proportion with common deaths, even on a large scale." The events surrounding the outbreak of the First World War provide just one striking instance of many in that tragic history. When the armies of the German Empire invaded Belgium in August 1914, one of their first victims was the University of Louvain, established by a papal charter of 9 December 1425. The burning of the university library cost the world of scholarship three hundred thousand books and more than a thousand original manuscripts (including the university's charter from 1425), and it has ever since symbolized the triumph of the irrational over the rational. As one historian has told the story, "In Brussels the Rector of the University, Monseigneur de Becker, whose rescue was arranged by the Americans, described the burning of the Library. Nothing was left of it; all was in ashes. When he came to the word 'library'—*bibliothèque*—he could not say it. He stopped, tried again, uttered the first syllable, '*La bib*—' and unable to go on, bowed his head on the table and wept."

This disaster from the First World War was rendered even more poignant by the reprise of the bombardment of Louvain in May 1940 during the Second World War, when the university library, which had been rebuilt in 1928, was destroyed once more. But for any university citizen anywhere, what dramatizes the symbolism of the burning of the books and library at the University of Louvain in 1914 still more sharply is the complicity of scholars and university professors in the atrocity, at any rate after the fact. Responding to the worldwide sense of outrage evoked by the news, a group of ninety-three intellectuals that included some of the most distinguished and erudite representatives of the German university system (among them Adolf von Harnack, the most eminent scholar the history of Christian doctrine has known) permitted themselves to issue a signed statement of moral and political support for the invasion of Belgium, on the unbelievable basis of the alleged threat it had posed to its larger and more powerful neighbor. Yet any assignment of blame in the story of 1914 is overshadowed by the grinding deprivation to which not only the University of Louvain but the University of Berlin and all its sister institutions in Germany were subjected during and immediately after the First World War. At the same time, it must be granted that this record does cast fundamental doubt on any lingering presumption, automatic though it might still seem to some academics, that the university and its scholars may somehow lay special claim to virtue, or that they can definitely be counted upon in the future to defend peace and international morality.

It is nevertheless difficult to imagine a substitute for the university as the primary staging area for peace through international understanding; to paraphrase Voltaire's familiar bon mot about the existence of God, if the university did not exist, it would be necessary to invent it. The record of the university in that capacity is, moreover, long and distinguished. In the shadow of the Thirty Years' War, the exiled Moravian bishop and educator John Amos Comenius, for whom the modern Slovak University of Bratislava is named, first set forth the vision of a *Collegium Pansophicum*, which would bring together scholars of all ages from all countries. Following almost every international conflict since that one, postwar planners have looked to cooperation between universities across national boundaries as a resource for healing the wounds of the past and for helping to prevent war in the future. If (as part II of this book argues) the advancement of knowledge through research, the transmission of knowledge through teaching, the preservation of knowledge in scholarly collections, and the diffusion of knowledge through publishing are the four legs of the university table, no one of which can stand for very long unless all are strong, it would follow that in the future even more than in the past they will all have to be represented in strength as components of any program of peace through international education: exchange of scholars and scientists in libraries and laboratories, exchange of students and teachers, and exchange and translation of books and journals. Such grave threats to the integrity of these programs as the brain drain are an issue not only for governments but for universities. Both at various universities and in such international agencies as UNESCO there have been repeated experiences of disillusionment with the practical devices for carrying out that aim. It is not the doomsayer but the realist who declares that the future of the university in all nations—indeed, the future of those nations themselves—will depend in considerable measure on finding structures in the twenty-first century to realize the ideals of Comenius's *Collegium Pansophicum* more fully.

Among the most dramatic though ambiguous outcomes of twentieth-century science has been the development of the means to stop the advance of Famine, the Second Horseman of the Apocalypse. That development, popularly called the green revolution, is a fascinating case study in the intellectual and programmatic interactions between the basic research carried on in the faculty of arts and sciences of the university (in this instance especially research in plant genetics) and the applied research located within the professional schools of the university (in this instance schools of agriculture and programs in nutrition). It is as well an instructive example of the interaction between university research of any provenance and the research enterprises of private industry, individual governments, and international agencies. The intricate patterns of funding for research within and across these several jurisdictions are also intriguing to study, and they are sorely in need of review and revision. But the important component also within the industrial, governmental, and international settings of research is the critical position of the university as the fulcrum for all of research. While some of the most decisive and abstract basic research was the result of work done in the laboratories of industry and government, these laboratories remain accountable to their chief executives, and ultimately to shareholders or legislators or taxpayers, who have the right to demand justification for any such basic research in relation to the primary mission of the institution. It is an oversimplification but not a distortion to point out that in the faculty of arts and sciences of the university basic research *is* a primary mission of the institution: to anticipate a later discussion, knowledge is its own end. Because the green revolution came out of the joint investigations of basic research and applied research and the interaction between them, the ambience of the university as a total and complex entity will continue to provide the natural opportunity for such joint investigations, because here basic research and applied research can interact. Of course, all of this assumes that in the future there will still be some sense in which we may speak about a *uni*versity at all.

That is by no means a safe assumption. The university has not discharged its intellectual and moral responsibility if, in its heroic achievement of attaining the possibility of putting bread on every table, it ignores the fundamental axiom, which may be biblical in its formulation but is universal in its authority, that man does not live by bread alone. The religions of humanity all have their special versions of that axiom, and both in its teaching and in its research the modern secular university often ignores these at its peril. But it is in keeping with Newman's "insisting simply on Natural Theology" (I.iii.10) to insist as well that this is the proper business not only of theologians but of scholars throughout the university, and in a particular way of scholars in the humanities. Now that they have been presented by their colleagues from the biological sciences with a new and unprecedented possibility that simultaneously amounts to a new challenge, those members of the university who study and teach literature, philosophy, history, and the arts will fail in their responsibility if they cannot find some way to break out of the cycle of angst and moral cynicism, to articulate a new sense of celebration in the joy and the tragedy of the human experience, including the human experience of their own traditions. One current critic of the university, Parker J. Palmer, has put this issue sharply, if rather one-sidedly: "These are people who go into this business out of some kind of passion. They now find themselves disconnected from the passions that brought them into the academy, disconnected from their students, from their souls, from each other. And the pain level has gotten so high that they are ready to listen to something different." But that listening to something different must not be achieved at the cost of scholarly discipline. Only the painstaking exercise of discipline illumined by imagination, and of imagination channeled by discipline, can lead to the rediscovery of an authentic humanism. Only such a humanism, in turn, will have something to say to those who, having finally found enough to eat, will recognize with shock that even in the midst of their famine they were yearning for a life, not only for a living. Here again, in profound and complex ways, the crisis in humanistic education at the university and the larger issues of the century in society as a whole do meet, but whether for deeper benefit or for even more bitter disappointment is by no means clear.

It seems safe to estimate that the university in the twentieth century has devoted more attention to Pestilence and Disease, the Third Horseman of the Apocalypse, than to the other three combined. The reform of medical education, not only in the United States and Canada but in many countries, has usually proceeded on the presupposition that an entire university, rather than merely a hospital or a school of medicine isolated from the university, is its only possible setting. This development has been steadily moving the institutions charged with preparing future physicians toward a deeper commitment to research into the underlying causes of disease rather than solely to instruction in the skills of coping with it once it breaks out. For one disease after another, the outcome has been a steep decline in incidence, together with the invention of new pharmacological, surgical, and above all preventive techniques. The statistics for deaths from the communicable diseases of childhood dramatically illustrate what has happened, but they are at the same time a dramatic illustration of the problem: a great gulf fixed, which is becoming ever more vast, between those who have access to these miracles of medical discovery and those who do not. Not accidentally, a graph of that contrast would coincide in many distressing ways with a chart of the difference between those in the general public throughout the world who have had access to the university and those who have not. Critics of the university, therefore, accuse it of being a principal bastion of the ruling class, not only in the restrictions on admissions and in selection of books that its students must study, but in the moral and intellectual concerns that fuel its scholarship and teaching, even in so universal a need as health care. Yet it can be argued in reply that if the university sacrifices quality to equality, it can jeopardize most those whom it is purportedly committed to helping.

When the writer of the Apocalypse identified the Fourth Horseman, Death mounted on a pale horse, with "wild beasts of the earth," he was reflecting the sense, widespread though not universal in late antiquity and well beyond, that humanity was pitting its superior intellectual capacity and technological skill against the forces of nature. That sense or something like it was at work in the distinction, which Newman quotes approvingly from Aristotle, between the liberal arts and the useful or mechanical arts (I.v.4). It was present also, at least according to the standard interpretations, in the command to Adam and Eve in the Book of Genesis to "have dominion" over the earth and to "subdue it." In his elevation of "the liberal arts" over "the useful or mechanical arts" Newman did not

want to be understood as disparaging the latter. "Life could not go on
without them," he acknowledged; "we owe our daily welfare to them; their
exercise is the duty of the many, and we owe to the many a debt of gratitude
for fulfilling that duty" (I.v.6). What he could not have foreseen in such a
statement, despite its "elitist" tone, was the extent to which, in the century
and a half that has intervened, it would be specifically the elites in the basic
and the applied sciences at the university—thus, by his definition and
distinction, chiefly in "liberal arts"—who would provide much of the
leadership for such "mechanical arts" and for the technology by which the
ancient imperative to subdue the earth would be carried out with a thoroughness far surpassing anything projected in Genesis or Aristotle or the
Apocalypse. During and shortly after Newman's lifetime, the "technische
Hochschule" in Germany, the institutes of technology in the United
States—Rensselaer Polytechnic Institute in 1824, the Massachusetts Institute of Technology in 1861, Purdue University in 1869, the Georgia
Institute of Technology in 1885, the California Institute of Technology in
1891, and the Carnegie Institute of Technology in 1900—and the schools
and faculties of engineering established within various universities everywhere were allying themselves with industry or government or both to
"have dominion over the earth and subdue it" through the interaction of
basic and applied research. The Manhattan Project at the University
of Chicago during the Second World War, which led to the harnessing of
nuclear energy for war and then for peace, stands as a monument to the
achievements of such an alliance. The alliance will become even more
momentous in the future, with the rapidly increasing involvement both of
universities as institutions and of individual professors as entrepreneurs in
the development of high-tech industry.

   Whatever chilling effect Newman's elitist words about the many whose
duty it was to carry on the mechanical arts so that the few could pursue the
liberal arts may evoke is greatly exceeded by the collective second thoughts
throughout the world at the close of the twentieth century about the consequences that have been brought on by such a "dominion over the earth."
Hardly a day passes without some new disaster to the environment being
brought to public attention. Apologists for capitalist private enterprise are
embarrassed to admit how rapaciously human greed and the capacity for
short-sighted exploitation have ravaged the planet, but socialist critics of
free enterprise capitalism are no less acutely embarrassed to learn what
ecological atrocities have taken place in the planned economies of Marxist
regimes. Anyone who cares simultaneously about the environment and
about the university must address the question whether the university has

the capacity to meet a crisis that is not only ecological and technological, but ultimately educational and moral. The appearance at many universities everywhere of courses, programs, departments, and entire schools bearing the title "environmental studies" is evidence that the question has begun to force itself upon the attention of educators. Just how much of this is a genuine wave of the future and how much is mere tinkering will depend at least in part on the readiness of the university community to address the underlying intellectual issues and moral imperatives of having responsibility for the earth, and to do so with an intensity and ingenuity matching that shown by previous generations in obeying the command to have dominion over the planet. Having once been the enemy, "the wild beasts of the earth" in the Apocalypse have become victims, or fellow victims, and what must now be "subdued" under the imperative of the Book of Genesis are the forces, most of them set into motion by human agents and some of them with the complicity of the university, that threaten the future of the earth—upon which, it must seem supererogatory to point out, the future of the university also hangs.

There are just Four Horsemen in the Apocalypse, but if there were a fifth it should probably be ignorance. As Newman's *Idea of a University* observed on its very first page (I.pr.) and as this book will also have occasion to observe more than once, knowledge and virtue are not identical, and the expulsion of ignorance by knowledge will not be enough to deal with the spiritual realities and moral challenges of the future. No one has to be literate to be trampled underfoot by any of the Four Horsemen, who often tend to be indifferent to the educational level of their victims. But to find ways of coping with the challenges represented by each of the Four Horsemen will require a triumph of literacy over ignorance. The university, too, will need to ask basic questions and to address such "first principles" (I.vii.4) as the interrelation between knowledge and utility, the problem of the intellectual virtues, and the nature of the university as community. These first principles, in turn, are in some special way central to the enterprise of going on to define "the business of a University" (I.vii.1) as well as its "duties to society" (I.vii.10). As a result of the crisis of confidence and the crisis of credibility described here, moreover, no university however distinguished—neither the university to which this book is dedicated nor the university whose press is the publisher of this book—can articulate the idea of the university to its own constituency without being obliged to reexamine the idea of the university as such, both within and beyond its own national boundaries.

3

PUSHING THINGS UP TO
THEIR FIRST PRINCIPLES

Except perhaps for big-time soccer, the university seems to have become the most nearly universal manmade institution in the modern world. There is, moreover, every reason to believe that in the future this idea of the university will continue to extend itself, if anything, even more universally than it has in the past century or so. But if it does, thoughtful university citizens everywhere will need to acquire what John Henry Newman, quoting his opponents with approval, styled "the invaluable habit of *pushing things up to their first principles*" (I.vii.4). Employing accents that nowadays would certainly be denounced as Eurocentric, perhaps even as racist, Newman, in a disquisition of 1854 on the idea of civilization that is now the first chapter of part II of *The Idea of a University,* looked briefly beyond the borders of Christendom and of Western civilization. "I am not denying of course," he said, "the civilization of the Chinese, for instance, though it be not our civilization; but it is a huge, stationary, unattractive, morose civilization." Then he assured his hearers that it was not his intention either to "deny a civilization to the Hindoos, nor to the ancient Mexicans, nor to the Saracens, nor (in a certain sense) to the Turks." Yet his conclusion was that although "each of these races has its own civilization," they are "as separate from one another as from ours. I do not see how they can be all brought under one idea. . . . None of them will bear a comparison with the Society and the Civilization which I have described as alone having a claim to those names" (II.i.2).

But today each of these civilizations—Chinese, Indian, Mexican, Arabian, and Turkish—does also have its own universities, and it can be instructive for our inquiry into first principles to look at them briefly, in the same order in which Newman lists them. As a recent publication by the State Education Commission of the People's Republic of China makes clear and as the events of 4 June 1989 confirm, the new society of the People's Republic takes university education very seriously indeed. The "Regulations concerning Academic Degrees" in that publication begin by specifying the aims and qualifications of the Chinese universities:

1. The Regulations are laid down to promote the growth of special talents in science, raise the academic levels of various branches of learning, and forward the development of education and science so as to meet the needs of socialist modernization.

2. All citizens who support the leadership of the Communist Party of China and the socialist system and who attain a certain academic level may apply for appropriate academic degrees in accordance with the requirements stipulated by the Regulations.

The official statement *National Policy on Education—1986,* issued by the government of India, after explaining that "there are around 150 universities and about 5,000 colleges in India today," laments "the existing schism between the formal system of education and the country's rich and varied cultural traditions," but promises that through the universities "education can and must bring about the fine synthesis between change-oriented technologies and the country's continuity of cultural tradition." The "Integral Program for the Development of Higher Education" of Mexico in October 1986 identified as the fourth point of its master plan "the importance of encouraging the increase of matriculation in the natural and exact sciences, in engineering and technology, as well as in the humanities." In Saudi Arabia, the catalog of the new King Faisal University for the year 1401/ 1982 opens with the affirmation: "Education is the cornerstone of our efforts properly to equip coming generations to bring about a bright future. University education in particular has a very important role to play in the enhancement of the welfare of the nation, economically, intellectually, socially, and culturally." And in Turkey—or, in Newman's somewhat condescending phrase, "in a certain sense [among] the Turks"—as a recent analysis by the president of the Council of Higher Education of Turkey acknowledges, "on the whole the numbers of publications and research projects were not up to the potential of the universities"; therefore a reform of university education was instituted in 1981, "to raise the standards of the institutions of higher education to contemporary levels, give more young men and women the opportunity for higher education, offer graduate training and encourage research."

These universities, far from being, in Newman's words, "as separate from one another as from ours," are in fact connected intellectually and technologically both with one another and with "ours" in a vast, if often imperfect, international network, as the enemies of free inquiry have repeatedly had to learn when they have stifled academic freedom in one part of the world, only to bring on themselves denunciations from all over the world. That special quality of being comprehensively universal while being intensively local, which is connoted by the term *catholic* as applied to the church, does seem to fit the university in a special way. As a catholic and international institution, the university continues to be the object of world-wide discussion and debate. Multivolume examinations of the university's mission and organization in many nations; statistical and demographic analyses of its problems and prospects; catalogs and programs of study; autobiographical memoirs and biographical studies about distinguished or controversial educators; collections of "secular sermons" by university rectors, presidents, and deans; and polemical discourses on the curriculum and faculty of the university—such works fill the shelves of the library (and the bibliography of this book).

All too often lacking in such studies of the university as *institution,* however, is a consideration of the university as *idea.* Commenting on the development of the natural sciences and technology during this century, as well as on the great revolutions of our time, Sir Isaiah Berlin has issued the reminder "that these great movements began with ideas in people's heads." It is noteworthy that in each of the five university systems just reviewed the concrete programmatic and institutional proposals are grounded in some very specific ideas of the university. There are nevertheless many circles, also within the university, where such considerations would be deemed quite irrelevant to the institutional realities of the university. It is symptomatic of where things stand that if we are to have those assumptions about the idea of the university explicitly raised at the end of the twentieth century, we are hard put to find contemporary expositions of them that are even nearly adequate, but are still obliged to turn to earlier discussions from the nineteenth century, and specifically to a book bearing that very title, John Henry Newman's *Idea of a University.* Speaking as a student of the American Revolution, David Brion Davis has suggested that "Book V of Aristotle's *Politics* . . . probably remains the best introduction to the causes of political revolution," and he feels able to say this even after there have been so many revolutions—and so many books about revolutions—in the past two centuries. It would not be presumptuous to suggest that in the discussion of the idea of the university Newman's work occupies a place analogous to that which Davis assigns to Aristotle's *Politics* in the discussion of revolution. Like Aristotle's Greece, the nineteenth century continues to occupy a special place in our intellectual conversation, as the place where ideas, including the idea of the university, were taken seriously.

As Thomas Mann observed about the nineteenth century (in the essay of 1933 that was to trigger his expulsion from Nazi Germany), "We shrug our shoulders both at its belief—which was a belief in ideas—and at its unbelief, which is to say its melancholy brand of relativism." In Newman's case, obviously, it is not a melancholy brand of relativism but his belief in ideas that stands out: his belief in many kinds of ideas, including, as chapter 1 has noted, his profound ideas about the very idea of the development of ideas, but, above all for our purposes here, his belief in the idea of the university. As he put it, "these Discourses are directed simply to the consideration of the *aims* and *principles* of Education" (I.pr.).

This was not because he was committed to abstract ideas at the expense of practical realities. "Necessity has no law," he mused (and would learn repeatedly as he tried to create the Irish Catholic University), "and expedience is often one form of necessity. It is no principle with sensible men, of whatever cast of opinion, to do always what is abstractedly best. Where no direct duty forbids, we may be obliged to do, as being best under circumstances, what we murmur and rise against, while we do it" (I.i.3). But he would have little patience with those who were "disposed to say that they are ready to acquit the principles of Education, which I am to advocate, of all fault whatever, except that of being impracticable" (I.i.4). He believed that it was fundamentally perverse to say that these principles were sound but could not be made to work; for ultimately if they could not be made to work, they were, in some basic sense, unsound. Mistaken assumptions and erroneous first principles could have, and have had, consequences both practicable and pernicious. In that sense, the conflict between "principle" and "practicality" poses a false alternative that is deleterious to both. "The invaluable habit of pushing things up to their first principles" (I.vii.4) was a habit to which Newman had been psychologically predisposed all his life. The very subtitle of the *Apologia pro Vita Sua* is "A History of His Religious Opinions"—not events, though there are many; not persons and institutions, though some of these are very prominent (above all, of course, Oxford University and the Church of Rome); but opinions and ideas and beliefs and first principles and even dogmas were fundamental to him: "I have changed in many things: in this I have not. From the age of fifteen, dogma has been the fundamental principle of my religion: I know no other religion; I cannot enter into the idea of any other sort of religion; religion, as a mere sentiment, is to me a dream and a mockery. As well can there be filial love without the fact of a father, as devotion without the fact of a Supreme Being." The eighteen propositions against theological liberalism that Newman appended to his

Apologia pro Vita Sua elaborate on his insistence upon the centrality of "tenets, doctrines, precepts, and truth" (to quote the terminology in various of the propositions). In contradistinction to the theological trends prevailing in much of the nineteenth and twentieth centuries, Newman as an Anglican, as an Anglo-Catholic, and as a Roman Catholic was committed without reservation to the doctrinal content of the Christian faith and to the dogmatic and creedal tradition of Christian-Catholic orthodoxy.

But that commitment was in fact part of a general mind-set or, as he calls it, "the concatenation of argument by which the mind ascends from its first to its final . . . idea," be that idea a religious idea or any other kind of idea, including the idea of the university. What Newman said of one of his colleagues in the Oxford Movement, R. H. Froude, applied in considerable measure to Newman himself: he "had that strong hold of first principles, and that keen perception of their value, that he was comparatively indifferent to the revolutionary action which would attend on their application to a given state of things." Later he would, in a special examination, probe the relation between kinds of assent and kinds of belief, as well as the place of first principles. This he did in the book that many students of his thought regard as his most original and profound, and that one such student has called "Newman's chief philosophical work . . . the realization of what he considered his life's work," the *Essay in Aid of a Grammar of Assent* of 1870—the very year of the First Vatican Council, whose approach to these issues of faith and knowledge differed so greatly from his own. Near the conclusion of the *Grammar of Assent* Newman stated the centrality of first principles: "If any one starts from any other principles but ours, I have not the power to change his principles, or the conclusion which he draws from them. . . . The fact remains, that, in any inquiry about things in the concrete, men differ from each other, not so much in the soundness of their reasoning as in the principles which govern its exercise . . . [and] that where there is no common measure of minds, there is no common measure of arguments." For him that applied to the first principles of thought about the natural world no less than to the first principles of revealed theology. As *The Idea of a University* makes abundantly clear, Newman believed that it applied with special force to an institution that was dedicated ex professo to learning and to ideas, and therefore to first principles.

All of this may well sound quite alien or at least quaint to present-day ears, even on the campus of the university. As Robert Maynard Hutchins was to discover, there is within some parts of the university a suspicion of what is seen there as "the menace of metaphysics." As deep-seated as it is widespread, this suspicion of metaphysics reacts negatively to any such talk of first principles, even when it comes from a highly respected figure. One highly respected figure who learned about this suspicion the hard way was Walter Lippmann. Lippmann's first book, *A Preface to Politics*, was published in 1913. It was, as his biographer has described it, "an intellectual potpourri," but it was "taut, perceptive and iconoclastic"; yet it was "not a systematic theory, but, as he called it, *A Preface to Politics*." In a sequel, *A Preface to Morals* of 1929, he diagnosed some of the underlying causes for the moral dilemmas of his generation. Believing that "our political thinking today has no intellectual foundations," Lippmann proposed a "humanism [that] was not so much a philosophy as a mode of conduct." As Ronald Steel puts it, "The book's stoicism, its bleak humanism, and its rewarding conclusion that he who had lost his religious faith could find salvation in a secular humanism that only innately superior sensibilities could glimpse" appealed to such readers as Justice Oliver Wendell Holmes, Jr., who called it "a noble performance." Lippmann's last book, except for collections of articles, speeches, and columns, was published in 1955, under the title *Essays in the Public Philosophy*. During a period of over four decades Lippmann had taken stands on many issues and many personalities (including his oft-quoted dismissal of Franklin D. Roosevelt early in 1932 as "a pleasant man who, without any important qualifications for the office, would very much like to be President"). But he found that his previous books and his concrete positions on the issues of the day had repeatedly raised for him fundamental questions of principle, and in *The Public Philosophy* he sought to address some of these questions. Yet, quoting yet again from Ronald Steel, "Lippmann's evocation of an undefined 'higher law' . . . actively irritated many," and there were dark mutterings that because of this quest for ultimate principles "it will be said that Lippmann has no logic for argument." Pragmatism, relativism, skepticism, agnosticism, and "bleak humanism" as voiced in his earlier books—all of these could be within the pale. It was only when he began to probe first principles that his reading public reacted with misgiving, irritation, and even alarm. Because that reaction of resistance to Lippmann's examination of first principles, and even more to Newman's, still expresses attitudes that sometimes seem to have become all but canonical within the university as well as beyond it, it may be useful to suggest the reasons for the resistance before going on to identify potential resources for addressing it.

Underlying many of the other reasons is a change of outlook through which we have all learned to be wary of statements of first principles, because they can so easily serve as a highblown justification for unacceptable practices and unjust structures. Our usual vocabulary for describing such statements is itself highly instructive. The word *rationalize* used to carry the positive meaning "to render conformable to reason" and to organize in a rational order or manner, as when Newman's contemporary Herbert Spencer said: "When life has been duly *rationalized* by science, care of the body is imperative." But today, as a recent psychoanalytic dictionary makes clear, the term *rationalization* is utilized, uniformly and almost exclusively, to refer to "a process by which an individual employs subjective 'reasonable,' conscious explanations to justify certain actions or attitudes, while unconsciously concealing other unacceptable motivations. Rationalization is always considered defensive." Because everyone would grant that the formulation of rational first principles is itself an act of "rationalizing" in the older sense of the word, the change in the very meaning of that word suggests a profound reorientation of the concept, by which it has now necessarily become a "rationalization" in the newer, psychoanalytic sense of the word. First principles, by this understanding of the process, are not really "first" at all, not "a priori" but "ex post facto"; what is "a priori" is not the principle, but the practice and the structure. Not only from Sigmund Freud, moreover, but also from Karl Marx everyone has learned how easily and how often specious philosophical and theological first principles have been employed in support of power and exploitation. Through much of Western history into the nineteenth century, for example, slavery was rationalized (in both the old and modern senses of the word) by a combination of Aristotle's teaching, that slavery is a natural condition because of the inherent inequality among human beings, with the doctrine of the Fall and the story of the curse of Ham from the Book of Genesis. Similarly, the authority of natural law came under a shadow because it was repeatedly invoked as a first principle, for example to undergird the divine right of kings and to strike down the concept of collective bargaining.

Common sense, mother wit, and poetic wisdom have all discovered that the human mind, like Milton's Belial, "could make the worse appear the better reason"; but it is especially to scholars from various departments and schools of the university that we owe the corollary discovery that first principles, far from being a conscious and rational presupposition on which actions are based, have often been invented after the fact. Thus the historical school of jurisprudence in the nineteenth and twentieth centuries has applied the methodology of social historiography to interpret how laws have arisen, with far-reaching results. Charles A. Beard's influential study, *An Economic Interpretation of the Constitution of the United*

States, together with his book of 1912 on the Supreme Court and his book of 1915 on Jeffersonian democracy, taught my entire generation of rising historians the importance of ferreting out the economic motives of interest groups and individuals that underlay not only political actions but especially political and philosophical theories. Beard's interpretations fell on soil that had been prepared also by the pragmatism of William James and others. But he made a major contribution to the current climate of academic opinion in which abstract first principles—of the kind that James sharply criticized when they were propounded by his idealist colleague Josiah Royce—are seen as far removed from reality.

William James insisted no less stoutly that his emphasis on the priority of experience over abstraction and on the bewildering variety both of experience and of interpretation did not make him either a relativist or a skeptic and agnostic. But it must be acknowledged that there are, especially in universities, those who, sometimes by invoking his authority, have elevated relativism, especially relativism about first principles, to the status of a first principle (about which it is not permitted to be a relativist). In Allan Bloom's widely debated (and occasionally studied) book of 1987, *The Closing of the American Mind: How Higher Education Has Failed Democracy and Impoverished the Souls of Today's Students,* the question of "relativism" occupies an important place. But here the issue of relativism is relevant as part of the explanation for the phenomenon of resistance to the notion of first principles. For relativism, too, can be seen either a priori or ex post facto. If it is a relativism ex post facto, it represents the admission that after thinkers or scholars or judges have done their best to be honest and not to intrude themselves and their prejudices on their material, the results of their research and thought will still be flawed and will bear the marks of the time and place and personality in which they have arisen. This is an admission that keeps scholars honest. But if it is a relativism a priori rather than ex post facto, it can bring on the "paralysis of analysis," bankrupting the entire intellectual enterprise; and it is this second approach, relativism as itself a first principle, that is responsible for the bankruptcy and for the resistance to first principles. As Hannah Arendt once said about Jacques Maritain, the French Thomist philosopher, "What Maritain wanted was one certainty which would lead him out of the complexities and confusions of a world that does not even know what a man is talking about if he takes the word truth in his mouth." When Maritain, in his lectures of 1943 on education, began his first lecture with a critique of what he called "the first misconception: a disregard of ends" and proceeded in the second lecture to formulate what he called "the fundamental norms of education," he was applying to the issues before us here the very quality of mind that Hannah Arendt admired in him and that others found so foreign. As he says near the end of the book, with that disarmingly sophisticated simplicity of his, "a good philosophy should be a true philosophy."

One of the reasons that Maritain's philosophy of first principles—and Newman's—seems so foreign is the lingering suspicion among some of its critics that in such a philosophy the existence of philosophical and religious pluralism is, at best, a problem to be suffered, rather than, as it has become more and more in contemporary societies, a resource to be celebrated. Newman's and Maritain's concern for some first principles that can form the basis of university education seems, just as Walter Lippmann's public philosophy did, to smack too much of uniformity and authoritarianism. At least until the Decree on Religious Liberty of the Second Vatican Council promulgated in 1965, there was, as the decree acknowledged, good reason to believe that not only in its concrete practice but in its official teaching the Roman Catholic church, which both Newman and Maritain joined as adult converts (Newman in 1845, Maritain in 1906), was willing to grant religious toleration and to accept religious pluralism as a provisional arrangement until it could achieve a majority in a society, but that once it became a majority it would legislate its teachings into a preferred position at the expense of others. When applied to the research and teaching of a university, that policy seemed to be a way of imposing a creedal test on professors and students; and the first principles of which Newman and Maritain spoke seemed to be uncomfortably close to the dogma that had, according to Newman's own words, been the fundamental principle of his religion from the age of fifteen, or to the Christian philosophy of Saint Thomas Aquinas, to whose exposition Maritain devoted his philosophical life. If, as Newman said in his lecture of 1855 on "Christianity and Scientific Investigation" for the School of Science, "the Church has a sovereign authority, and, when she speaks *ex cathedra*, must be obeyed" also by the university (II.viii.2), this has made it seem better to disdain the entire quest for first principles altogether than to jeopardize the university at its very heart, which was freedom of inquiry.

This reexamination of the idea of the university is based on the assumption that in spite of these problems the modern university is not as bereft of positive resources for an inquiry into its first principles as many critics would have us believe. For if it is the case, as I believe, that first principles and assumptions are always present whether they be recognized or not, one methodology that can be followed is to tease out such presuppositions from the concrete life of the university in today's world and then to ask whether they are defensible. To mention one striking example, the present-day athletic practice of many American universities, pragmatic and indeed cynical though it sometimes is, is nonetheless grounded in some first principles, principles that just happen to be erroneous and downright dangerous. It does not call for educational legerdemain or philosophical divination to recognize what those principles are; but it does call for educational and moral courage to articulate them and to act against them—more courage than some university athletic associations, some university boards of trustees, and, alas, some university presidents have been willing to manifest. Another first principle at work in this book is the conviction that the tradition out of which the modern university has come is not to be dismissed as a quaint museum piece, with the ease and glibness that sometimes proceeds as though we in the present generation were free to define the university in any way we wish without attention to its heritage. It can even be argued that there is in the internal life of the modern university more of a consensus than many might suppose about "the intellectual virtues," and therefore that it is possible to begin to define some of those virtues. Much of that defining may turn out to be something quite different from Newman's own specific ideas and proposals. But if, as he insisted, "the true and adequate end of intellectual training and of a University . . . is [that] we must generalize, we must reduce to method, we must have a grasp of principles, and group and shape our acquisitions by means of them" (I.vi.7), such a departure from his conclusions will itself still be faithful to his own deepest intuitions and intentions, and thus also to his invaluable habit of pushing things up to their first principles.

4

KNOWLEDGE
ITS OWN END?

The first principle underlying all other first principles in the reexamination of the idea of the university is formulated by Newman in the title of his fifth discourse, "*Knowledge Its Own End.*" In support of this principle Newman cites the authority of Cicero, who, as Newman puts it, "in enumerating the various heads of mental excellence, lays down the pursuit of Knowledge for its own sake, as the first of them" (I.v.3). Cicero does this in a number of places, most familiarly in the first book of his treatise on duties, *De officiis*, where he declares that "only man possesses the capacity to seek and pursue truth," and elaborates on this capacity. Newman quotes from this portion of *De officiis*, adding that this passage "is but one of many similar passages in a multitude of authors." As Dwight Culler has observed, "the most directly pertinent passage . . . is that in the first book of the *Metaphysics*" of Aristotle, from which, among other sources, Cicero had presumably taken it. "All men by nature desire to know": these familiar opening words of Aristotle's *Metaphysics* (which, over the centuries, teachers of the young have repeatedly had reason to question) continue to state the underlying rationale of university education. When this principle was combined, as it was in Hellenistic Judaism and then in patristic Christianity, with the biblical doctrine of the image of God, it identified the desire to know, together with the capacity for self-transcendence implied by it, as the distinctive quality of the human species. Because of this quality, although the birds may sing more beautifully than we do, only we, as far as we know, can write a history of music—or for that matter a history of birds. Unobjectionable though the general thesis may be, it becomes much more problematical when it is taken to mean, in Newman's words, "that Knowledge is, not merely a means to something beyond it, or the preliminary of certain arts into which it naturally resolves, but an end sufficient to rest in and to pursue for its own sake" (I.v.2).

In Newman's time, and not only in his time, this polemic against utilitarianism had a special edge because of the campaign to eliminate from the curriculum, also in the university, traditional fields of inquiry that could not be justified on the grounds of their usefulness. Between 1808 and 1811 the *Edinburgh Review* had fiercely lampooned the undergraduate curriculum at British universities as having lost touch with reality and therefore as not being able to prepare young men for the real world. As tends to happen at universities in any age from medieval Paris to modern America, alumni, faculty, and undergraduates all became embroiled in the controversy. The principal defender of Oxford education was Edward Copleston, Fellow of Oriel; Newman, who was elected to Oriel in 1822, admired Copleston "for the distinction which his talents bestowed on it, for the academical importance to which he raised it, for the generosity of spirit, the liberality of sentiment, and the kindness of heart, with which he adorned it" (I.vii.3). Whatever may have been his generosity of spirit, liberality of sentiment, and kindness of heart, Edward Copleston proved to be a formidable controversialist in his *Reply to the Calumnies of the Edinburgh Review*, issued in 1810 and celebrated in Oxford undergraduate doggerel:

Since the cold cutting gibes of that Northern Review
Have tormented and teased Uncle Toby and you,
I'm exceedingly happy in sending you down
A defence, which is making much noise in the town,
Of all our old learning and fame immemorial,
Which is said to be writ by a Fellow of Oriel.

Almost half a century later, Newman still felt the memory of that controversy keenly enough to employ it as the foil for his defense "of all our old learning," which is based on his definition of liberal knowledge: "That alone is liberal knowledge, which stands on its own pretensions, which is independent of sequel [that is, of consequences], expects no complement, refuses to be *informed* (as it is called) by any end, or absorbed into any art, in order duly to present itself to our contemplation" (I.v.4). As the German scientist Rudolf Fittig once put this principle, "Our establishments are establishments for teaching and research, independently of any application of their findings."

This definition does not imply, as many of its critics and even some of its defenders have occasionally supposed, that the liberal learning which is the university's reason for being must never produce anything useful or have any "sequel" or consequence; it means only that its pursuit is not to be justified principally on those grounds. Yet today it is necessary to sharpen, more than Newman did, the polemical point that utilitarianism is a threat to utility, and that therefore a rigid application of the utilitarian criterion could deprive the next generation of the very means it will need for the tasks that it will face, which will not be the tasks that this generation faces and which therefore cannot be dealt with by those particular instrumentalities that this generation has identified as "useful." I was nurtured, as were others of my generation, on the eleventh edition of the *Encyclopaedia Britannica*. Having gone on to serve as one of the editors for the fourteenth edition, I have frequently pointed out that the handsome morocco-bound double volumes of my father's set (which I still have and use) devote nine folio columns to the topic "Delian League" (by John Malcolm Mitchell, joint editor of Grote's *History of Greece*), and not quite two columns to the topic "Uranium." From the latter article, which is unsigned, it is clear, moreover, that there appeared to be no significant use for this "metallic chemical element." Nevertheless, it obviously possessed qualities that were so intriguing to basic scientific research that uranium deserved to be investigated as an object of interest in its own right. As a reminder of those qualities, the article "Relativity" in the expanded version of the eleventh edition spoke about the revolutionary insights into the relation between mass and energy that had come out of recent scientific study, above all through the researches of Albert Einstein, but the investigation still had a long way to go. It is no exaggeration to say that the practical consequences of those investigations of uranium and of relativity have remade the world. It is worthwhile to contemplate the damage both to "knowledge its own end" and to the utility of knowledge if the editors of the old *Britannica* or their counterparts in the universities had been successful in eliminating "Uranium" from the encyclopedia and from the laboratory, or, for that matter, if their modern counterparts *are* successful in eliminating "Delian League" from the classroom and the library. Behind this observation, which as it is formulated could sound utilitarian, there does stand a fundamental and nonutilitarian perspective, which is informed as well by a definition of knowledge on the basis of a set of distinctions: between knowledge and information; between knowledge and wisdom; between knowledge and intuition; and between knowledge and faith. This set of distinctions is not derived directly from Newman, but they are fundamentally congenial to his outlook.

It is difficult to get anywhere in any discussion of knowledge, whether as an end in itself or as a means to some other end, without introducing the distinction between knowledge and information. Thus a dictionary of synonyms—and does a dictionary contain knowledge or information?—explains that whereas *information* often "suggests no more than a collection of data or facts either discrete or integrated into a body of knowledge," the term *knowledge* "applies not only to a body of facts gathered by study, investigation, observation, or experience but also to a body of ideas acquired by inference from such facts or accepted on good grounds as truth." When pressed to explain the distinction, some discriminating speakers of English have suggested that the telephone directory contains information but the encyclopedia contains knowledge—although, at least when it comes to the classified pages, the task of organizing information in the telephone directory does call for a measure of reflection and sophistication about categories that goes well beyond such a simplistic distinction. The distinction between knowledge and information, as applied both to the research and to the teaching of the university, does seem to imply that the accumulation of information through research and the transmission of information through teaching are not adequate to define the mission of the university, which must, in its teaching but also in its research, press beyond information to knowledge. Another way to put the distinction—which can be helpful but may also be misleading—is to say that information tells us the What and knowledge tells us the How.

All of that leaves, of course, the Why, which, ever since the Hebrew Bible and the Greek thinkers, has been the province of wisdom. Newman usually refers to this as "philosophy," meaning by that term not exclusively what is done by professional philosophers or by professors in an academic department of philosophy, but "a science of sciences" charged with "the comprehension of the bearings of one science on another, and the use of each to each, and the location and limitation and adjustment and due appreciation of them all, one with another" (I.iii.4). Significantly, he does not call this activity "theology," despite his view that theology is indispensable to the university as a whole as well as to each of the disciplines of knowledge (or, as Newman calls them, "sciences," meaning more than simply the natural sciences). He does not even call it "natural theology," a term he sometimes invokes in a positive sense (I.iii.10). The distinction between knowledge and wisdom in relation to the learning of the university has engaged critical and reflective minds in all ages, and at no time more than in Newman's nineteenth century. The most universal mind of that age opened his most universal work with critical reflection on that issue, as the aged philosopher Faust recalls having traversed all four of the traditional faculties of the university but not having found the answer to his quest for wisdom in any of them:

I've studied now Philosophy
And Jurisprudence, Medicine,—
And even, alas! Theology,—
From end to end, with labor keen;
And here, poor fool! with all my lore
I stand, no wiser then before:
I'm Magister—yes, Doctor—hight,
And straight or cross-wise, wrong or right,
These ten years long, with many woes,
I've led my scholars by the nose,—
And see, that nothing can be known!
That knowledge cuts me to the bone.

Doctor Faust's discovery that knowledge defined as university erudition is fundamentally different from wisdom as a treasure that no amount of learning can guarantee represents a form of "knowledge" in itself, but one that cuts him to the bone.

It also cuts to the bone of the university's commitment to knowledge. For it would be misleading in the extreme either to claim that the university's pursuit of knowledge through research and instruction is the royal road to wisdom or, in contrast, to claim that when it does lead to wisdom it is being untrue to itself. Even apart from the cumulative experience that comes from sitting through university faculty meetings or chairing them, there is anecdotal evidence in abundance to corroborate a sharp distinction between knowledge and wisdom. The university depends for its integrity on various kinds of testing, not only of students but also of professors. What it tests for can, indeed must, go beyond information to knowledge, to the classification and correlation of the information that is known into at least preliminary patterns of meaning, lines of development and influence, forms of analogy and contrast. All of this still comes under the heading of knowledge, as more than information yet less than wisdom. Such knowledge does mark the boundaries of what the university has the absolute right to expect from its students and, conversely, what the students have the absolute right to expect from the university and its faculty. In that sense, Newman's (and Cicero's, and Aristotle's) principle that knowledge is an end in itself defines and limits the university's character. This implies that a scholar, whether junior or senior, may possess in outstanding measure a knowledge that transcends information and yet may at the same time not have, or at any rate not manifest, a wisdom that transcends knowledge.

Nevertheless, after even a bit of recollection anyone would be obliged to affirm that some of those to whom the term *wisdom* most appropriately belongs have been at the same time scholars of great learning, and moreover that their wisdom has been grounded in their erudition. The so-called lessons of history are by no means obvious or simple, and there is no direct means of verification by which they can be credited or discredited; yet the essays of reflection in which historians like Lord Acton or Sir Isaiah Berlin have pondered their accumulated experience of the past stand as monuments of wisdom. The same would be true of Alfred North Whitehead among physicists, or of Joseph Schumpeter among economists, or for that matter of mentors and colleagues whom, as the prayer says, each of us could name in our hearts. When such wisdom appears, it is to be welcomed and cherished, but it would not be right to vote a promotion, much less a degree, up or down on the basis of its presence or absence: to decide that vote, we look for knowledge, and knowledge as an end in itself, not as a means to utility and not even as a means to wisdom. It also bears mentioning that the university is by no means the natural habitat of wisdom; for, in Newman's words, "Works of genius fall under no art; heroic minds come under no rule; a University is not a birthplace of poets or of immortal authors, of founders of schools, leaders of colonies, or conquerors of nations. It does not promise a generation of Aristotles or Newtons, of Napoleons or Washingtons, of Raphaels or Shakespeares, though such miracles of nature it has before now contained within its precincts" (I.vii.10). And it still does contain them within its precincts.

The validity and adequacy of the criterion of knowledge as its own end have, however, been attacked from quite another quarter as well, and particularly in recent times. An overemphasis on intellectual knowledge, many today would charge, has made the university sterile and two-dimensional, depriving it, and human society through it, of the depth dimension that comes from other ways of knowing, especially ways of knowing that would be regarded as instinctive or intuitive or poetic. Newman once observed, a bit wistfully: "Alas! what are we doing all through life, both as a necessity and as a duty, but unlearning the world's poetry, and attaining to its prose! This is our education, as boys and as men, in the action of life, and in the closet or library; in our affections, in our aims, in our hopes, and in our memories. And in like manner it is the education of our intellect" (II.iv.1). But, to quote the most eloquent statement of the contrary position, "The heart has its reasons which reason knows nothing of." As applied to the university, this criticism has now acquired several settings within the university curriculum itself. Sometimes it concerns itself with the place of the arts in human life and culture, for which the conventional tools of scholarly knowledge have proved inadequate. Until Adolf Hitler in his blindness made a gift to American scholarship of such scholars as Erwin Panofsky, the history of art as a discipline was struggling to be born in the American university. Much of the pioneer work was done by the Andrew W. Mellon Lectures in the Fine Arts at the National Gallery of Art, which were inaugurated by a Thomist and rationalist who had an antenna tuned in many directions, Jacques Maritain. As a result of the changes of the last half-century, no cultural historian or social historian or intellectual historian today would dare to ignore the place of the arts, and therefore the place of the methodology of the art historians. That methodology, as Maritain already made clear in his Mellon Lectures, *Creative Intuition in Art and Poetry* published in 1952, practices its rationality so thoroughly as to go beyond reason in recognizing the irreplaceable function of intuition and imagination.

This critique can also come from those who have studied other cultures, finding in their ways of knowing a directness, depth, and spontaneity that, they charge, cannot be squeezed into the categories of Western, Hellenic-Germanic intellection. It has sought scientific validation by reference to the physiology of the brain, in which, it was discovered as late as 1863, the two hemispheres function differently and therefore achieve at least two different kinds of "knowledge," both of which are equally entitled to be called knowledge. Above all, of course, the critique has invoked the authority of Sigmund Freud, who, as a "conquistador" (to use his own term for himself), explored the hidden workings of the subconscious and the unconscious, with which reason can only partially come to terms. As history of art and history of music, as anthropology, as neuroscience, and as psychiatry and psychoanalysis, these four perspectives all hold a distinguished place in university research and teaching today across a spectrum of departments and schools, and all of them would in one way or another raise questions about the undue preoccupation of the traditional university curriculum with abstract knowledge, with analysis, ultimately with reasoning as an end in itself. All of these fields, however, have made their point, at any rate within the university, by means of analysis, reasoning, and abstract knowledge. That "apparent paradox" has been well stated in a recent observation by Freud's biographer: "Freud, who more than any other psychologist concentrated on the workings of unreason, detecting sexual motives and death wishes behind the masks of polite manners and untroubled affection, was one of the great rationalists of the modern age. He waded into the sewers of irrationality not to wallow in them, but to clean them out." Similar paradoxes could, of course, be found in the scholarship of art historians, anthropologists, and neuroscientists. Their discoveries have profoundly changed the very definition of knowledge, not by spurning analysis, intellection, and reasoning, but by applying them, inductively as well as deductively, to new and hitherto unexplored fields—which is precisely what the university has the task of doing.

There is a somewhat analogous paradox in the relation between knowledge and faith, as this concerns the university. To Newman, this was the most important of all these distinctions, not only for the life of the university and for the life of the mind, but for the life of the soul and for human life as such. Like many believing scholars before and since, he was simultaneously engaged in balancing against each other two seemingly contradictory assignments: insisting against the secularists that "University teaching without Theology is simply unphilosophical [and that] Theology has at least as good a right to claim a place there as Astronomy" (I.ii.9) while defending the integrity of the university as such against the encroachments of the ecclesiastics who could not understand that, fundamentally and in its essence, "it is not a Convent, it is not a Seminary; it is a place to fit men of the world for the world" (I.ix.8). In that two-front battle, the distinction between knowledge and faith was fundamental. It was a distinction, not an identity; but it was also a distinction, not a separation. It is, however, essential to transfer this issue to another venue from the one in which Newman was discussing it; for while it was his assignment then and there to present the rationale for a university that was Catholic and Irish (and, in so doing, to define the university), the assignment of reexamining the idea of the university here and now needs to concentrate on defining what a university is as such. For that assignment, too, the distinction between knowledge and faith has several far-reaching implications.

When the distinction between knowledge and faith, or for that matter the separation between church and state, is interpreted as a justification for a professed "knowledge" about human life and society, about human history and culture, that is as ignorant about the faith-dimension as is much of the current scholarship of humanists and social scientists in many universities, in the Soviet Union and in Western Europe and in the United States, such knowledge is fundamentally deficient—deficient as knowledge and as scholarship, completely apart from what it may or may not mean for the life of faith. This may put professors of English into an enviable position pedagogically, of being able to teach Milton's *Paradise Lost* to students who do not know how the story comes out, and therefore wait in suspense to see whether Adam and Eve eat the apple. But such reductionism can easily distort the persons, societies, and texts with which it deals by requiring them to conform to its own inability to imagine that anyone could ever have really believed any of this, and therefore to its assumption there must be some other explanation. By its very nature, of course, the knowledge and scholarly study of faith can be not only controversial but contagious: it can lead lifelong believers to surrender cherished tenets of faith, or it can engage students existentially in such a way that, having come to observe and criticize, they remain to pray. The university must not pretend that either of these outcomes cannot happen within its walls; nor should it, in its care for its members as human beings, dismiss such concerns as trivial. But for the pursuit of knowledge as an end in itself, the university is at the very least obliged to pay attention also to the knowledge of this dimension of its subject matter.

In addition to the clarifications of Newman's thesis about "knowledge its own end" that can come from these several distinctions, there are as well a number of equally fundamental questions about the future of the university that come from a critical reexamination of Newman. As good a place as any to begin that reexamination is with two gloomy comments from his book. One was made in an address of 1858: "This is that barren mockery of knowledge which comes of . . . mere acquaintance with reviews, magazines, newspapers, and other literature of the day, which, however able and valuable in itself, is not the instrument of intellectual education" (II.ix.7). The other appears in the final paragraph of his preface to *The Idea of a University*:

> One other remark suggests itself, which is the last I shall think it necessary to make. The authority, which in former times was lodged in Universities, now resides in very great measure in that literary world, as it is called [or, as we would call it today, the world of journalism]. . . . This is not satisfactory, if, as no one can deny, its teaching be so offhand, so ambitious, so changeable . . . [and if its writers] can give no better guarantee for the philosophical truth of their principles than their popularity at the moment, and their happy conformity in ethical character to the age which admires them (I.pr.).

Almost a century and a half later, the situation Newman lamented has deteriorated still further, with the result that we would have to paraphrase him to say that "the authority, which in former times was lodged in universities and then was transferred to newspapers as the successors to universities, now resides in very great measure in the nonliterary world of television."

Newman's preface, which closes with that prophecy, opens with his root definition: "The view taken of a University in these Discourses is the following:—That it is a place of *teaching* universal knowledge." As breathtaking a statement of the scope of the university's task as this is, with that language about "universal" knowledge, it does need to be understood on Newman's own terms. Already in 1852—or, as a modern would be tempted to put it, even in 1852—the sheer quantity of information available in the civilized world was so formidable as to be utterly daunting, and it would be fatuous to read Newman's definition of "universal knowledge" as either an assignment or a promise or a claim. Before the preface is finished, he has made clear that he does not have in mind producing scholars "who can treat, where it is necessary, *de omni scibili,*" on every subject in the world and perhaps beyond this world. Yet even when Newman's term "universal knowledge" has been relieved of that burden, the differences in this respect between the university of the past and the university of the present and future can hardly be exaggerated. The realities of knowledge as research and teaching in the university compel every university to make difficult choices, and to do so repeatedly, about which disciplines to include—and which to exclude—from within universal knowledge. Such choices, however, dare not be left any longer to the capricious processes of decision-making that are characteristic of the university in many lands. Universal knowledge as an ideal is, obviously, not a realistic goal for any one university, but it is in considerable measure realistic as a goal for the university community worldwide. That choice will call repeatedly for the academic equivalent of national and international summit conferences of university educators, involving the allocation of fields of knowledge, periods of history, laboratory instrumentation, and library resources—ultimately, perhaps, even of faculty. Otherwise, the world of scholarship could wake up some cold morning to find that no one is collecting materials or doing research or teaching courses in ancient Egyptian mathematics or in the dialects of Galicia. If approached in this rational manner, universal knowledge can and must remain an ideal for the university of the future.

In at least one respect these ideals of "universal knowledge" and "knowledge as its own end" do seem to have become more realistic rather than less realistic since Newman: the impact of technology, and above all of the computer, on university research and teaching. As Alfred North Whitehead once observed, "Throughout the Hellenic and Hellenistic Roman civilizations—those civilizations which we term 'classical'—it was universally assumed that a large slave population was required to perform services which were unworthy to engage the activities of a fully civilized man." It is noteworthy that, without always being spoken in that context, this universal assumption also underlay the classical definitions of liberal knowledge cited earlier. The Aristotle who at the opening of the *Metaphysics* declared that "All men by nature desire to know," asserted near the opening of the *Politics:* "The one who can foresee by the exercise of mind is by nature intended to be lord and master, and the one who can with his body give effect to such foresight is a subject, and by nature a slave." Newman certainly cannot in any way be read as an apologist for slavery. Indeed, the British campaign for the abolition of slavery was led by the great Evangelical Anglican lay theologian William Wilberforce, whose son Robert Isaac was, as Newman says in the *Apologia pro Vita Sua,* his "intimate and affectionate" friend at Oriel College, eventually following him in 1854 into the communion of the Roman Catholic church. Just as certainly, however, the fifth discourse of *The Idea of a University,* "Knowledge Its Own End," does proceed on the basis of an ideal of education that to a superficial reading may seem to be related, if not to a slave structure, then at any rate to a class structure. "You see, then, here are two methods of Education," Newman writes there. He might have said instead, "here are two classes"; for he continues, "the end of the one is to be philosophical, of the other to be mechanical." That impression is substantiated when the paragraph concludes: "Not to know the relative disposition of things is the state *of slaves or children;* to have mapped out the Universe is the boast, or at least the ambition, of Philosophy" (I.v.6). As chapter 14 will suggest, however, Newman's concrete plans and program for the Catholic University of Ireland looked to "the extension of knowledge among those classes in society" (II.ix.4) to which educational opportunity had previously been denied, as "the one remarkable ground of promise in the future" (II.ix.3). The more recent evolution of technology in the service of scholarship does carry the promise of instruments that can, to repeat Whitehead's words about slaves, "perform services which were unworthy to engage the activities of a fully civilized man." Among other benefits, the arrival of that technology, which Robert Maynard Hutchins before the age of the computer described as "the substitution of machines for slaves," has raised with new force the distinction between knowledge and information mentioned earlier, and if properly handled it can assist the university in the evaluation of knowledge as an end that has been attained by going through information but beyond it.

But anyone who grew up, as I did, reading Aldous Huxley's *Brave New World,* published in 1932, and who then in adulthood read and reread George Orwell's *Nineteen Eighty-four,* published in 1949, may be pardoned for a certain amount of skepticism about such promises, which often seem not to have factored Original Sin and the Fall into their calculations. There is no guarantee that the university will not, as it has all too often in the past, permit itself to be corrupted also in its cultivation of this technology. To be specific, the principle at the heart of this chapter and of Newman's fifth discourse, "Knowledge Its Own End," is liable to such corruption. After quoting the opening discussions both of Aristotle's *Metaphysics* and of his *Politics*, it may be helpful to recall the opening discussion of the *Nicomachean Ethics,* which is devoted to means and ends: "If, then, there is some end of the things we do, which we desire for its own sake (everything else being desired for the sake of this), and if we do not choose everything for the sake of something else . . . clearly this [end] must be the good and the chief good." But if knowledge is defined as this chief good and end in itself, "everything else being desired for the sake of this," the moral consequences can be frightening. Scholars in all fields, myself included, have often defined the purpose of research as the single-minded pursuit of truth at any price, or almost any price, and have cited the principle of knowledge its own end in justification. But during the twentieth century—partly, it is obvious, as a consequence of the Holocaust, but also as a consequence of more general reflection—it has become clear to all of us that such a definition is both simplistic and dangerous, leading, as it can, to the torture or the pharmacological manipulation of witnesses in order to obtain accurate "knowledge." The principle of knowledge its own end, then, must be integrated with a larger and more comprehensive set of first principles, which can be summarized under the heading (likewise Aristotelian) of "the intellectual virtues."

5

THE IMPERIAL INTELLECT
AND ITS VIRTUES

One of Newman's most arresting terms for the university is "the philosophy of an *imperial intellect*," which, he warned, did not require one discipline, such as theology, to lord it over the others, but rather mandated
"religious writers, jurists, economists, physiologists, chemists, geologists,
and historians, to go on quietly, and in a neighbourly way, in their own
respective lines of speculation, research, and experiment" (II.viii.3–4).
And if there was an "imperial intellect," there also had to be (to borrow
Aristotle's term) *"intellectual virtues."* John Henry Newman was both the
author of *The Idea of a University* and, in the words of the Lutheran
archbishop of Uppsala, Nathan Söderblom, writing in 1910, "England's
outstanding theologian and Catholicism's—at least besides Leo XIII—
most significant personality in the last century." As such, Newman was
acutely conscious of what he called, in the titles of the third and fourth
discourses of *The Idea of a University,* the "bearing of theology on other
knowledge" and the "bearing of other knowledge on theology," but no less
conscious of the distinction between theology and other knowledge.

The most fundamental implication of his definition of the university,
"that it is a place of teaching universal knowledge," was, as he himself said
on offering the definition, "that its object is . . . intellectual, not moral"
(I.pr.). A tutor at the Catholic University of Ireland, according to its Rules
and Regulations, was to be responsible for "certainly the moral, but more
directly the intellectual care of his pupils." In describing how students "are
sure to learn one from another, even if there be no one to teach them," he
quickly added the explanation: "I am not taking into account moral or
religious considerations" (I.vi.9). Similarly, in attacking an idea of the
university under which "the moral and mental sciences are to have no
professorial chairs," he immediately defended himself strenuously against
the charge that he was "supposing that the principles of Theology and
Psychology are the same" (I.iii.5–6). Even when he did come to discuss

such principles of theology in his *Grammar of Assent* of 1870, moreover, the distinction "intellectual, not moral" from *The Idea of a University* reappeared. Examining the nature of moral duty on the basis of the Aristotelian concept of *phronesis,* or judgment, he applied that same distinction, concluding that "in this respect . . . the law of truth differs from the law of duty, that duties change, but truths never." That is the philosophical context within his system for the axiom that the university "is not a Convent, it is not a Seminary" (I.ix.8).

At the same time he was well aware that although "Academical Institutions (as I have been so long engaged in showing) are in their very nature directed to social, national, temporal objects in the first instance," nevertheless, "if they deserve the name of University at all," it was to be expected that they "of necessity have some one formal and definite ethical character, good or bad, and do of a certainty imprint that character on the individuals who direct and who frequent them" (I.ix.2). Although the ancestors of the modern university are multiple and complex, including as they do the seats of learning in many ancient cultures, there is no denying that the university has deep roots also in the monastery and the church. Indeed, most historians would look to the Catholic Middle Ages as, in Newman's phrase, "the very age of Universities" (II.viii.5). The medieval university was the foundation of the university as we know it, and many of the most eminent modern universities—Bologna, Oxford, and Prague, among others—can trace an unbroken, or almost unbroken, continuity to the Middle Ages, from which large parts of the customs (and costumes) and prerogatives of the modern university are also derived. One has only to witness an academic convocation for the conferral of degrees to be reminded in countless large and small ways how much the church has been the mother of the university. Newman's ninth discourse, "Duties of the Church Towards Knowledge," draws upon the accumulated memory shared by the university and the church. At times the university occupied a decisive place in the life and polity of the church. During the stormy trials of fifteenth-century schism and heresy, with the papacy and the religious orders in disarray, the universities of the church, above all the University of Paris, which Newman hails as "the glory of the middle ages" (I.i.7), filled at least part of the vacuum, becoming, under the leadership of Pierre D'Ailly and Jean Gerson, almost a kind of corporate pope. John Wycliffe at Oxford, Jan Hus at Prague, and Martin Luther at Wittenberg all addressed the church and called it to account from within the privileged sanctuary of the university, whose academic freedom and rights provided them with at least some protection against both church and state.

Eventually, of course, the requirements of academic freedom clashed with ecclesiastical authority so repeatedly and so fundamentally that a declaration of educational independence was called for. Such declarations came at various times over a period of many centuries in Europe and North America, by a process that John S. Whitehead has called "the separation of college and state." There would be considerable merit to the thesis that the history of the process of secularization in the West can be traced more thoroughly through the history of education than through that of any other area of society (except perhaps family life). Not only did the process of separation occur at different times in different lands and even in different institutions within the same land, but it moved at different speeds and achieved different degrees of thoroughness. For example, in the system of some universities all the trustees and the chief executive officer were clergymen at first; then the clergy members became a simple majority; then they were a minority; and finally, at many places, they disappeared altogether. The movement was not all in the same direction, for the church has continued to maintain some of its universities and to found many others, as Newman's experience in Dublin documents. But Newman's experience and the classic on university education that came out of that experience also demonstrate the shift that occurred when the very nature of the university, whatever its origins, came to be defined by its nonecclesiastical embodiments, to which in one way or another the church's universities had to accommodate themselves. As Newman acknowledged, it was Anglican educators at Oxford "under the shadow of whose name I once lived" when he himself was an Anglican, but "by whose doctrine I am now profiting" in his discourses as a Roman Catholic for the Catholic University of Ireland (I.vii.3).

A basic reason for that shift is the sheer quantity and quality of those universities that do not look to the church for their certification, or do not look to it any longer; rather, the church looks to them in the modern era, just as it did in the ancient era. It probably sounds less generous than it is intended to be when Newman acknowledges that "in the early ages the Church allowed her children to attend the heathen schools for the acquisition of secular accomplishments" and that "the gravest Fathers [of the church] recommended for Christian youth the use of pagan masters" (I.i.3). But he makes this acknowledgment in order to justify his applying to the Catholic University of Ireland intellectual norms that are derived from the experience and practice of non-Catholic, that is, "Protestant" and Anglican—and therefore, in his present judgment, functionally secular—universities, above all of Oxford. In one academic discipline after another, such norms can be traced to origins and inspirations that arose within the communities of Jewish and Christian humanism but that are now primarily the concern of secular scholarship. A striking example is textual criticism, the science (or art) of comparing readings that come from manuscripts and other evidence to determine the best possible "authoritative" text of some work. The preparation of critical scholarly editions of writers ancient and modern, to which university presses have made and continue to make such a monumental and abiding contribution, depends for its validity on the rigorous and sophisticated application of the techniques of textual criticism, which are by no means as simple and commonsensical as the lay reader would imagine. But most of the editors and other philological scholars who use these techniques to publish the works of poets and thinkers may not even be aware that many, perhaps most, of them were developed in confronting the overwhelming welter of textual evidence with which editors of the New Testament, going back to Erasmus of Rotterdam in the sixteenth century and even to Origen of Alexandria in the third, have to deal; and these Christian textual critics of New Testament manuscripts, in turn, were adapting philological methods that had originally been developed to cope with textual problems in Homer and the Greek classics.

As a consequence of this process of secularization, the very right of religious communities to found and maintain universities has often been questioned in various lands. Whatever other ideological and political sources there may be for this opposition, it also rests on an intellectual assumption. The history of religious polemics—and of antireligious polemics—shows that it is always easier to recognize what Whitehead calls "assumptions [which] appear so obvious that people do not know what they are assuming because no other way of putting things has ever occurred to them" in the positions of others than in one's own position. With a naïveté matching that of many believers, the secularist critics of religious belief have sometimes proceeded as though assumptions a priori that cannot be proven were exclusively the property of believers, and therefore as if their scholarship and their university were free of presuppositions. On the basis of such a perspective, for example, one prominent twentieth-century American scholar and university professor—and he was probably not alone—did not find it inconsistent to vote down a distinguished candidate for an appointment in theology on the grounds that, being a Roman Catholic priest, he would not be free to carry out his scholarly responsibilities because he was under authority, and subsequently to vote affirmatively to appoint another distinguished scholar who was a Marxist to a professorship in political science.

In spite of such incidents and the ideological confusion they manifest, it is an unjustifiable capitulation to intellectual and moral relativism to conclude, as many contemporaries seem to have done, that a consensus about what seem almost unavoidably to be called "values" is beyond our grasp, and therefore that the university cannot draw on any such consensus to shape the decisions that affect its common life. On the contrary, the methodology of teasing out such presuppositions and values from the concrete life of the university in today's world, and of then asking whether they are defensible, carries the promise of transcending such cynicism and relativism and of defining a set of "intellectual virtues." Also when speaking about such virtues, Aristotle was for Newman "the oracle of nature and of truth" (I.v.5). Whether or not Newman himself held to it consistently in his later discourses, the principle necessarily underlying a catalog of intellectual virtues is a doctrine "of nature and of truth" rather than a doctrine "of revelation and of truth." The virtues therefore are based upon the principle voiced at the beginning of the first discourse: that they "are attainable . . . by the mere experience of life" and "do not come simply of theology"; and "therefore, though true, and just, and good in themselves, they imply nothing whatever as to the religious profession of those who maintain them." Therefore "it is," Newman concludes, "natural to expect this from the very circumstance that the philosophy of Education is founded on truths in the natural order" (I.i.2). In clarifying the imperial intellect and its virtues, it may be helpful, in addition to repeating Newman's distinction between "the law of truth" and "the law of duty," to adapt a distinction from classic jurisprudence, which makes the "law of persons" a distinct category, but to speak first about a corresponding "law of studies."

It should perhaps go without saying, but unfortunately the history of the university past and present makes it all too obvious that it does not, that the two fundamental intellectual virtues in the "law of studies" are free inquiry and intellectual honesty. The freedom of inquiry is an intellectual value upon which the life of the university as a center of research and teaching depends. But it is both intellectually and politically dangerous simply to identify it, as its latter-day defenders sometimes do, as a corollary derived from the right of free speech guaranteed by the First Amendment of the Constitution of the United States and by equivalent political constitutions in other states; for the free inquiry of the university is essential to it also, perhaps even especially, in the tyrannies where no such constitutional guarantee exists. In a paradoxical way one could argue that the freedom of scholarly inquiry, like the freedom of artistic expression, has special importance for such political orders, as a means both of relieving the internal pressures in the society and of protecting the regime from the fatal disease of self-deception. Philosophically, of course, the right of free speech in the several constitutions and the virtue of free inquiry in the university share a common foundation, in a doctrine of the worth of the human being and therefore of respect for the integrity of the human person both in the society at large and in the academy. But the justification for the freedom is different in the two cases, as becomes evident also from the definition of its scope and limits. To invoke the dictum of Justice Oliver Wendell Holmes, Jr., "the most stringent protection of free speech would not protect a man in falsely shouting fire in a theater, and causing panic." Such protection does not extend to shouting fire in a university theater any more than it does to doing so in a Broadway theater; but free speech does not apply to whispering answers to a classmate during an examination either, because it negates the very processes and principles on which the examination is based and to which the student has freely submitted by freely entering the university and then by freely taking the examination.

Therefore, in a special way that does not have a simple and direct corollary in civil society except perhaps for the laws of libel and slander, the "law of studies" in the academy does link free inquiry inseparably with intellectual honesty. There appears to be no means of determining historically and statistically whether the popular impression is correct that the incidence of scholarly and scientific fraud has risen in recent years. Nor is it possible to apportion the blame for that increase, if any, among such factors as the pressure generated within the university for scholars to produce, the demand for tangible results originating from public and private funding agencies, the competition among researchers for positions and for grant support, and the reduced standards of personal honesty and integrity that some observers claim to be able to discern in modern Western society at large. The awareness that scholarly fraud undermines the foundations of the university in a manner and to a degree that even the most heinous and disgusting political libel does not undermine the foundations of the state has made, or should make, the academic community eternally vigilant against it. Because knowledge is its own end for the university quite apart from its utility, such vigilance is necessary even when the falsification of the results of research does not lead, as it sometimes does, to the production of medicines or the enactment of social policies that will do great harm. With unforgettable vividness, as the deranged widow of the perpetrator of an academic fraud screams out, "He told a lie about someone else who was dead and dust hundreds of years ago. Nobody was the worse for that. Was a dirty bit of paper more important than all our lives and happiness?" the denouement of *Gaudy Night* has depicted the tragic human consequences that the university's seeming pettifoggery in insisting upon scholarly honesty can bring on. No one should blandly voice such principles without being conscious of those potential consequences. Yet without that insistence on scholarly integrity the university will not only damage itself, it will destroy itself; and the question must be asked whether in the future that is now being created by modern social and technological forces the university will have the resources, including the moral resources, to continue to balance free inquiry and intellectual honesty.

A third intellectual virtue is a sustained, if now significantly chastened, trust in rationality and its processes. For a variety of reasons already reviewed, such a trust in rationality has been challenged, not only in the general society but specifically in the academy, by an awareness of its fallibility and limitations. It seems imperative for the university to develop a deepening appreciation for other ways of knowing and thinking, which cannot be accommodated easily to the criteria of Enlightenment rationalism. The trust in reason has traditionally been associated as a first principle with a trust in the consistency of the world, just as the rejection of reason in favor of a reliance on the irrational can be associated with a recognition of the dominance of randomness in the universe. These associations are not at all simple, however, as is evident from a recent book that combines meticulous examination of the Burgess Shale and of its fossil remains with a spirited rejection of rational patterns and of any teleology or "progress" in the history of evolution. Nevertheless, as the methodology of that book also demonstrates, research in any field of knowledge is still predicated on the assumption that it could be authenticated through repetition by any other trained investigator with access to the same data. It may have been true of George Eliot's Edward Casaubon, as was said of him, that "he dreams footnotes." But the footnote as an artifact is the very opposite of the dream: it is eminently public while the dream is ineluctably private; in Freud's classic phrase, "dreams are a product of the dreamer's own mind." But the footnote invites reenactment and points beyond itself, and beyond the subject, to a source or text or body of data that can be shared and can presumably be reinterpreted through a challenge to the interpretation that has been offered. Behind this epistemological assumption is the even more basic metaphysical assumption or article of faith that this is how the universe itself is constructed: in Whitehead's words, "the instinctive faith that there is an Order of Nature which can be traced in every detailed occurrence." That body of assumptions has obvious and direct moral implications for free inquiry and for intellectual honesty.

It also implies the moral obligation to convey the results of research to others. There is an imperative of communicating that corresponds to the indicative of knowing. As chapter 12 will argue, the university as an institution as well its individual members both junior and senior stand under this obligation, and the institution and the individuals have the collegial duty of enforcing it upon themselves and upon one another. Research, teaching, and publication are ultimately inseparable for the university, because they are all functions of this single obligation. It may be true that I publish the results of my research in articles and books in order to have my peers review and correct the results, while I publish them in classroom lectures and seminars in order to have my students learn about them; but concretely that distinction repeatedly breaks down in both directions. The moral obligation to convey the results of research to others has one other exceedingly important implication for the university: that, at any rate in principle, both the results of university research and the data on which it is based should be public, or at the very least should be accessible to those who are qualified to evaluate them. Some of the most difficult academic and political choices faced by the university continue to be those dealing with classified research, a category that has to be broadened to encompass the delicacy of personal data, whether locked in documents and papers in the library or coded in patient files. Modern technologies of information retrieval make these problems infinitely more complex for the modern university, but they do not invalidate the fundamental principles of communication and of public verifiability.

By its insistence on the communication of the results of research, the university likewise proclaims the intellectual virtue of affirming the continuity of the intellectual and scholarly life, upon which each generation builds and to which it contributes in turn. The architectural solidity of Academic Gothic is in some ways a facade, not only because the future of the university depends so vitally on the repair and rehabilitation of the physical plant, at an estimated total cost for American universities alone that will be astronomical, but because, even more fundamentally, the continuity with the past and the continuity into the future symbolized by all that granite can in fact be easily lost. Those who have rebelled against the continuity as a repressive authority have often discovered, to their dismay, that it is held together by tissues that are as fragile, and as tough, as the intellectual virtues being described here. But to an extent that each new generation of researchers finds it difficult to comprehend, all of us are, as the traditional phrase has it, dwarfs standing on the shoulders of giants—a phrase that, as the delightful researches of Robert Merton into its history have shown, is itself a documentation of the very principle it enunciates. The debt and the continuity can be recognized more easily in some disciplines than in others. Professors of philosophy in the university of the twenty-first century will still have to deal with Plato and Aristotle, not as museum pieces but as teachers and colleagues. In the sciences it is possible to suppose that earlier work is largely the dead hand of the past, but historians of science have been probing beneath the surface of research in the physical and biological sciences to trace the lines of continuity not only from teacher to teacher but from generation to generation and even from century to century.

Indeed, the history of science as a young but vibrant scholarly discipline provides considerable justification for the oxymoron that scientific discontinuity can sometimes be convincing evidence for scientific continuity. One of the figures from the history of science to whom fundamental research has been addressed in the past few decades is Galileo. As Newman's uncomfortable references to him make clear (II.viii.6; I.ix.3), he has long stood as a symbol of the virtues of free inquiry and intellectual honesty, and of intellectual and moral courage, for his refusal to capitulate to the authority of the Inquisition. None of that is taken away by the discovery of just how profound his continuities with earlier centuries were. That applies even to the medieval scholasticism from which he has been seen as diverging in a fundamental way, when in fact he was and continued to be, philosophically and theologically, a pupil of the Dominican scientific tradition represented by Thomas Aquinas and Albertus Magnus. The common teacher of Thomas Aquinas and Albertus Magnus, but also of Galileo, was Aristotle. When Galileo declared, on the basis of his observations through the telescope, that the earth moves around the sun, he was opposing the authority of the results of Aristotle's observations (without a telescope) as set forth especially in the *Physics*. But with his telescope he was doing in his own time what Aristotle had done in his: collecting the most complete and most accurate data available and attempting to make rational sense of them. Can anyone imagine, Galileo was arguing, that if Aristotle had had access to a telescope, he would have refused to use it—this painstaking scientist whose patron assembled for him a vast collection of biological specimens for observation and research? Who, then, was affirming the continuity of scholarship the more faithfully, those who took the results of Aristotle's studies as unquestionable authority or the one who picked up Aristotle's method where he had left off and came to divergent results?

In the "law of studies" there is one other intellectual virtue that pertains as well to the "law of persons." It has never been completely absent from the life of the university, but the university is now finding new ways of applying it ever more creatively: the principle that the whole world and all of humanity are the only appropriate ultimate context of scholarship. The fourth movement of Beethoven's *Ninth Symphony*, as one of the noblest expressions of the humanistic and cosmopolitan tradition, has become virtually an anthem of that principle, a new and more authentic *Internationale*. The affirmation of the unity of the human race is, for the university and its scholars, both an ideal and a fact: a fact without which, as that kind of ultimate context, research into this or that particular and local phenomenon is fatally skewed; and an ideal that cannot be realized without just such research into this or that particular and local phenomenon. The relation between those two poles of the one truth has often been ignored on both (or the several) sides of the arguments about the place of "Western civilization" in the university curriculum. But the ancient Greeks and ancient Hebrews, for all their annoying ethnocentrisms, knew both poles very well, and they have taught them to all of us, including both the champions and the critics of "Western civilization."

Yet as a table of intellectual virtues for the university, the public law of studies is incomplete and distorted without some attention to a corresponding private law of persons, to what William DeVane called the university's duty "to correct the mass tendency and to make our graduates real three-dimensional persons of wisdom, individuality, and conscience." Much of this is not confined to the university nor even distinctive of it, but pertains to personal ethics in general, and is thus not as germane to our assignment. Nevertheless, it is clear what happens to the morality of research if the personal dimension is ignored. This was dramatized by the case of the Nazi doctors during the Holocaust, but in less forceful ways it could probably be documented from the inner history of any university. If the pretensions of the university to be a free and responsible community are not to be a mockery, it must constantly reaffirm and reapply the distinction between the scholar and the scholarship. The pursuit of scholarly excellence, on which the very future of the university quite literally depends, requires the continuous and unsparing evaluation and criticism of scholarship, one's own and that of others. But it is not only in academic novels that this pursuit has been invoked to justify bullying and exploitation. If modern studies of personality, which presumably apply also to the scholars of the university, have produced any reliable conclusion, it is that aggression and what Nietzsche called "the will to power" can appear in many guises, not least in the aggressive vindication of a scholarly position against other positions. As those who have gone on from the university to national and international politics have repeatedly noted, the reason why conflicts in the academy are often so bloody is that the stakes are often so small.

The inability to distinguish between the idea being attacked and the person espousing that idea is even more inexcusable when that person is junior to the attacker, for one of the moral principles at work in the university ought also to be a recognition of the various levels at which persons stand and a concern for them as persons. There do not seem to be extensive statistical reviews of the evidence, but anecdotal evidence abounds for the trauma than can be inflicted by a brutal or sarcastic teacher. On the more positive side, there is likewise anecdotal evidence for the healing power of compassion in the life of an entire university campus when, as happened in 1990 at the University of California at Berkeley, it has been traumatized by the kind of terrorism and irrationality that so often seems to make a university its target. Chancellor Chang-Lin Tien, recognizing that "this is a time for our community to draw together and provide every kind of support for those who were directly involved and for others who were affected," urged professors at the university to be sensitive in their enforcement of academic expectations, and he called for "the personal caring and comforting of friends." Any definition of the university that does not explicitly incorporate this dimension of personal caring betrays the deepest traditions and highest ideals of the university and is woefully inadequate, and any citizen of the university who feels squeamish about a definition of the university that includes this dimension should reexamine both the intellectual and the moral imperatives that underlie the university as community. At the same time it bears repeating that the caring and compassion of the university, like that of the family and the church it resembles, must also express itself in the obligation of holding people to the consequences of their actions, including their intellectual and academic actions. A refusal to enforce that obligation is not evidence of sensitivity and love but a betrayal both of the university and of its members (including the members to whom it may be necessary to give a failing grade in a course or to deny academic tenure).

Closely related to this dimension of personal caring but by no means identical with it is a virtue that ought to be especially in evidence at the university and by which the university can serve as a model for the society at large: the ability to tolerate fundamental diversity of beliefs and values without sacrificing conviction. Conviction without toleration is, as history shows, all too easy. Toleration without conviction is more difficult, but relativism has, especially since the eighteenth century, been the most common basis for an armistice between warring opinions. It is, unfortunately, an extremely vulnerable armistice; for, as the example of Nazi Germany suggests, the displacement of the relativism by a new set of convictions, even of demonic convictions, will destroy the toleration as well. As has been well said, "If you don't stand for something, you will fall for anything!" What is needed is the skill and the art of holding views strongly and yet of respecting views that are diametrically opposed. This skill is one with which the university has had rich experience. It involves a civility of discourse that is all too often overlooked in discussions of free speech, inside or outside the university. Civility in discourse is sometimes treated as though it were at best an arbitrary convention, and hypocrisy at worst. But the discourse that goes on within the university may serve as the most impressive exhibit available to prove that civility is in fact the best means that human reason has devised, over centuries of warfare and aggression, for coping with fundamental difference.

Perhaps the most distinctively academic of all the private virtues is the virtue of discipline, or, as Newman called it in the title of the ninth of his "occasional lectures and essays" (addressed to the evening school), "discipline of mind." As he observes, "A man may hear a thousand lectures, and read a thousand volumes, and be at the end of the process very much where he was, as regards knowledge. Something more than merely *admitting* it in a negative way into the mind is necessary, if it is to remain there. It must be not be passively received, but actually and actively entered into, embraced, mastered" (II.ix.4). For as one great German scholar put it, "To be a scholar, it is necessary to be part monk . . . and to get an early start." This emphasis on self-denial and discipline is still one of the most intriguing vestigial remnants of the ecclesiastical and monastic backgrounds of the university, and one with which the biographies of great scientists and scholars are replete. We who have spent a lifetime in research and teaching, and who have found in it such fulfillment and joy that we cannot imagine having done anything else, have the obligation, in recruiting and training the next generation of scholars, to stress the correlation between the fulfillment that comes out of scholarship and the ascetic discipline that goes into it. To anticipate a later discussion, the interrelation between the law of studies and the law of persons has one direct programmatic corollary: it seems difficult to avoid the conclusion that if both of these tables of intellectual virtues possess validity and are to be carried out in practice within the life of the university, research and teaching must likewise be correlated. For most of these virtues pertain both to teaching and to research, some of them more to the one than to the other. But collective experience in the university suggests that the dangers and excesses to which each of these virtues is liable can be addressed best if the claims of these two poles of its common life are both being taken seriously.

6

THE MANSION-HOUSE
OF THE GOODLY FAMILY
OF THE SCIENCES

A consideration of the intellectual virtues suggests that among the many clichés about the university, perhaps none is more worth keeping than the definition of it as a "community of scholars." In a discourse of 1852 entitled "General Knowledge Viewed as One Philosophy," which was not included in the collection that forms part II of *The Idea of a University,* Newman attacked critics of the university who "do not rise to the very idea of a University." He charged them with considering it "a sort of bazaar, or pantechnicon, in which wares of all kinds are heaped together for sale in stalls independent of each other," and in which "all professions and classes are at liberty to congregate, varying, however, according to the season, each of them strange to each." To the contrary, Newman insisted, "if we would rightly deem of it, a University is the home, it is *the mansion-house, of the goodly family of the Sciences,* sisters all, and sisterly in their mutual dispositions" (II.app.i).

Elsewhere, in a lecture on "Christianity and Scientific Investigation," he expanded on this definition in glowing language that has probably never been surpassed either for its substantive grasp of the central genius of the university or for its eloquence in voicing that ideal:

What an empire is in political history, such is a University in the sphere of philosophy and research. It is, as I have said, the high protecting power of all knowledge and science, of fact and principle, of inquiry and discovery, of experiment and speculation; it maps out the territory of the intellect, and sees that the boundaries of each province are religiously respected, and that there is neither encroachment nor surrender on any side. It acts as umpire between truth and truth, and, taking into account the nature and importance of each,

assigns to all their due order of precedence. It maintains no one
department of thought exclusively, however ample and noble; and it
sacrifices none. It is deferential and loyal, according to their respective weight, to the claims of literature, of physical research, of history,
of metaphysics, of theological science. It is impartial towards them
all, and promotes each in its own place and for its own object
(II.viii.2).

An "empire," yes, yet an empire marked by the mutual respect that characterizes a republic and by the universal participation that characterizes a
democracy—in short, the university must be a community of scholars, but
a community that is simultaneously free and responsible, "the mansion-
house of the goodly family of the Sciences, sisters all, and sisterly in their
mutual dispositions." That definition applies to all the components of "the
business of a university" to be discussed in part II of this book.

   To begin with the definition of the university from the opening sentence
of Newman's preface, as "a place of teaching," it is integral to the idea of
the university that it be a free and responsible community of scholars in its
teaching. This has implications for the relation both between teacher and
student and between teacher and teacher. Because it is in some ways correct
to say, with A. E. Taylor in his biography of Socrates, that Plato's Academy
was "the first European University," the Platonic and Socratic ideal of the
teacher has always hovered, be it ever so ineffectually, over even the most
authoritarian of university lecture halls and classrooms. In a memorable
chapter titled "Socrates the Teacher," Werner Jaeger has reviewed the principal components of his unique gift as teacher. At center was the respect of
the teacher for the pupil and the cultivation of the belief in both of them
that they were engaged together in a common quest for learning. There are
almost infinite opportunities for fakery in the espousal of such a belief, and
critics of Socrates from his time to our own have suggested that he was
actually exercising a subtle form of power over his pupils by his avowed
refusal to dominate them. Nevertheless, it remains the case, also for the
university, that the attitude of mind which develops in a senior scholar out
of the experience of authentic scholarship, an attitude that moderates confidence in the results of study with a continuing skepticism about them,
does lead to a sense of sharing in the quest, in which the senior can also
learn from the junior. For Plato and—if Plato's account of his doctrine is
historically accurate—also for Socrates, that sense of the quest for knowledge was related to, or even rooted in, the doctrine of recollection, or
anamnesis, expressed in Plato's assertion that "all inquiry and all learning

is but recollection" of that which the soul had known all along. The vocation of the teacher, therefore, was not to implant knowledge in the pupil but to permit the knowledge that was already there to come to light; in the familiar metaphor of Socrates, the teacher was not the father of the truth but its midwife. But even without the Platonic doctrine of anamnesis, the Socratic method of teaching through participation in a common inquiry is (with some not insignificant variations among fields of scholarship and intellectual inquiry) a powerful expression of community between teacher and pupil.

There is, however, no variation among the fields of intellectual inquiry in one implication of the Socratic method for the idea of the university: that the teacher should teach students, not recruit disciples. This is a problem for all forms of teaching, but it seems to have special relevance to the temptations that attend the teaching of graduate students, because of the position of power occupied by the teacher as the student's mentor. If, as Newman says in the context of an ominous warning about the extremes to which "Intellectualism" can sometimes lead, "Knowledge, viewed as Knowledge, exerts a subtle influence in throwing us back on ourselves, and making us our own centre, and our minds the measure of all things" (I.ix.2), it is at the very least my moral obligation as a teacher that I do not instead throw my students back on myself, making myself the students' center and my mind the measure of all things for my students. Such a caution is not easy to combine in practice with my assurance as a scholar that through the long hours of my research I have arrived at results that are in some significant sense a new discovery, and thus with the irresistible desire to let others in on the secret through publication and through instruction; research, teaching, and scholarly publication would all collapse without some such sense. It would, moreover, be fatuous in the extreme to ignore the positive contributions that the imitation of the master can make as an essential part of the student's process of growing to scholarly maturity. The moment of truth comes, however, when, in the exercise of this maturity, the student begins to arrive at conclusions different from those of the master, as the largely unilateral power relation of an apprenticeship gradually yields—or should yield, in a healthy relationship—to authentic community and to a deepening collegiality between teacher and student, eventually perhaps to a dependence of master upon pupil that exceeds that of pupil upon master. For someone who has experienced it, either as teacher or as student or as both, it is a rite of passage filled with joy and fulfillment for all concerned, as well as with moments of deep anxiety. But this community will not simply happen in the instant of independence, unless it has in fact been happening from the beginning of the process; and it is, by the nature of things, chiefly the mentor's responsibility to see to it that it does happen.

In the graduate context and perhaps even more in the undergraduate context, the community of teacher and student depends for its integrity also upon the community of teachers with one another, upon the recognition, in Newman's words, that "the Sciences [are] sisters all, and sisterly in their mutual dispositions." But as Ernest Boyer has observed in his study of faculty members, "there is a yearning for community, although each individual goes on in his or her individualistic competitive way." Academic folkways being what they are, this competitive individualism often expresses itself in the language of methodological or, especially in recent times, ideological and political differences. When such differences are aired in the classroom, undergraduates sometimes express confusion and dismay, but they are in fact being introduced to an important dimension of authentic academic community. If, as seems incontrovertible, the university everywhere is in the process of becoming far more international and far more diverse and pluralistic than any university ever seen before, even in the twentieth century, it will have to refine still further the mechanisms for coping with pluralism while cultivating community. The fundamental differences of outlook and conviction about ultimate issues and about proximate means will need to be made the subject of explicit and public discussion among teachers. Where an official ideology is said to define the university, be it Marxist or Muslim or Christian, pluralism will often go underground; it will not disappear, but each contending position will strive to define itself somewhere within the spectrum and to prove that it belongs there. The future of the university will not depend, as the secularist ideology of the Enlightenment fondly expected, on the obliteration of all ideologies and of all presuppositions, especially religious presuppositions, but it will depend on the university's acknowledgment of the fact of pluralism both between and within ideological positions. "Great minds need elbowroom," Newman warned, doing so, it should be noted, in the course of affirming the authority of the church. "If you insist that in their speculations, researches, or conclusions in their particular science . . . they must get up all that divines have said or the multitude believed upon religious matters, you simply crush and stamp out the flame within them, and they can do nothing at all" (II.viii.7). Whatever its ideological orientation, the university must be the kind of free and responsible community where that does not happen, and it repeatedly becomes necessary to remind the university, as well as the church, the state, and private donors, that this is so.

This implies, to a degree and at a depth that may not have been necessary in the past (though it would probably have been useful at any time), that university teachers will have to carry out their work as pedagogues in sensitive awareness of other fields of research and other courses of instruction. In Newman's metaphor, all the sister sciences will have to learn to be "sisterly in their mutual dispositions." In 1798 Immanuel Kant wrote a short book entitled *The Conflict among the Faculties [Der Streit der Fakultäten]*. In the first of its three sections, because of his work as a metaphysician and his investigation of the relation between reason and faith, he was especially concerned with the conflicts between the theological faculty and the philosophical faculty. The first section concludes with the admonition: "And so the theologians have the duty, and thereby also the authorization [*Befugnis*], to uphold faith in the Bible. But they must do so without impairing the freedom of the philosophers to subject [this faith] continually to the critique of reason." The admonitions of Kant's essay of 1798 will be even more pertinent in 1998, and well beyond, not only to the philosophical faculty and the theological faculty, but to all the faculties of the university, to all the sister sciences, and to the community between teacher and teacher.

It is also an important implication of the definition of the idea of the university as a free and responsible community of teaching that it will need to make room, in its programs and in its expectations, for self-education. Newman is obviously mirroring his own experience as an Oxford undergraduate in his observation that "when a multitude of young men, keen, open-hearted, sympathetic, and observant, as young men are, come together and freely mix with each other, they are sure to learn from one another, even if there be no one to teach them." In this community, as he describes it, "the conversation of all is a series of lectures to each, and they gain for themselves new ideas and views, fresh matter of thought, and distinct principles for judging and acting, day by day." Such a "youthful community," he continues, "will constitute a whole, it will embody a specific idea, it will represent a doctrine, it will administer a code of conduct, and it will furnish principles of thought and action." Thus, he concludes, "independent of direct instruction on the part of Superiors, there is a sort of self-education" (I.vi.9). By a crude mathematical formula, it can be suggested that what students teach students should be one-third of an undergraduate education, what professors teach students should be another third, and what each student does alone in the library, the laboratory, and the study should be the remaining third; if any of those three fractions deviates significantly from that norm by approaching one-half, there is an unhealthy imbalance. (In graduate study the component of what each student does alone in library, laboratory, and study should be noticeably larger than either of the other two, perhaps larger even than the other two combined, certainly at the dissertation stage.) This emphasis on what students learn from other students implies that the residential dimension of undergraduate education is crucial, as recent studies have also indicated. But it requires imagination to create formal and structured instructional opportunities in university residences, not to take the place of, but to give discipline to, the informal processes that, in Newman's happy turn of phrase, continue to "give birth to a living teaching, which in course of time will take the shape of a self-perpetuating tradition" (I.vi.9).

Just as the reexamination of the idea of the university implies new attention to university's definition of itself as a community in its teaching, so the definition of the university as a community of research requires significant reconsideration in the light of the "sisterly disposition" of the sciences toward one another. That applies in the first instance to those departments, agencies, and personnel of the university who usually stand outside the classroom but without whom research would halt. Because of its unique position among these as the heart of the university, the university library, as I shall assert more explicitly later, must be seen as a collegial part of a total university network of support services for research, and the network in turn must be seen as a free and responsible community if it is to be equal to the complexities that are faced by university-based research. Indeed, even such a term as "providers of support services" is becoming far too limited to describe both the skills and the knowledge required of those who hold such positions. Scholars and scientists in all fields have found that the older configurations of such services, according to which the principal investigator has the questions and the staff person provides the answers, are no longer valid, if they ever were; as both the technological expertise and the scholarly range necessary for research grow, it is also for the formulation and refinement of the questions themselves that principal investigators have to turn to "staff," whom it is increasingly necessary— not a matter of courtesy, much less as a matter of condescension, but as a matter of justice and of accuracy—to identify instead as colleagues in the research enterprise.

Collaborative research in the strict sense of the word is a distinct problem unto itself, a problem that seems to grow with the number of collaborators; one study has suggested "that the optimum group size is about five to seven scientists, and that when groups grow larger the quality of their performance suffers more than the quantity of their output of publications." Comparative studies of various countries indicate that research in the natural sciences tends to create a communal atmosphere between the principal investigators and their collaborators far more readily and more frequently than does research in the humanities. In part, of course, this is due to the cooperative nature of much scientific research: in a project requiring many pairs of hands and instant responses, everyone must be part of a team, and such barriers as rank and title will tend to fall, for the alternative is a failed experiment—or serious injury to persons and property. Those scholars in the humanities who regularly work in a team, for example on a scholarly edition or in the production of such a joint enterprise as *The Cambridge Medieval History*, may have a similar experience, although in the case of that composite work, which was caught in the political crossfire of the First World War, one study has concluded "that the two editors exchanged views only through the medium of the publishers." On the other hand, the unforgettable portrait by his granddaughter of how James A. H. Murray enlisted the services of his family and other staff of the Scriptorium, together with readers from all over, in the preparation of *The Oxford English Dictionary*, suggests rather the image of the single-minded scholar who is a benevolent despot. It is sometimes impossible, in a paper carrying the names of multiple authors (these being perhaps listed alphabetically, to complicate matters further), to determine which of the collaborators did what and therefore which qualities of whose mind went into the work. Those who review charges of research fraud have discovered that in those rare instances where actual fraud has taken place in a collaborative project, this has sometimes been due to the carelessness or preoccupation or haste of the responsible investigator, who has signed the results without adequate scrutiny and who, it seems necessary if harsh to conclude, must now be held accountable also for the falsifications or the plagiarism that may have crept in unawares. This, too, raises questions about the size and the number of projects for which any single investigator should be permitted to accept authority and responsibility (and funding).

It does seem likely, nevertheless, that any blueprint for university-based research must envisage the rapid increase in the amount of collaborative research. For it is as true of senior scholars, both women and men, as it is of the "young men" to whom Newman was referring explicitly, that "when a multitude of young men, keen, open-hearted, sympathetic, and observant, as young men are, come together and freely mix with each other, they are sure to learn from one another," so that "there is a sort of self-education" also through scholarly and scientific collaboration (I.vi.9). That collaboration, moreover, cannot be—and is not now—confined to one university or to one region or even to one country. In commenting on the presumed decline of the sense of community within a university faculty, critics have frequently observed that when professors speak of "my colleagues," they are referring nowadays to scholars who do the kind of research they do, wherever such scholars may be, rather than to professors who teach at the same institution, whatever their research may be. Short of sending out vast numbers of questionnaires, there appears to be no empirical means to verify this observation, but the impression is shared by colleagues (in both of the senses just indicated) that this phenomenon, which was once regarded as peculiar to the natural sciences, has spread to all disciplines. While this raises grave questions about the preservation of institutional loyalty, even about the very governance of the university, it remains the case that some of the most important scientific and scholarly discoveries of the past decades have taken place on the borders between two or more of the conventional disciplines rather than within their walls; and there is every reason to believe that this is where they will continue to appear. If so, then not only biochemistry and mathematical economics but comparative literature and women's studies will oblige scholars in such hyphenated fields to find their collaborators wherever they can. The integrity of the idea of the university as a community of research lies to a considerable extent in the development of mechanisms for such collaboration, not only across disciplines and across campuses, but across national boundaries and across continents, also because much of the collaboration, in all fields but perhaps above all in the social sciences, involves joint work with scholars and thinkers outside the academy. Despite the modern technologies of communication and transportation, collaborative research of that kind and on that scale creates serious difficulties for the teaching responsibilities of the researchers. Yet if the university is to attract and hold for its teaching mission those who are engaged in this pioneering research work, as it must, it needs to become more imaginative about devising new systems and new standards for its faculties.

At the same time, it should not be seen only as a hopeless remnant of nineteenth-century Romanticism if this emphasis on community in research and on "the family of the sciences" is coupled, as any healthy understanding of the family must be, with a reminder about the need to respect and to cultivate creative solitude. Ralph Waldo Emerson, who is perhaps best known in this regard for his Phi Beta Kappa address of 1837, "The American Scholar," and who published a book called *Society and Solitude* in 1870, spoke in 1838 about the two questions of the scholar and solitude together. "I would not have any superstition about solitude,"

Emerson warned, but he urged that the scholar "must embrace solitude as a bride. He must have his glees and his glooms alone. . . . And why must the student be solitary and silent? That he may become acquainted with his thoughts." When Newman for his part speaks about "a philosophical habit of mind" (I.iii.4); or about "an acquired faculty of judgment, of clearsightedness, of sagacity, of wisdom, of philosophical reach of mind, and of intellectual self-possession and repose," adding that "the eye of the mind, of which the object is truth, is the work of discipline and habit" (I.vii.1); or about "formation of mind" as "a habit of order and system, a habit of referring every accession of knowledge to what we already know, and of adjusting the one with the other; and, moreover, as such a habit implies, the actual acceptance and use of certain principles as centres of thought, around which our knowledge grows and is located" (II.ix.7)—he is in each of these apostrophes describing qualities that are indeed a gift from a community, and ultimately a gift from God, but that must be cultivated in solitude. Therefore it will always be necessary in the university for us to counsel those students who think that they would like to become scholars to find out early for themselves whether they can bear to be alone as much as a scholar must be alone; for many find that they cannot, and it is just as well for them to learn this about themselves, and the earlier the better. It is not an inconsistency to insist that the healthiest community of scholars is one in which scholars are not obliged to be in the community incessantly, and therefore that one of the functions of the community of scholars is to protect the right and need of the scholars in the community to be by themselves. Anyone like myself, whose scholarship deals with the minds and works of the past, has special reason to testify that in the deepest sense the community of scholars is, in a favorite formula of Edmund Burke, "a partnership not only between those who are living, but between those who are living, those who are dead, and those who are to be born."

In its teaching as well as in its research, the community of scholars that is the university will need to affirm old ways of being both free and responsible, and to learn new ways of doing so, also because of the alarming increase in the tendency to politicize the university. For it remains true that "a liberal education is an education for freedom," but also that "the order necessary to keep that freedom from collapsing into merely competitive appetites or colliding gusts of anarchy is, in this country, a respect for law and the processes of law." Therefore it is necessary to preserve the "essential, grand connection" which affirms: "Order is the precondition of humane freedom, freedom the goal of responsible order." Such a view of freedom and order is consonant with Newman's idea of the university. He was an ardent convert to Roman Catholicism who would eventually be named a cardinal of the church (and may someday be canonized as a saint); but he insisted that the university "maps out the territory of the intellect, and sees that the boundaries of each province are religiously respected, and that there is neither encroachment nor surrender on any side," and that in doing so the university is "deferential and loyal, according to their respective weight, to the claims of literature, of physical research, of history, of metaphysics, of theological science," deferential but "impartial towards them all," yes, also towards "theological science," which, despite supernatural revelation, remains a discipline of the human mind (II.viii.2).

This discussion of the "first principle" that the community of the university is "the mansion-house of the family of the sciences" prompts me to confess to a potentially dangerous propensity of mine, which is, as should be evident by now, one I share with John Henry Newman. As Ian Ker has said of Newman, with apposite quotations,

> Newman's idea of the Church is couched in terms noticeably similar in some respects to his idea of the university. The former is "the representative of the religious principle," the latter "the representative of the intellect." The "University is an intellectual power . . . just as the Church is a religious power." The Church "is imperial, that is, One and Catholic," while the university is "an empire . . . in the sphere of philosophy and research." The Church is the "guardian" of the "circle of . . . dogmatic truths," the university "the high protecting power" of "the whole circle of . . . knowledge." If "among the objects of human enterprise . . . none higher or nobler can be named than that which is contemplated in the erection of a University," the Church in her turn is "a supereminent prodigious power sent upon earth to encounter and master a giant evil." . . . What is so striking is the extent to which Newman's description here of the university reminds one of the terms in which he speaks elsewhere of the Catholic Church.

Because I have been disappointed so often in institutional Christendom and because, by contrast, the university has been for almost half a century the chief repository of truth and the community of wisdom to me personally, and is (in a metaphor that is eminently applicable both to the church and to the university) my spiritual mother who has reared and nourished me, my "Alma Mater" (I.vi.8), I have sometimes been in danger of regarding it as the embodiment of the One Holy Catholic and Apostolic Church affirmed in the Nicene Creed. It is *not* that; and if we act as though it were, we shall send a charge through the wires that the wires cannot carry, ending in idolatry or disaster. But if, as Newman said, "among the objects of human enterprise,—I may say it surely without extravagance, Gentlemen,—none higher or nobler can be named than that which is contemplated in the erection of a University" (II.viii.2), then it follows that the university is, in God's good world, the principal community through which human rationality can examine all existing communities, families, and structures—including itself, but also including the One Holy Catholic and Apostolic Church—and thus can help them to become what they are. For that reason, too, the identification of the university as "family" and community does belong to the first principles of the idea of the university.

II

7

THE BUSINESS OF
A UNIVERSITY

In the introduction to his seventh discourse, under the general title "Knowledge Viewed in Relation to Professional Skill," Newman defined liberal education and the university, and did so perhaps more succinctly than he did anywhere else:

> This process of training, by which the intellect, instead of being formed or sacrificed to some particular or accidental purpose, some specific trade or profession, or study or science, is disciplined for its own sake, for the perception of its own proper object, and for its own highest culture, is called Liberal Education; and though there is no one in whom it is carried as far as is conceivable, or whose intellect would be a pattern of what intellects should be made, yet there is scarcely any one but may gain an idea of what real training is, and at least look towards it, and make its true scope and result, not something else, his standard of excellence; and numbers there are who may submit themselves to it, and secure it to themselves in good measure. And to set forth the right standard, and to train according to it, and to help forward all students towards it according to their various capacities, this I conceive to be *the business of a University* (I.vii.1).

Newman's prescription of the business of a university does call for critical reexamination, as the following chapters will repeatedly be obliged to make clear, because in crucial respects it does not seem to define sufficiently the idea of the university at this juncture in its history. Yet the questions he asked were and still are the right ones, without which neither the idea of the university nor its vocation can be charted or even reasonably discussed, much less critically reexamined.

It is, of course, a play on words, but also far more than that, to note, in introducing a discussion of the business of the university, that the university *is* business, and big business. Each year the debates over the budget for higher education in various countries and in individual states make it clear all over the world that the university must be included in the catalog of major industries in any modern society, involving a significant percentage of its income and expenditure and occupying an important place in the service (or the "not-for-profit") sector of its economy. The most successful leaders of modern universities have been those who have come to their task from the "business" of teaching and research, but have then learned to administer the university as "business" without being overwhelmed by it. Deserving of special mention among these are three university presidents who have decisively shaped the American university (and who have, as will already have become evident by now to many readers, no less decisively shaped the thought and study going into this book): Daniel Coit Gilman, who at age twenty-five laid out the basic scheme for the Sheffield Scientific School at Yale, but in 1872 became president of the University of California, then three years later the first president of the Johns Hopkins University (often called the first genuine university in the United States) for the next twenty-six years, then the first president of the Carnegie Institution of Washington from 1901 to 1904, and finally president of the National Civil Reform League; Andrew Dickson White, who, after membership on the faculty of the University of Michigan, went on to found Cornell University as its first president from 1868 to 1885, graduating after that to a career in diplomacy, which included the chairmanship of the American delegation to the Hague Peace Conference in 1899; and William Rainey Harper, the wunderkind who received his Ph.D. from Yale at the age of nineteen, returning there as professor of Hebrew, until he became in 1891 the first president of the University of Chicago.

Conversely, the roadside of the history of university administration is littered with the debris of institutions and of educators who have come to grief because, sometimes from the highest of motives, they have ignored these fiscal realities or have supposed that whatever it is in the university that can be called "business" was beneath their intellectual station or would somehow take care of itself. A considerable amount of such debris, however, has also been deposited by institutions and educators who were less than worthy and who, knowing all too well that the university is a business, have sought to exploit it for profit, often by perpetrating the hoax on unsuspecting applicants that because upward mobility in almost any modern society does come through its universities and colleges, students have only to "pay your money and take your choice." Scandals associated with college athletics and with student loan programs have shown how easy it has been for unscrupulous profiteers to move into the university business. An unavoidable corollary of that experience is the necessity for a more thorough monitoring of higher education precisely on the score of its financial management. It is part of the definition of the university as a free and responsible community and a "family," as set forth in the preceding chapter, that its fiscal housekeeping must be beyond reproach, and that there must be within the community of higher education as a whole an atmosphere of accountability that will discourage financial abuses and if need be take action against them. For it is a lesson of educational history in many lands that if the higher education community, individually and collectively, declines to carry out this responsibility, there will be other agencies, both private and public, that will all too willingly assume it, and with it a significant share of authority over the *real* business of the university.

Use of the word *business* in conjunction with the word *university* likewise calls to mind the deep and long-standing dependence of the modern university on the business community. Both the university and the capitalistic system have their origins in the Middle Ages, but both grew to maturity only after the Middle Ages. Moreover, they grew up side by side, not exactly as twins nor even as siblings, but as cousins who have only sometimes been close and who have more often been quarrelsome, but who recognize that in telling ways they do belong together. Any statistical comparison worldwide between private and public universities, as to numbers of students served or degrees conferred or faculty employed, would certainly show that neither business nor private capital nor philanthropy but government is by far the most important source of financial support, and therefore the most important base of power, for the modern university seen on a global scale; the "private university" is largely an American phenomenon. As a leading American educator warned in 1943, "industry and government will control education, and it is evident that these customers will have little use for many of the wares which the institutions of higher learning value exceedingly." Moreover, many private universities, while decidedly and even militantly private in their outlook and in their governance, have become highly dependent on government for a large part of their financial support, above all in scientific research. Their freedom depends in part on the goodwill of the government agencies from which that support derives. But if one is naturally suspicious of such goodwill, as the university in a worldwide context and in historical perspective has every reason to be, it is prudent to protect that freedom by other devices, for example, by avoiding so thoroughgoing a dependence on any one government agency—the military in the case of some universities, energy or health care in the case of others—that a withdrawal of support from the university by the agency or a declaration of independence from the agency by the university would cripple the total enterprise of research and teaching at the university. Yet private financial support for the university has historically been an important bastion of freedom against government intrusion. All universities regardless of location or governance, moreover, are the beneficiaries of the atmosphere of freedom created at the independent institutions by such support. In addition, some public universities have succeeded in having it both ways, being part of the publicly supported system of higher education but gaining private support and a university endowment that ranks with those of their leading private partners. And despite some flagrant and well-documented cases of interference by business donors in the internal academic affairs of the university, especially in the past, the record is increasingly and impressively weighted in the opposite direction, and such interference has come to be the exception rather than the rule.

These two issues, the responsible management of the university as business and the dependence of the university on support from business, intersect in an area that has received less attention than it merits—namely, the position of university trustees. Any consideration of the topic of university governance must pay special attention to the relation among the several bases of university governance, specifically, the faculty, the administration, and the board of trustees, each with its own constituencies. In the present context, that relation raises the special question of the decisive contribution that trustees representing the business community have historically made to the university as business. In the history of various universities, this contribution has at certain crucial junctures rescued the institution from bankruptcy or scandal, by providing the kind of technical business skills and personnel that academics tend to treat with condescension or contempt. One has only to read around in the memoirs of university rectors, vice-chancellors, and presidents in various lands to learn, even apart from these crises, about the benefits that have accrued to the university from these technical business skills and personnel in such a field as the investment of endowment. Where the process of trusteeship has broken down and has changed into either indifference or interference, a significant part of the blame for the breakdown must often be assigned to the university administration and faculty for not responsibly engaging in intellectual dialogue with the trustees about the idea of the university (for which they could do worse than to read Newman). Conversely, where the trustees have put the idea of the university, rather than only dollars and cents or bricks and mortar, on their agenda, they have been in a position to make decisions informed by such discussion.

All of that needs to be said when the phrase "the business of a university" is under consideration; but when Newman says that "to set forth the right standard, and to train according to it, and to help forward all students towards it according to their various capacities, this I conceive to be the business of a University" (I.vii.1), he is, obviously, using the word *business* in its older and more generic sense. At least since the word *multiversity* was introduced into the vocabulary in 1963 or so, the members of the university community in the United States—but also throughout the contemporary academic universe—have become increasingly conscious of the almost infinite diversity of institutions calling themselves "universities," and thus of the correspondingly infinite variety of activities devoted to teaching, research, professional training, collection building, and publication in which those institutions are engaged. As is evident from the experience of students caught in the process of applying to university, whether for undergraduate, graduate, or professional study, that variety can be confusing, even paralyzing. The diversity and variety will almost certainly increase in the next century, especially if the context of the inquiry is, as it has been here, worldwide. For example, such areas as national and provincial history, folklore and ethnomusicology, and the data of local and regional linguistic phenomena will be a continuing assignment for university scholars, teachers, students, libraries, and publishers in every country.

No one would question that it is the business of a university in a particular nation and culture to chart such phenomena and to publish such scholarly works, and that in a world of multiversities someone should be doing such research and teaching on this or that language. The same will also be true not only of folklore or history or natural resources, but of a vast range of specific topics. But given all that attention to national cultural particularity and, as a consequence, given all that diversity, is it hopeless even to ask today whether Newman's description (or prescription), "to set forth the right standard, and to train according to it, and to help forward all students towards it according to their various capacities, this I conceive to be the business of a University," makes any sense? For ultimately the question of the business of a university is not the university as business, nor all the other kinds of "business" and "busy-ness" at a university, but rather: In which kinds of "business" must the university be engaged if it is to have the right to be called "university," and by whose definition of the idea of the university? No one institution can do it all: teach all the languages spoken on the globe, survey all the geography of this and all other planets, investigate the history and prehistory of the entire human race, undertake a taxonomy of all the phyla and species, construct laboratories and machines for research into all the elements and forces of the material world, or prepare for every job that calls itself a profession. But are there any activities or fields whose absence or neglect should disqualify the institution from a claim to the name "university"? In short, is there or can there be a definition of the university?

Obviously, this book is based on the assumption that there can be, and that the components of such a definition should probably include the following: advancement of knowledge through research; extension of knowledge through undergraduate and graduate teaching; training that involves both knowledge and professional skill in the professional programs or schools of the university; preservation of knowledge in libraries, galleries, and museums; and diffusion of knowledge through scholarly publication. A university may do many other things, and all of them do. There are also some additional things that any one university must do as part of its "duties to society" (I.vii.10), which will differ from one society to another, from one time to another, and from one university to another; but these are the things it ought to be doing if it wants to be a university—and I suppose, a bit hesitantly, that I am saying that in one way or another it probably ought to be doing all of them to qualify. As the number of educational institutions in the world laying claim to the name "university" has increased steadily, sometimes it seems exponentially—with "universities" in some place or other devoted to the martial arts, to almost every job or vocation, and to every conceivable ideology and belief—confusion on this point of the relation between the advancement of knowledge and the extension of knowledge has produced the new tautology of distinguishing between a "university" as such (meaning, apparently, any institution in which postbaccalaureate teaching is carried on, even perhaps only an institution in which several kinds of bachelor's degrees are offered) and a "research university" (meaning a university in which an ongoing program of research and publication is expected of all the faculty, not only as a means of initially qualifying for appointment or for conferral of tenure but as a continuing responsibility and a part of the professor's job description).

Needless to say, this distinction is fundamentally alien to the central position of this book, although I have found it necessary to resort to the nomenclature of "research university" from time to time; for the first principles that have primarily engaged our attention do appear to lead to a definition of the university, and of the business of the university, like the one just proposed. It would require at least another such book to define the business of the college as distinct from that of the university. In the universities that Newman knew best, "Colleges arose and became the medium and instrument of University action" (II.i.1), all the while retaining a considerable measure of academic and administrative autonomy. Elsewhere, for example in the United States, the transformation of "college into university" has often accomplished the change of designation and sometimes of little else, at great cost to the essential business of the college and not always with a clear sense of the business of a university. As various of the following chapters will suggest, the university does not and should not hold any sort of patent on the education of the young, and the subordination of its collegiate responsibilities to the other parts of its mission has often led to educational disaster. For the college continues to function as a corrective on the university. Nevertheless, there remains a fundamental distinction between "the collegiate and university models of higher learning," and that distinction remains fundamental also to this reexamination of the business of a university.

8

THE ADVANCEMENT
OF KNOWLEDGE
THROUGH RESEARCH

At least one major implication of Cardinal Newman's first principle of "knowledge as its own end" needs to be pressed much further than Newman pressed it. That implication is, moreover, fundamental to the definition of the university and its vocation, as well as to the divergence of this reexamination of the idea of the university from Newman's vision of the university. Newman's familiar definitional vision is set forth already in the opening words of the preface to *The Idea of a University*:

> The view taken of a University in these Discourses is the following:—
> That it is a place of teaching universal knowledge. This implies that its object is, on the one hand, intellectual, not moral; and, on the other, that it is the diffusion and extension of knowledge rather than *the advancement [of knowledge]*. If its object were scientific and philosophical discovery, I do not see why a University should have students; if religious training, I do not see how it can be the seat of literature and science.

In his notes to that passage, Ian Ker has quite rightly pointed out in extenuation that "Newman not only planned research in science, technology, archaeology, and medicine . . . but was explicit about the research duties of university professors." Elsewhere Newman also spoke about "the sphere of philosophy and research" at the university (II.viii.2). He made it clear that scholars should be permitted to proceed freely "in their speculations, researches, or conclusions in their particular science" (II.viii.7). And he called upon "religious writers, jurists, economists, physiologists, chemists, geologists, and historians, to go on quietly, and in a neighbourly way, in their own respective lines of speculation, research, and experiment" (II.viii.4).

Yet it is striking that so many of the fields for which he insisted on such research duties belonged to the natural sciences and their application. The very need to defend him as vigorously as Ker and others have done indicates that he did not specify at all explicitly just how, even in those fields, these research duties of the advancement of knowledge were to be related to the diffusion and extension of knowledge through teaching, which was for him the primary purpose of the university. In setting forth the thesis that on the basis of Newman's own first principles it is necessary to revise his formulation of the objects of the university, therefore, it does seem attractive to apply to his view of the university the familiar principle he defined in his *Essay on the Development of Christian Doctrine* of 1845. A "great idea," Newman observed there, referring not only to Christian doctrine but expressly to any great idea, "changes in order to remain the same. In a higher world it is otherwise, but here below to live is to change, and to be [mature] is to have changed often." For I would propose that there is no better way to protect Newman's principle of "knowledge its own end" in the teaching of undergraduates than to "develop" it into the principle that in the university the teachers who "extend" the knowledge to students should also be investigators who "advance" the knowledge. The history of the university during the twentieth century well illustrates the development of doctrine that took place when that principle of knowledge as its own end was pressed to its fullest conclusions: on the one hand, that the advancement of knowledge as an end in itself should be pursued even if the results turn out not to be capable of being translated, now or ever, into the diffusion and extension of knowledge to students; but on the other hand, that such diffusion and extension is infinitely more rich and profound when it is in the hands of professors who were and still are engaged in the advancement of knowledge through research, even though there appears to be at any given time a small pool of candidates who can carry out both assignments.

Earlier I have briefly examined the question of what Newman may have meant by his distinction that the object of the university is "intellectual, not moral," as well as the question of whether that distinction is still an adequate basis for the idea of the university in an era when other agencies of moral formation cannot be relied upon to reach some of the very populations that are the primary constituency of the university. But the other distinction in his definition is perhaps even more fundamental, also for him: "that [the university's] object is . . . the diffusion and extension of knowledge rather than the advancement [of knowledge]. If its object were scientific and philosophical discovery, I do not see why a University should have students." For if that distinction were to be accepted just as it stands and if, as the authors of some present-day protests seem to be urging, it were to be ruthlessly carried out to its final consequences, faithfulness to the idea of the university would seem to require the dismantling of the vast research programs for the advancement of knowledge that now occupy such a major part of the university's facilities and budgets all over the world, and returning the university to a primary, or even an exclusive, concentration on "the diffusion and extension of knowledge rather than the advancement [of knowledge]." The academic trade union mentality that sees any such demand as an unwarranted intrusion into the privileged territory of the guild fails to recognize the valid concerns being expressed by these protests. In its answer to the criticism of university research, therefore, it has largely failed to formulate a convincing response to the concern about university teaching. On intellectual and indeed on moral grounds no less than on pragmatic and pedagogical ones, this concern about teaching at the university needs to be addressed, and in being addressed to be affirmed, if the idea of the university is to stand. The bulk of the next chapter will attempt to do just that by reexamining "the extension of knowledge through teaching."

But the first question here, even before considering the future of the business of the university as teacher, is the issue of the advancement of knowledge, together with its place in the definition of the idea of the university and of its mission and future. The case against combining the advancement of knowledge through research with the extension of knowledge through teaching, both in the definition of the mission of the university and in the definition of the vocation of the university professor, was trenchantly stated by Newman in his preface:

> The nature of the case and the history of philosophy combine to recommend to us this division of intellectual labour between Academies [for research] and Universities [for teaching]. To discover and to teach are distinct functions; they are also distinct gifts, and are not commonly found united in the same person. He, too, who spends his day in dispensing his existing knowledge to all comers is unlikely to have either leisure or energy to acquire new. The common sense of mankind has associated the search after truth with seclusion and quiet. The greatest thinkers have been too intent on their subject to admit of interruption; they have been men of absent minds and idio-

syncratic habits, and have, more or less, shunned the lecture room
and the public school.

Any reexamination of the idea of the university and any statement of the
case in favor of that combination that does not want to be battling against
straw figures, then, may well consist in a review of Newman's fundamental
objections, adapted to the present-day situation of the university worldwide. For these objections were, according to Newman, based not on
personal opinion but on the formidable convergence of "the nature of the
case and the history of philosophy."

Of Newman's three objections, the last reads: "The greatest thinkers
have been too intent on their subject to admit of interruption; they have
been men of absent minds and idiosyncratic habits, and have, more or less,
shunned the lecture room and the public school." This objection would
seem to have received more reinforcement from the development of research since his time than have the other two, but it pertains less directly to
the question of why teachers should be scholars than to the question of why
scholars should be teachers, and therefore it is better deferred to the next
chapter. On the other hand, the most basic of Newman's objections was the
assumption that "to discover and to teach are distinct functions." Or, as he
put it later, "he, too, who spends his day in dispensing his existing knowledge to all comers is unlikely to have either leisure or energy to acquire new
[knowledge]." Anecdotal evidence abounds in support of this objection.
The successful and challenging teaching of undergraduates is at least as
demanding for the teacher as it is for the student; it is also not one whit less
demanding than basic research. In the classroom, but also outside it, instruction that goes beyond rote recitation is a full-time job. As critics of
university research have pointed out, there has been entirely too much of
the kind of research and writing, necessitated by the requirements for
promotion, that has been squeezed into the interstices of the teacher's job,
when, in Newman's phrase, the teacher "is unlikely to have either leisure or
energy to acquire new [knowledge]." At least part of the answer to Newman is to be found when Newman himself speaks of the teacher of undergraduates as one "who spends his day in dispensing his existing knowledge
to all comers." Behind this objection, however, appears to be the assumption that as new knowledge is gained through advanced research, which is
being carried on by somebody else and even somewhere else, undergraduate teachers will add it to their "existing knowledge" and in turn dispense it
to their students.

But Newman's grasp of the mystique of the teaching process was clearly far more subtle than that formulation would suggest. He rejected the idea that the mere communication of knowledge could be equated with "that sense of enlargement or enlightenment" for which education strives. On the contrary, he insisted, "the enlargement consists, not merely in the passive reception into the mind of a number of ideas hitherto unknown to it, but in the mind's energetic and simultaneous action upon and towards and among those new ideas, which are rushing in upon it" (I.vi.5). Such an action of the student's mind, and even more of the teacher's mind, would appear to demand that the passive reception of communicated knowledge be replaced, or at any rate be accompanied, by an active participation in the very processes by which knowledge is advanced. It is important not to speak pretentiously about how deeply the average student in secondary school or college can genuinely participate in the processes of research and discovery, but it is even more important to recognize that for such a student the learning process does not mean, or does not mean only, learning the What of existing knowledge but learning the How of as yet unknown knowledge. Only by entering into the How will the student become anything more than an authority on the state of knowledge in a field during the semester in which the course happens to have been taken. But for the teacher to communicate that, it simply is not enough to have someone at the head of the classroom "who spends his day in dispensing his existing knowledge to all comers."

From this assumption that "to discover and to teach are distinct functions" it followed, according to Newman, that discovery and teaching "are also distinct gifts, and are not commonly found united in the same person." Again, "I do not say that there are not great examples the other way, perhaps Socrates, certainly Lord Bacon; still I think it must be allowed on the whole that, while teaching involves external engagements, the natural home for experiment and speculation is retirement." The collective experience of countless search committees from many universities in many countries, criss-crossing the world in the quest for those elusive "scholar-teachers" and then bidding for their services in the academic auction, would seem in many ways to corroborate this depressing observation, that the combination at the highest level is to be found only occasionally. Newman's two examples are instructive in themselves: Socrates, to whom in his *Grammar of Assent* he attributed "clear and strong notions, nay, vivid mental images" of many basic religious truths, but who, as he put it in *The Idea of a University,* was one of "those heathen philosophers who in their disadvantages had some excuse for their inconsistency" (I.v.8); and Francis Bacon, the man whom Newman, being himself a convert from Protestantism to Roman Catholicism, called with obvious admiration "the most orthodox of Protestant philosophers" (II.iii.3.5), but whom he could also disparage as one who typified "the intellectual narrowness of his school" (I.v.8). Yet are not the points he scores here in some respects more rhetorical than philosophical? For if "perhaps Socrates" is to serve as proof that the combination of teaching and speculative thought or research is exceedingly rare, though possible, why should not the example of Socrates be taken as proof that great teachers as such are also almost impossible to find—which would defeat the purpose of the entire argument? The answer to Newman's rhetorical point must be that as the combination has been known to occur sublimely in Bacon or "perhaps Socrates," so it can "perhaps" be found in other measures and in other mixtures in a sufficiently large number of other men and women within each generation to equip the universities simulta- neously for the extension of knowledge through teaching and for the ad- vancement of knowledge through research. The examples Newman cites in the first discourse of *The Idea of a University*, of "an heterogeneous and an independent body of men, setting about a work of self-reformation" (I.i.1), and then, in the fifth discourse, of an "assemblage of learned men, zealous for their own sciences, and rivals of each other," who gradually learn "to adjust together the claims and relations of their respective subjects of inves- tigation" (I.v.1), do seem to describe a faculty of scholar-teachers not alto- gether dissimilar from the one being projected here.

In advancing these objections to support his insistence upon teaching as the exclusive or all-but-exclusive mission of the university, moreover, Car- dinal Newman seems to have restricted himself too rigidly to the pattern then prevalent at Oxford and Cambridge. In spite of his reference else- where to the University of Paris as "the glory of the middle ages" (I.ii.7), all the examples he cites in these objections are either British or classical, as when he speaks of ancient Athens as "the University of the world" (I.v.7). He betrays some sensitivity to the possibility of such a charge when he suggests that "some persons may be tempted to complain that I have servilely followed the English idea of a university" (I.pr.). Students of New- man are not agreed as to just how well he could ever read German, since he had admitted in 1845, "I . . . don't know German." Therefore it is not clear whether his generous references to such German thinkers as Johann Adam Möhler of the University of Tübingen, for example in his *Essay on Development* of that same year, may be taken to indicate a specific intellec- tual and scholarly debt to them; he probably had read Möhler in a French translation. Here in his *Idea of a University* the German university as a model is significantly absent, except perhaps for the comment about "the

open development of unbelief in Germany" (II.v.1.1), which is paralleled
by a comment in his *Apologia pro Vita Sua* about "the perils to England
which lay in the biblical and theological speculations of Germany." Both of
these remarks seem to be aimed at faculties of Protestant theology in German universities and to be based on the study of those faculties published in
1828–30 by Newman's sometime mentor, E. B. Pusey, *An Historical En-
quiry into the Probable Causes of the Rationalistic Character Lately Predominant in the Theology of Germany.*

Yet it was above all at the German university that the "research university" in the form we know now had been invented, early in Newman's
lifetime. In 1810 the establishment of the University of Berlin under the
leadership of Wilhelm von Humboldt (for whom the University of Berlin
was eventually named) set the pattern, with the philosopher Johann Gottlieb Fichte as the first rector. It was, moreover, from the German university,
including not only Berlin but especially also the University of Göttingen,
that the Ph.D. degree was adapted when it was introduced in the United
States in 1860. Superimposing a German understanding of the university
defined by the doctorate upon the British and American understandings of
the college defined by the baccalaureate has created some of the ongoing
educational and intellectual tensions we are examining in this book. Nowhere are those tensions more evident than here in the question of the place
of the advancement of knowledge through research and its relation to the
extension of knowledge through teaching. At several crucial junctures, that
question has forced itself even upon the attention of the German university
system. In the decade after the collapse of the German Empire at the end of
the First World War, there followed a searching reexamination of the universities. One of the most eminent of German scholars in the humanities,
Adolf von Harnack of Berlin, spoke on 23 October 1929, in what was the
final year of his long scholarly life, for the dedication of a research institute
in Münster:

> I begin with a statement of faith: *Never must our German universities
> and institutions of higher learning change their character of being
> devoted both to instruction and to research.* It is in the combination
> of research and instruction that the distinctiveness of German institu-
> tions of higher learning is expressed; but this distinctiveness, in which
> research and instruction mutually fructify each other, would be com-
> pletely destroyed if this combination were dissolved. . . . [In some
> countries] the chief emphasis lies on introducing students to the
> results of scholarship. But at our universities we want to introduce

them to scholarship itself, and to teach them how one arrives at the reality and truth of things and how one can advance the progress of scholarship.

Noting the anomaly of his speaking at the dedication of a research institute that was to be separate from teaching, Harnack concluded: "For fifty-five years I have been active at the university in this way. How could anyone believe that I would ever do anything that would handicap the research character of the institutions of higher learning!" Such was the judgment of the scholar who, on the side, had written the history of the Prussian Academy of Sciences and had been the director of the Prussian State Library, and who therefore could not be accused of a narrowness of view about the various component elements of the business of a university. But the relation of teaching and research again became the central question of university reform after the Second World War, also in Germany.

One of the most pungent comments about the danger of the emphasis upon research came from the eminent Oxford scholar of classics, Newman's somewhat younger (and theologically much more liberal) contemporary Benjamin Jowett, Regius Professor of Greek, Master of Balliol College, and Vice-Chancellor of Oxford University. As reported by Logan Pearsall Smith,

> The word "research" as a university ideal had, indeed, been ominously spoken in Oxford . . . but the notion of this ideal, threatening as it did to discredit the whole tutorial and examinational system which was making Oxford into the highest of high schools for boys, was received there with anger and contempt. In Balliol, the birthplace and most illustrious home of this great system, it was regarded with especial scorn. . . . This ideal of endowment for research was particularly shocking to Benjamin Jowett, the great inventor of the tutorial system which it threatened. I remember once, when staying with him at Malvern, inadvertently pronouncing the ill-omened word. "Research!" the Master exclaimed. "Research!" he said. "A mere excuse for idleness; it has never achieved, and will never achieve any results of the slightest value."

As the translator of Plato and of Thucydides, but also of the *Politics* of Aristotle, Jowett knew that with this exaggeration he was in fact contradicting his own classical tradition. The formula quoted earlier from the opening words of Aristotle's *Metaphysics*, "All men by nature desire to know," was, in the context of that Aristotelian treatise, a justification for his lifelong effort to chart the several kinds of knowing and the relations among them. But in the context of Aristotle's oeuvre, this formula reaches even further: into the *Logic*, the *Topics*, and the other parts of the *Organon*, which investigate the principles and rules of knowing and reasoning that discipline and govern the desire to know; and into the vast scientific and empirical corpus of Aristotle the zoologist, physicist, and meteorologist—so influential in the history of early modern science, but now sometimes neglected even by classical scholars. Yet in the modern period this Aristotelian axiom, "All men by nature desire to know," has vindicated itself in decisive ways, in the research explosion of the nineteenth and twentieth centuries. The staging area of that explosion all over the globe has been the university—including, eminently, the University of Oxford.

It seems fair to argue that anyone who would, in a laudable concern for the sake of the quality of teaching in the university, subordinate research to teaching bears the obligation to specify alternate venues for research and the advancement of knowledge—unless, of course, the real opposition is not to the dominance of research in the contemporary program of the university but to the central importance of the research enterprise for the nation and the international community. The recent experience of Eastern and Central Europe can be instructive here. For the relation between research and teaching articulated by Harnack was not an exclusively German model, but became the Central European model. Although academies of sciences had long existed in those countries, their mission began to undergo a fundamental redirection after the Second World War. Following the model of centralized planning of the entire society, the concentration of research in the academies of sciences increasingly ran the danger of peripheralizing the universities as centers of research, by comparison with the high standards of research activity for which they had long been celebrated. Scholarly publishing, even when the author happened to be a university professor, was taken to be the responsibility not of the university but of the academy of sciences; the university published materials primarily intended for its own administrative and pedagogical needs, not for a wider national or international scholarly audience. The members of the academy, conversely, when they did engage in teaching, did not have this as an essential component of their job description. Although one serendipitously beneficial result of this allocation of tasks and resources was that certain topics excluded from the curriculum of the universities continued to be studied by the scholars of the academies of sciences, recent changes in Eastern and Central Europe have included a concerted effort to bring the academies of sciences and the universities closer together again, and thus to reintegrate research and teaching for their mutual improvement, as an essential part of the rebuilding of the university and of the nation.

In Newman's exposition, as noted earlier, the principle of "knowledge its own end" is a highly ascetic doctrine, but it has sometimes been permitted to become an apologia for self-indulgence and greed. No defense of the principle will stand unless it begins with the acknowledgment that at least some of what passes for research—at any rate in other people's fields, and at other people's universities—is trivial, largely self-referential, and devoted to belaboring the obvious. Yet the full dimensions of the crisis are only beginning to make themselves visible. The universities are not the only place where such basic research goes on; but they are effectively the only place where the researchers come from, and therefore they must also be the major centers for the research as well as the training. That is as true, moreover, in the humanities and the social sciences as it is in the natural sciences: to revert to an example cited earlier, textual criticism seems as irrelevant as uranium did in the days of the eleventh edition of the *Britannica,* but in philology no less than in physics we may find ourselves grinding the seed corn into flour, as generations of basic research are applied and exploited but not extended and deepened.

"Knowledge its own end," then, is a first principle for the university that must not only be reaffirmed but must be applied more thoroughly than ever. For some reason, it seems to be easier to make the case for the advancement of knowledge in the natural sciences as the mission of the university than it is to assert that research and scholarly discovery in the humanistic disciplines are necessary parts of the same mission, and easier still to make the case for applied research in medicine or in engineering than for the basic research underlying these professional activities; Newman's attention to medicine at his university is a suggestive example, but also a caution (II.x). As Newman's usage in his *Idea of a University* indicates (I.iii.2), the ambiguity of the term *science* in English usage is, though not a cause, then certainly a symptom of the problem. *Science* in French or *Wissenschaft* in German or *veda* in the Slavic languages continues to refer to scholarly and in that sense "scientific" research regardless of discipline, and various of the "academies of sciences" have included the particles of Greek grammar no less than the particles of nuclear physics in their research agendas. But during the century or so since Newman, *science,* which in English used to refer to "a particular branch of knowledge or study, a recognized department of learning," has come to be, "in modern use, often treated as synonymous with 'Natural and Physical Sciences,' and thus restricted to those branches of study that relate to the phenomena of the material universe and their laws." German, for example, has avoided the problem by distinguishing between *Naturwissenschaften* and *Geisteswissenschaften*, both of them being entitled to the name *Wissenschaft*, or science. At the risk of imposing a theistic criterion on fields in which theism is not always an explicit presupposition, one could get the impression that in the English language *science* seems to have come to be reserved for the study of the works of God, not for the study of such human works as history, language, and the arts. Although Newman could speak of "Social Science" as part of his comparison of "the physical with the social laws" (II.viii.3), the social sciences, individually and collectively, may be said to have constituted a special case in the development of the modern university. As their very name suggests, they have sometimes sought to align themselves with the natural sciences and to distinguish themselves from the humanities on the basis of their precision of methodology. That precision has been thought to rest on at least two foundations. Like the physical and the biological sciences, the social sciences proceed by the collection of precise data obtained through controlled observation; also like those other sciences, they have come increasingly to rely on primarily quantitative research. But within the social sciences, there has arisen an ominous distinction between those that are "hard" (as mathematical as possible) and those that are "soft" (still related to the humanities in presuppositions, methods, and "values").

In all of these ways it does seem necessary to propose a revision and expansion of Newman's opening sentence in the preface to *The Idea of a University,* to make it read: "The view taken of a university in *these* discourses is the following: that it is a place of teaching universal knowledge, but also of advancing knowledge through research and of diffusing knowledge through publication, as well as of relating such advancement, teaching, and diffusion to the training of professionals."

9

THE EXTENSION
OF KNOWLEDGE
THROUGH TEACHING

The actual title of the lecture series constituting the first and principal section of Newman's *Idea of a University* is "University Teaching Considered in Nine Discourses," an indication of the centrality of teaching to his very definition of the university. Newman went on to define the university as "a place of *teaching*. . . . Its object is the diffusion and *extension of knowledge*" (I.pr.). But in the preceding chapter I have argued that, whatever the qualifications for teachers may be at colleges, free-standing professional schools, or other educational institutions, it has become a distinctive and defining characteristic of professors who teach at the university that they be scholars, who have been and are still engaged in the advancement of knowledge through research and scholarly publication even while they are engaged in the extension of knowledge through teaching. The parallel to that proposition is this: that, whatever the qualifications of scholars and researchers may be at academies of sciences, free-standing laboratories, or other research institutions, it is a distinctive and defining characteristic of professors who carry on their scholarly and scientific investigation at the university that they be teachers. Whether or not it is a parallel, this thesis does not, however, follow automatically from the first; the case for the requirement that university scholars be teachers, therefore, while certainly related to the requirement that university professors be scholars, must be supported on other grounds.

In this form, the case for such a combination once again stands in opposition to Newman's judgment about the relation between teaching and research, as formulated in the preface to *The Idea of a University*, that "to discover and to teach are distinct functions; they are also distinct gifts, and are not commonly found united in the same person." He continues:

"The great discoveries in chemistry and electricity were not made in Universities. Observatories are more frequently out of Universities than in them, and even when within their bounds need have no moral connexion with them." For although the resistance to teaching by scholars receives far less publicity, either in the public media or in the educational journals or in the undergraduate press, than does the campaign against the criterion of research and publication for teachers, the demand that scholars teach if they are to be professors in the university is by no means self-evident. The entire system of professors, docents, and assistants in the European university was designed in part to protect against any such demand. At the University of Uppsala in Sweden, to cite just one example, the teaching of undergraduates is in the hands of university lecturers, while the professors and even the docents devote their time almost exclusively to graduate students and to their own research. There are, after all—although, to be sure, more in some disciplines than in others—alternative ways for scholars of excellence to make a decent living without being reduced to the teaching of undergraduates.

The biography of one leading American archaeologist who worked in Egypt at the beginning of this century describes in fascinating detail the necessity of working in situ for months and even years at a time, with great difficulties for his family and for his undergraduate students (if any), his graduate students being perhaps in a better position, at any rate so long as they, too, were working in situ on some part of the master's dig. In all three of the disciplines of the physical sciences that Newman cites explicitly in the passage just quoted—"chemistry" (including now biochemistry), "electricity" (now physics as a whole), and "observatories" (observational astronomy, together with astrophysics)—the separation of major centers of research from university campuses has often been a practical necessity, whatever the theoretical arguments or even the educational arguments pro and con may be. As the phenomenon that has been called "sophistication inflation" has made the instrumentation for scientific research in all of these fields increasingly complex and expensive, it exceeds the capacity of any single university; or at any rate, the notion that every research university should have every instrument approaches the bizarre. Even in medicine, for example, competition has sometimes led neighboring hospitals or medical schools to acquire, sometimes beyond the limits of defensible need, the massive devices of diagnosis and treatment without which any one of them would seem to be at a competitive disadvantage in health care or in research. The alternative to such internecine competition, however, is the creation of national and international instrumentation centers to which scientists from an entire consortium of universities would have access. One of the most important of these is the Conseil Européen pour la Recherche Nucléaire, usually identified by its acronym, CERN, in Geneva. As a consequence of these developments in instrumentation, many universities are facing the logistical problem of how, without jeopardizing their teaching, those who regularly instruct undergraduates in the natural sciences are to visit such centers to engage in the research projects, some of them of many months' duration, on which the advancement of scientific knowledge— and, not incidentally, the careers of the faculty members—depend. Team teaching has often helped considerably. Nevertheless, the theoretical interdependence of research and teaching does seem to break down in the face of such a logistical problem.

For these and other reasons, some well-informed and sober observers of the educational scene today share Newman's judgment that "to discover and to teach are distinct functions, they are also distinct gifts," and therefore have concluded not only that they "are not commonly found united in the same person," but also that they should not commonly be found in the same institution. It is, of course, possible to take such a position for a variety of reasons. One can make the case that to protect what Newman calls the "seclusion and quiet" of "the search after truth" and the integrity of the research enterprise in all disciplines, scholars need to be protected from the intrusive demands of teaching. Or, alternately, one can demand that because, in Newman's opening definition, "a University . . . is a place of teaching universal knowledge" (I.pr.), professors get back to doing what they are paid to do instead of diverting so much of their time and attention to research. That demand was voiced with characteristic acuteness a quarter-century ago in the polemical article of John H. Fischer, "Is There a Teacher on the Faculty?" More recently it has been articulated with vigor and eloquence in the annual report for 1990 of the chairman of the National Endowment for the Humanities. Nor is the concern restricted to the demand for undergraduate teaching; it addresses itself also to professional education. Thus it is widely perceived among hospital patients and public critics of the university that a preoccupation with the advancement of knowledge and with scientific discovery is adversely affecting not only teaching, in this case the training of future physicians who are learning to regard pure research as preferable to the practice of medicine, but the quality of medical care in hospitals, where the sick are sometimes made to feel that their illness is of interest chiefly because it provides data for research. Such a criticism of the primacy of research over teaching is sounded far more stridently by aggrieved undergraduates who have lost a beloved instructor to the university's scholarly requirements. The criticism cannot be shaken off by a defensive "professoriate" (to invoke Fischer's favorite epithet) as the philistinism of (invoking an epithet from Sinclair Lewis) "sewing machine salesmen and college presidents."

On a more personal scale, the issue of the relation between scholarship and teaching at the university presents itself every year to millions of prospective students and their parents, as they ponder the confusing menu of universities and colleges before deciding where to apply. For many in this situation, the best starting point, before discussing any specific college or university, is to draw the distinction between a university college and a free-standing college on this very basis. Any university professor who has participated as an outside examiner in the honors program at one of the leading undergraduate colleges will have come away from the experience deeply moved by the loyalty and dedication of the professors there to their students—deeply moved, and struck by the humbling realization that no university professor, no matter how devoted to undergraduate teaching, would or could make the major investment that the tutorial instruction and close scrutiny of the students' progress in such a program demands. Comparing the best with the best, applicants should ask themselves whether they are coming to college with the expectation that their faculty will be as accessible and as involved as that. For at the university, they will ordinarily be obliged to share their professor's time with the graduate students to whom the professor also has an ongoing obligation. Thus, to put it in crudely quantitative terms, the undergraduate in the college is entitled to all of the professor's student time, while the undergraduate in the university is entitled to only half of the professor's student time. It is even more important, and more pertinent to the issue at hand, that at the university the students, both undergraduate and graduate, are together entitled to only half of the professor's total professional time, the other half of which is owed to scholarship and writing. It is a tribute to the faculty at the best university colleges that, despite this rough quantitative division, even some of those professors who are the most productive as scholars and authors may end up devoting far more than that one-fourth of their time to their undergraduate students; but the point is valid nevertheless.

At the same time a prospective undergraduate must recognize that the quantity of access to faculty may not be the only index to faculty-student relations, but that the quality of such access may be far more important. At a time of rapidly breaking changes in scholarship, most dramatically in the natural sciences but not exclusively there, students need to ask whether they will run the danger that their intellectual and scholarly needs will outgrow their faculty. Even with computerized card catalogs and faster interlibrary loan service, moreover, the university undergraduate has far easier access to the libraries and to the laboratories of the university than does the college undergraduate, and this may more than make up for less ready access to the teacher-scholars of the faculty. Now if it is true also for undergraduates, to quote what I said earlier, that passive reception of communicated knowledge must be replaced or at any rate accompanied by active participation in the processes by which knowledge is advanced; and if therefore the learning process does not mean simply learning the What of existing knowledge, but learning the How for as yet unknown knowledge—it seems to follow that it is not enough to have someone at the head of the classroom who, in Newman's words, "spends his day in dispensing his existing knowledge to all comers" (I.pr.). Rather, the university teacher, also the university teacher of undergraduates, must at the same time be adding to existing knowledge *for* others, and not simply receiving it *from* others. Many college professors certainly fit that description, and brilliantly; but by this definition, all university professors must fit it.

In an effort to break free of some of the implications of this dichotomy and in the belief that "the time has come to move beyond the tired old 'teaching versus research' debate," the Carnegie Foundation for the Advancement of Teaching has proposed, in a "special report" under the title *Scholarship Reconsidered,* a new and a "broader, more capacious" classification of four kinds of scholarship: "the scholarship of *discovery*; the scholarship of *integration*; the scholarship of *application*; and the scholarship of *teaching*." The first of these, "the scholarship of discovery," was the primary topic of chapter 8, although the second category, "the scholarship of integration," is more closely related to the first than is often realized. The third, "the scholarship of application," is in part the topic of chapter 10, "Knowledge Viewed in Relation to Professional Skill." But it is the fourth, "the scholarship of teaching," that represents the main point of the Carnegie Foundation report. For "although," the report continues, "teaching is often viewed as a routine function, tacked on, something almost anyone can do," it is in fact both "a scholarly enterprise" and "a dynamic endeavor," because it "means that faculty themselves are learners." Moreover, "in the end, inspired teaching keeps the flame of scholarship [meaning here, apparently, the scholarship of discovery] alive." Whatever may be one's evaluation of this provocative proposal, it does rest on another distinction, one that is above all fundamental to my reexamination of the idea of the university: the distinction between what the report itself identifies at the very outset as "the collegiate and university models of higher learning." It is, of course, only with "the university model" that my reexamination of the idea of the university is dealing, also here in its consideration of under-graduate teaching. Staying with the several distinctions of the report, then, the specific question here can be formulated this way: Can "scholarship as teaching" be carried on by those who are engaged in "scholarship as discovery," and within the context of the "university model of higher learning," and why should professors who carry on their scholarship in the university—"scholarship as discovery"—even bother to be teachers?

Although the complaint is frequently voiced, and with good reason, that prospective college teachers working for their Ph.D. in graduate school do not receive adequate preparation for their eventual work in the classroom, it is no less true that their preparation for the work of scholarly publishing is also inadequate, or at best haphazard and uneven; I shall return to this issue later. Because graduate professors are chosen, and should be chosen, for their scholarly standing in the field of their research and because they in turn evaluate the work of their students by the criteria appropriate to that definition of the field, they frequently contribute unwittingly to the per-petuation of an impenetrable writing style infected with trendy buzz words and scholarly jargon. The amusement with which professors at a university commencement read the titles of the dissertations that have been directed by their colleagues from other departments is in part a defensive reaction, but it is also a symptom of the quality of scholarly and scientific writing. Indeed, some of that sort of writing is probably acceptable in a dissertation and in the equivalent specialized articles that a scholar produces later on, but it afflicts the writing of many scholars even when they are addressing their work to a nonspecialized audience. To this latter kind of writing, at any rate, Newman's definition would seem to apply: "Thought and speech are inseparable from each other. Matter and expression are parts of one: style is a thinking out into language" (II.ii.4). Usually, the counterpart to the audience for this kind of writing that a publishing scholar can find is the class at an undergraduate lecture. If the students there are well in-formed in general but poorly informed in particular, if they are bright and interested and ignorant, they correspond to the readers, or at any rate the potential readers, of a scholar's books. The scholar can have no better practice for the writing of such books than a continued exposure to under-graduate teaching. For when undergraduates are puzzled, their wrinkled brows show it; when readers are puzzled, they decide not to buy the book.

One fundamental reason for the contribution that undergraduate teaching makes to scholarly writing and publishing is that both of these activities call for going beyond the data and details of research to hypothesis and generalization, in the terminology of the Carnegie Foundation, from "the scholarship of discovery" to "the scholarship of integration." The very task of organizing the material of an undergraduate course into discrete units, like the task of dividing the results of an investigation into an outline and individual chapters, requires critical reflection about such hypotheses and generalizations. For although it is still sometimes customary to call the doctoral dissertation a "thesis," many dissertations seem in fact not to have a thesis at all, but to leave the products of the candidate's digging uninterpreted, by doing the mining without going on to the minting. In a research seminar, for graduate students but also for advanced undergraduates, that may often be enough: in an entire semester that is devoted to a discussion of and commentary upon some crucial text, it is probably sufficient if the students have parsed the author's sentences (in whatever language) and prosecuted the course of the author's argument, without necessarily developing a larger hypothesis about the work, much less about the larger questions with which it deals. But when the results of that commentary are incorporated into a course, the professor is obliged to draw connections and contrasts and to locate the work in its broader context. Eventually it is the professor's obligation to carry out that same assignment of drawing connections and contrasts and of locating the work in its broader context also as a scholarly author. The professor comes to that obligation of the scholar far better prepared after having first taken it on as an undergraduate teacher.

The teaching of undergraduates from all over the college, rather than the teaching exclusively of graduate students from the professor's field and department, is likewise the best possible forum for relating one scholarly discipline to another. In an eloquent description of what a university does, Newman declares that

> . . . it is pledged to admit, without fear, without prejudice, without compromise, all comers, if they come in the name of Truth; to adjust views, and experiences, and habits of mind the most independent and dissimilar; and to give full play to thought and erudition in their most original forms, and their most intense expressions, and in their most ample circuit. Thus to draw many things into one, is its special function; and it learns to do it, not by rules reducible to writing, but

by sagacity, wisdom, and forbearance, acting upon a profound insight into the subject-matter of knowledge, and by a vigilant repression of aggression or bigotry in any quarter (II.viii.2).

Newman could have added that this it does above all in undergraduate
teaching, for that is undoubtedly what he had in mind. One of the most
positive results of that process for the scholar and researcher is that from
the interplay of ideas so eloquently described by Newman will come the
analogies and distinctions between disciplines, the definitions and comparisons of methodologies, and perhaps above all the illustrations and
metaphors from other disciplines that will illumine the subject matter of
the scholar's own discipline in a new way. Even discoveries that are entirely
or largely confined to the proper subject matter of a discipline have frequently drawn on other fields for the key metaphors in which they have
been articulated. Thus Sigmund Freud, a physician, learned about the
Oedipus complex not from reading medical journals but from reading
Greek literature; as his biographer has noted, "Freud was an educated
European speaking to other educated Europeans and had raided Sopho-
cles" for such allusions. But also in a personal and professional way,
teachers need to be increasingly aware of what is being taught in the
departments and courses of their colleagues, so that they may draw correla-
tions and contrasts, instead of leaving that entire task to the students
themselves, as they have all too often tended to do. They will often tend to
do that the most effectively in their own scholarship through having
learned from their undergraduate students.

Conversely, however, it is and must be in the undergraduate context that
the university and its scholars pay attention to the university's function of
transmitting, cultivating, and criticizing "a common learning." As one
educator has recently put it, "A liberal education needs to create a challenge to the ideas, habits, and attitudes that students bring with them."
But, he continues, "if the students are to educate one another in this way"
by issuing such a challenge, "some part of their studies must be in common." Whatever it may mean for undergraduates themselves, moreover,
the absence of a common body of learning also raises grave questions for
the future of scholarly research. For the difference between bad scholarship
and good scholarship is the result of what a student learns in graduate
school, but the difference between good scholarship and great scholarship
is, as often as not, the general preparation of the scholar in fields other than
the field of specialization and is thus the result of what a student learns in
college. (There is an analogous relation between common learning and

artistic performance.) This is, moreover, a process that does not end with the scholar's formal education but continues; and it is the ongoing responsibility of undergraduate teachers for the common learning of their students that also continues to supply those teachers as scholars with the ideas and images for interpreting their own special disciplines.

For that reason, by stimulating intellectual dialogue and thus becoming the chief unifying force in the common life of the faculty and the university, the teaching of undergraduates and the sharing of responsibility for that teaching can be the principal agency through which, in the words of Newman quoted earlier, "the goodly family of the Sciences" can become "sisters all, and sisterly in their mutual dispositions" (II.app.i). Thus I was shocked to discover, on becoming dean of the graduate school at Yale, just how limited the range of intellectual discourse between the members of the graduate faculty of the university can be. The reason is that the arena of intellectual discourse is in the departments and programs of the graduate school, not in the faculty as a whole. The graduate school and its faculty as a unit can only prescribe certain minimums—for example, in residence requirements, in the language examinations for the Ph.D., or in the form of the dissertation. But it is there in the departments or interdepartmental graduate programs, and not in the graduate faculty, that the definition of scholarly research, the determination of standards for admission and for completion, the relation of the graduate curriculum to the present and future discoveries of the fields, and the identification of methods and criteria are all worked out. In the college of the university, by contrast, as also in any good college apart from the university, these issues over which professors debate within graduate departments are, or at any rate should be, the concern of the faculty as a whole. To the extent that the clarification of such issues is, for scholars, a responsibility and an opportunity for them to clarify as well as they can the larger implications of their scholarship, scholars carry out their task as scholars better if they are forced to confront these issues not only with their fellow chemists or historians inside one graduate department, but with chemists and historians and psychologists as part of the total college faculty of the university.

The involvement of scholars in the teaching of undergraduates likewise remains the best possible way for them to carry on one activity in which, if they are committed to their scholarly disciplines, they must be vigorously engaged: the recruitment of the next generation of scholars. It has been well said that "excellence is transmitted within colleges and universities (and all other schools) through individuals." The autobiographies of scientists and scholars are replete with anecdotes of how they were inducted into the mysteries of their discipline already as undergraduates by some more or less eminent scholar who took the time to communicate to them not only the facts but the methodology, and not only the methodology but the excitement of the field. One such eminent scientist, J. Robert Oppenheimer, said at the bicentennial celebration of Columbia University in 1954:

> The specialization of science is an inevitable accompaniment of progress—yet it is full of dangers and it is cruelly wasteful since so much that is beautiful and enlightening is cut off from most of the world. Thus, it is proper to the role of the scientist that he not merely find the truth and communicate it to his fellows, but that he teach—that he try to bring the most honest and most intelligible account of new knowledge to all who will try to learn.

That is as true of Greek literature or of economics as it is of Oppenheimer's field of physics, and the need to find the posterity to which each generation of scholars will hand on the torch of the discipline ought to be incentive enough all by itself for distinguished scholars to want to carry their share of the responsibility for undergraduate teaching.

Although it remains true, as has been said earlier, that the requirement for teachers to be scholars and the requirement for scholars to be teachers are by no means identical, they do coincide at certain fundamental points. One of these is the "statement of faith" quoted earlier, that "it is in the combination of research and instruction that the distinctiveness of [our] institutions of higher learning is expressed. . . . We want to introduce [our students] to scholarship itself and to teach them how one arrives at the reality and truth of things and how one can advance the progress of scholarship." That applies not only to the German university in which it was spoken but to the university everywhere, to undergraduate teaching no less than to graduate teaching—and, in Newman's terminology, to the "extension of knowledge" through teaching no less than to the "advancement of knowledge" through research.

IO

KNOWLEDGE VIEWED
IN RELATION TO
PROFESSIONAL SKILL

When the scholar Faust, at the opening of Goethe's "subversive classic," wanted to catalog all the fruitless paths he had traveled in his futile search for wisdom, he had simply to recite the titles of the four faculties of the medieval university: "Philosophy and Jurisprudence, Medicine,—and even, alas! Theology." By "Philosophy," moreover, he was referring not only to what is now the curriculum of the philosophy department, but to the entire program of what is now called the faculty of arts and sciences, which even in Goethe's time had begun to dominate the German university as a whole, especially with the founding of the University of Berlin in 1810. Three of the four faculties through which this eternal student had passed, therefore, would now be called professional schools, constituting the three traditional learned professions, which were law, medicine, and divinity. It would therefore be a disastrous foreshortening of perspective if a reexamination of the idea of the university like this one were to concentrate exclusively on the faculty of arts and sciences at the expense of the professional schools of the university, just as it is a foreshortening of perspective, and for that matter ultimately an impoverishment of the faculty of arts and sciences, when the university is defined or organized without professional education as a constitutive part of the enterprise.

Although the seventh of Newman's original discourses does bear the title I have borrowed for this chapter, "*Knowledge Viewed in Relation to Professional Skill*," there are some grounds for having to attribute such foreshortening of perspective also to Newman himself. In a lecture of November 1854 to the School of Philosophy and Letters he comments: "It is indeed not a little remarkable that, in spite of the special historical connexion of University Institutions with the Sciences of Theology, Law, and Medicine, a University, after all, should be formally based (as it really is), and should emphatically live in, the Faculty of Arts; but such is the deliberate decision of those who have most deeply and impartially considered the subject." He nevertheless goes on to speak of "the reasonable association . . . which exists in our minds between Universities and the three learned professions" of law, medicine, and theology (II.i.1). In voicing such a judgment, Newman is, as he acknowledges, following the lead of Victor-Aimé Huber's *English Universities:*

> The studies of Law and Medicine grew up by the side of Arts, but never gained strength to compete with the last; nor has the principle ever been attacked, *that the University has its foundation in Arts.* Yet this apparent preeminence concealed a real inferiority. The Students in Arts always maintained (more or less successfully) that their studies were an indispensable preparation for the Faculties. What else was this, but to assign to the Arts a lower position, as being merely preliminary?

This does reflect in considerable measure the special origin and history of the university in England; but it is a mistake—historically, and also educationally and intellectually—to treat the English experience as universal and thereby to provide, in Newman's words, grounds "to complain that I have servilely followed the English idea of a University" (I.pr.). Yet this is what Newman appears to be doing when he states, without qualification, that "Arts existed before other Faculties" (II.i.1). In other places and at other times, *pace* Newman's statement, other faculties existed before the arts faculty did; and, conversely, more than a few of the fields of study that we now associate with the faculty of arts and sciences had their beginning in those other faculties and continue to be strongly based in them.

In "An Address to the Students of Medicine" delivered in November 1858, Newman explores the meaning and status of the concept of "profession," especially as it affects professional education within a university context. "All professions have their dangers," he warns. "Every professional man has rightly a zeal for his profession, and he would not do his duty towards it without that zeal" (II.x.2). This lecture is in turn an echo of the seventh discourse of Part I, "Knowledge Viewed in Relation to Professional Skill." There he is, as he puts it, "arguing . . . against Professional or Scientific knowledge as the sufficient end of a University Education," but with the explicit reassurance that thereby he does not intend "to be disrespectful towards particular studies, or arts, or vocations, and those who are engaged in them" or "to imply that the University does not teach Law or Medicine." But wherein, he asks, lies the distinctiveness of how "a Professor of Law, or of Medicine, or of Geology, or of Political Economy" functions in a university context? Newman's answer is "that out[side] of a University he is in danger of being absorbed and narrowed by his pursuit, and of giving Lectures which are the Lectures of nothing more than a lawyer, physician, geologist, or political economist." Inside the university, on the other hand,

> he will just know where he and his science stand, he has come to it, as it were, from a height, he has taken a survey of all knowledge, he is kept from extravagance by the very rivalry of other studies, he has gained from them a special illumination and largeness of mind and freedom and self-possession, and he treats his own in consequence with a philosophy and a resource, which belongs not to the study itself, but to his liberal education.

For that kind of professional training, what is needed first is the liberal education of "the man who has learned to think and to reason and to compare and to discriminate and to analyze, who has refined his taste, and formed his judgment, and sharpened his mental vision," in short, the education of one who has been "placed in that state of intellect in which he can take up any one of the sciences or callings I have referred to, or any other for which he has a taste or special talent, with an ease, a grace, a versatility, and a success, to which another is a stranger" (I.vii.6). The "philosophy and resource" of which Newman speaks expresses itself also in the recognition of the moral issues in the practice of any profession. For "it may easily happen," he observes, speaking specifically about medical ethics, "that what is in itself innocent may not be innocent to this or that person, or in this or that mode or degree" (II.x.3).

From the correspondence and other documents surrounding the founding of the Catholic University in Ireland, it is clear that it was the professional mission of the university that bulked largest in the minds of the Irish hierarchy and people. One of the primary desiderata for them was the need to have a place where British Roman Catholics, especially in Ireland, could be prepared for the learned professions of law and medicine in an atmosphere that was not hostile to their beliefs and church. To receive such a training in the Universities of Oxford and Cambridge, they would have been obliged to sign an affirmation of the Protestant faith. Many Cambridge or Oxford students who made such a pro forma affirmation, whether Anglicans or Dissenters or Roman Catholics or Jews or agnostics, were clearly doing so with enormous reservations about the Thirty-nine Articles, and the requirement of accepting that creed or any creed was by this time a dead letter. Roman Catholics, too, could therefore go through the formality of declaring their allegiance to the Protestant Anglican faith while keeping their Roman Catholic faith and practice intact, and many of them were doing just that. But for John Henry Newman—who from his own experience of the early 1840s knew something about the existential anguish and moral ambiguity of what he calls in his novel *Loss and Gain* "signing the Articles" as a mere formality, that is, officially affirming one system of faith while personally accepting another—such a pretense was simply unacceptable. "Paris is worth a Mass!" Henri IV was reputed to have said. It was not so for Newman: doctrine was too important, and the implications of its truth or error too awesome, to be trivialized for the sake of expediency—or for the sake of a professional career. The only solution for the predicament of Roman Catholics at British universities was to establish a Catholic university, and in the political situation of the time such a university was most appropriately situated in Ireland. While all of that was true for every field of learning, it bore special practical significance for professional training, because of the need for Roman Catholic lawyers and physicians in Ireland. Newman was, therefore, addressing a central issue in the very idea of a university, or at any rate in the idea of such a university, when he sought to clarify the place of professional studies in it (I.vii). As George N. Shuster has suggested, however, it is "somewhat ironical that the greatest practical achievements of this unusual Rector, who was concerned above all with the relationships between theology and what he called 'liberal education,' were the development of a School of Medicine, which for the first time gave young Irish Catholics ample opportunities to become masters of the art of healing, and the establishment of a pioneer chair for Celtic studies." As rector of the Catholic University, Newman in the summer of 1854 purchased the medical school of the Dublin Apothecaries' Hall, opening it that November as the medical school of his university.

When he entitled his seventh discourse "Knowledge Viewed in Relation to Professional Skill," Newman was also addressing the issue that, more than any other, raises fundamental and troubling questions about his principle in the fifth discourse of his book (and in the fourth chapter of this volume), "Knowledge Its Own End." For as the president of Dartmouth College, Nathan Lord, put it in his inaugural address of 1828,

The examples of other times, when the learning of universities all had respect to the future political and ecclesiastical relations of the student, and these institutions became little better than panders to allied despotism and superstition, may teach us to cultivate our youth in the elements of general knowledge, and impart vigor and force to their minds in the course of sound fundamental study, before they are permitted to engage in any merely professional acquisitions.

Both historically and intellectually (not to say administratively), therefore, the place of "professional skill" in the context of the university and of the college is at best ambiguous. On the one hand, it is instructive to note that when *The Oxford English Dictionary* defines "trade school" as "a school in which handicrafts are taught," it supports that definition with two apposite quotations: one from 1898, referring to "the Proficiency of the Trade School Plumber"; the other from 1906, which speaks of "the day trade-schools provided by the Council for the training of boys and girls in certain trades after they leave the elementary schools." On the other hand, one of the most thoughtful discussions of the university since Newman's, Alfred North Whitehead's *Aims of Education,* carries the reminder that "at no time have universities been restricted to pure abstract learning. . . . The justification for a university is that it preserves the connection between knowledge and the zest of life, by uniting the young and the old in the imaginative consideration of learning," also, though not exclusively, in its professional training. For it may come as a surprise to some partisans of the faculty of arts and sciences to learn that Whitehead's essay is based on a lecture that he delivered at Harvard in 1928 for the business school. What he calls "the connection between knowledge and the zest of life," which he identifies as the very "justification for a university," necessarily implies the movement of questions and ideas in both directions between (to use the historic medieval designations of the four faculties) the university's centers of professional training in the faculties of medicine, law, and divinity (together with whatever other professional faculties and schools may develop) and the centers of research and teaching in its faculty of philosophy.

Yet even a cursory examination of a dozen or so current university catalogs will reveal a bewildering variety of professional schools now hovering in and around various universities in various countries; in addition, and more disquieting still, there are the professional and quasi-professional undergraduate majors for which students may receive a bachelor's degree—even at times the degree of Bachelor of Arts. Recalling some observations he had made already in 1935, Robert Maynard Hutchins observed in 1941, with typical but appropriate hyperbole:

> I attacked triviality, and forty-two students enrolled in the Oklahoma University short course for drum majors.
>
> I attacked vocationalism, and the University of California announced a course in cosmetology, saying, "The profession of beautician is the fastest growing in this state."

As one alarmed European observer has summarized the situation, not only in his own country but generally, the historic pattern by which lectures and seminars in the university were "imbued with the latest advances in science [scholarship] and, at best, the personality of the professor" has been threatened by "the impending division of the university into two halves, [one devoted to research] . . . and the other—which has wiped out the old concept of a University—to the acquisition of professional knowledge." In the evaluation of all professional schools in the university, it deserves to be noted that the most important review of professional training ever carried out for any of them was the Flexner Report of 1910, *Medical Education in the United States and Canada*. Its diagnosis of the scientific deficiencies in the curriculum and the laboratories, as well as in the research background of faculty, at American schools of medicine was an indictment of any system of preparation for any profession that amounts to little more than a glorified apprenticeship. Most of the recommendations of the Flexner Report became basic for the quantum leaps that have been taken by medical education in the United States and Canada and in other countries during the twentieth century, which have in turn become the starting point for the reconsiderations of medical education now being undertaken by several projects and panels in several nations. The resulting literature on the reform of professional training at schools of medicine and of baccalaureate preparation for it has been expanding rapidly.

Many of Flexner's proposals for revisions of the medical curriculum were the outcome of advances in the art, technique, and technology of healing, to which medical students needed to be introduced during their primary training, as well as of changes in the organization and funding of medical education. But the most fundamental proposals were made possible and even urgent by the advances in the basic sciences of human biology in the departments to which schools of medicine still refer as "preclinical." It was no longer possible, if it ever had been, for these sciences to be taught to future doctors in isolation from the centers of biological research within the rest of the university. Whether or not one accepted all the conclusions of Darwin's *Origin of Species* and *The Descent of Man,* one implication was clear and unavoidable: human biology must be studied within the total context of biology, and those who are being prepared to apply the information and insights of human biology to the art of healing must be at home within that larger context or they will not be professionally (not to say scientifically) equal to their tasks. At the very time that Flexner was formulating his case for embedding professional medical education within the scientific faculties of the university rather than isolating it in the ghetto of the professional school, the twentieth-century science of biochemistry was coming into its own, out of the work of chemists, biologists, and physicists chiefly though not exclusively in university laboratories, to revolutionize all of the biological sciences—and the teaching of medicine.

A similar review has been taking place in legal education. Preparation for a career as a lawyer, too, had, both in England and in the early history of the United States, grown away from the university and was carried out in an apprenticeship system of "reading law" with an experienced jurist. But then the American law schools, one at a time, began their migration back to the university—which, after all, they had helped to create. At the *Universit' degli Studi di Bologna,* contrary to Newman's account of the historical sequence (II.i.1), it was the study of law, specifically of Roman law, that originally defined the university (although Bologna now has ten other faculties, though not any longer a faculty of theology). At worst, this relocation of professional education in the law within university walls has tended simply to perpetuate the ghetto, to the detriment not only of the law school but of the university. For as Edward H. Levi insisted in an analysis of "The Choices for a University," responding to this ghetto mentality, "The professional school which sets its course by the current practice of the profession is, in an important sense, a failure." The reason for that severe judgment, he continued, is that "the professional school must be concerned in a basic way with the world of learning and the interaction between this world and the world of problems to be solved." That, Levi argued, is why the professional school and the university need each other. Indeed, opposing the customary snobbery of the faculty of arts and sciences, he even suggested that "viewed in terms of its larger responsibilities, the professional school inherits and exemplifies much of the disappearing tradition of the liberal arts college. As such it represents some of the highest values in a university." In an earlier talk entitled "The Law School within the University," Levi had concluded with the observation:

When I was a law school dean I had to say, or so I thought, that law and law schools were of the greatest importance to the larger community and to the universities of which they are a part. Now that I am in a sense free, I find that what I said was true. I had not fully realized, however, how intertwined the roles of law school and university were, nor had I appreciated that so much of the humanistic tradition is kept alive in the professional course of liberal arts which is the law. And that is the sense of values, which while so frequently formally eschewed, helps give the law schools their distinction.

Levi added: "It is good to hope that the values and ways of life of law schools and universities will gain from each other."

Several decades after the Flexner Report, and not in any sense set forth as a mere adaptation of it, the review of theological education directed by H. Richard Niebuhr and two colleagues reached conclusions that were fundamentally similar to Flexner's and Levi's. Niebuhr, too, found that the scholarly equipment of seminary professors varied widely, many of them, even in the theological equivalent of "preclinical" scholarly disciplines, having had no formal preparation or experience in basic research beyond that which their own seminarians would reach by graduation; in effect, therefore, such professors were self-taught as scholars. That lack of background was still more of a problem in the students coming to seminary, growing numbers of whom had not studied philosophy, history, social science, and languages, the branches of the liberal arts that pertained the most directly to the traditional content of the theological curriculum. Both for the remedial needs of such students and for the continuing scholarly and professional maturity of their professors, it was, in Niebuhr's judgment, mandatory that schools of preparation for the ministry find creative ways of relating themselves to the university, whether by becoming (or becoming again) faculties of the university or any rate by situating themselves in such a way, academically and geographically, as to facilitate an easy interchange between the fields of theological study and the disciplines of the humanities and social sciences corresponding to them.

The field of theological education is also an intriguing case study with which to illustrate the general problem of "knowledge and professional skill." Arguably the most important action of the Council of Trent—which met from 1545 to 1563 in response to the Protestant Reformation and of which, while he was still an Anglican, Newman declared that "the Church of Rome was bound up with the cause of Antichrist by the Council of Trent"—was neither the decree of its fourth session on Scripture and Tradition nor its attempt in the decree of its sixth session to formulate a balanced statement of the doctrine of justification, the two issues on which I had to concentrate in my interpretation of Trent in volume 4 of *The Christian Tradition,* but the legislation of its twenty-third session of July 1563, bearing the title "Forma erigendi seminarium clericorum." Whatever may have been its intended scope, the result of the decree was, for most countries, the concentration of theological education in diocesan institutions of clerical training that were isolated from the university. That had grave consequences for the life and thought of the Roman Catholic church, as well as for the university. By a historical twist that is genuinely (to use an overworked word) ironic, an American Protestantism that strove so assiduously to cast off what the Puritans called "the remnants of popery" adopted, and even exaggerated, this unfortunate "remnant of popery" by creating a vast network of church seminaries, as well as of church colleges, a few of which laid claim to the title "university" but were often able to do so credibly only by casting off their ties to the church. I am a graduate of such a seminary, and because of the exigencies of my schooling I was registered simultaneously as a candidate for the degree of Bachelor of Divinity at Concordia Seminary in Saint Louis and as a candidate for the degree of Doctor of Philosophy at the University of Chicago, receiving both degrees in 1946. Whatever other symptoms of intellectual and educational schizophrenia that experience may have precipitated, it did give me an abiding sensitivity to the fundamental issues raised by Newman's Discourse VII on "Knowledge and Professional Skill."

To consider the place of professional education within the university in critical perspective, I have sometimes put two unabashedly rhetorical questions, which still, I think, formulate the issue quite directly. One is to ask: "Should the university establish a school of mortuary science, perhaps across the street from the school of medicine?" The other, still reflecting that preoccupation with lugubrious thoughts, is to inquire: "If the bubonic plague were to strike the university tonight and wipe out the entire faculty (save for thee and me and the endowment), would we, after burying our dead, proceed to replicate all the dozen or so professional schools that happen to be here now?" If the immediate answer to both questions is an obvious No, the underlying justification for such an answer is considerably less obvious. For although it is true historically that many universities have, with greater or lesser hesitation, adopted the professional schools that happen to have been left at their fiscal and educational doorstep, there is some definition of the idea of the university implicit in any such decision. It is probably easier to specify the definition of "professional skill" and of professional training that is implicit there: the recognition that to qualify as a "profession," an occupation or activity must involve some tradition of critical philosophical reflection, and probably the existence of a body of scholarly literature in which such reflection has been developed and debated. But the corollary of that thesis is probably a definition of the university as the only possible setting in which such reflection on a profession, and therefore the training informed by such reflection, can be carried on in its full intellectual context—and hence also a definition of the university that includes such training as a necessary element.

If the university understands the crisis in which it is living and if the university is the key to educational reform throughout the various societies in which it exists all over the world, the reexamination of the relation between its professional mission and its research and teaching in the faculty of arts and sciences may well be its most fundamental assignment. Limning the contours of a "University of Utopia" or setting forth "fanciful speculation" about an "innovative academy" is a time-honored pursuit. When Newman declared that "to set forth the right standard, and to train according to it, and to help forward all students towards it according to their various capacities, this I conceive to be the business of a University" (I.vii.1), he may not have been using the word *train* in the strict sense of professional education; but "the business of a University" does involve the several "learned professions," regardless of which of these may be on any individual university's roster. Robert Stevens once hazarded the prediction that someday there would be law schools in which "research . . . uses and teaches law in the framework of the social sciences and humanities." More hazardous perhaps, but inherent to my argument, is the prediction that, at any rate for some professional schools and for some universities, such a recognition will lead to the conviction that this framework calls for a fundamental reorganization not only of the professional schools but of the whole university.

The division of the biological sciences may serve yet again as a model for such a reorganization; for it now crosses the boundaries not only between such traditional disciplines as biology and chemistry but between the school of medicine and the faculty of arts and sciences. It is, then, at any rate on some university campuses, an academic entity which not only combines fundamental research with teaching (as, in one way or another, all the divisions and departments and professional schools are expected to do), but which in that teaching takes responsibility for undergraduates in the college, for Ph.D. students in the graduate school, and for professional students in the medical school. The administrative, financial, and intellectual toil involved in such an arrangement is enormous, as administrators can attest. But it can be, in Newman's phrase in the final sentence of *The Idea of a University* (and in a lecture to the school of medicine), "arduous, pleasant, and hopeful toil" (II.x.5), because of the potential intellectual benefits if fundamental research, professional training, graduate study, and undergraduate teaching are all being carried on in continuing interaction with one another.

Is it possible, is it even conceivable, that the entire university could be reorganized on that model? This would happen not only by integrating B.A. and Ph.D. studies under the aegis of the several departments of the faculty of arts and sciences, as has been done almost universally, but by providing for the structural (as distinguished from the merely informal) integration of both of these with the faculty and program of one or more professional schools that are germane to such study, and conversely the integration of those professional schools with one or more of the divisions to which they have intellectual and scholarly affinities: "law in the framework of the social sciences and humanities"; medicine in the framework of the biological and social sciences; the claims of "theological science" in creative tension with those "of literature, of physical research, of history, of metaphysics" (II.viii.2); and Faust's "Philosophy," which means the faculty of arts and sciences with all its departments and fields, asking the kinds of questions, if not providing the kinds of answers, that can qualify philosophy to be, as Newman said it should be, "a sort of science distinct from all of them, and in some sense a science of sciences, which is my own conception of what is meant by Philosophy, in the true sense of the word" (I.iii.4).

II

THE EMBALMING OF
DEAD GENIUS?

In his rather loosely organized *Rise and Progress of Universities* of 1856, which was published between the first and the second parts of *The Idea of a University,* Newman described the ancient library of Alexandria as a major precedent for the rise of the university; for it was there that "for the first time, a great system was set on foot for collecting together into one, and handing down to posterity, the oracles of the world's wisdom." Over time, various gifts and accessions expanded "this noblest of dynastic monuments." As "the two great conceptions brought into execution by the first Ptolemy," therefore, Newman put the support of teaching as "the endowment of living [genius]" and the establishment of a library as *"the embalming of dead genius."* He may have regarded this as an especially appropriate metaphor for an Egyptian institution, but he was also anticipating George Eliot's characterization of Edward Casaubon's scholarship as "a lifeless embalmment of knowledge." Nevertheless, John Henry Newman—in his successive careers as Oxford don, as Tractarian, as convert to Roman Catholicism, as theologian, and as university rector—became what he was largely as a consequence of all the time he had spent sequestered in the library and the study. Already as an undergraduate at Trinity College, he "put in an average of twelve hours of study" a day, and later in his life, despite all of his travels, "the only true voyage was that which he took in the silence of his own heart or among the works of his beloved Fathers."

Therefore Newman's *Apologia pro Vita Sua,* which is in many ways patterned after Augustine's *Confessions*—which is in turn patterned after Paul's narrative of his own conversion—is nevertheless the account of a transformation that came not from a voice in the garden that said "Tolle, lege! Take and read!" nor from a voice on the road to Damascus that said "Saul, Saul, why persecutest thou me?" but from his solitary reading and scholarly research. During the Long Vacation of 1839, Newman writes, he returned to the course of reading which I had for many years before chosen as especially my own. I have no reason to suppose that the thoughts of Rome came across my mind at all. About the middle of June I began to study and master the history of the Monophysites. I was absorbed in the doctrinal question. This was from about June 13th to August 30th. It was during this course of reading that for the first time a doubt came upon me of the tenableness of Anglicanism. . . . My stronghold was Antiquity; now here, in the middle of the fifth century, I found, as it seemed to me, Christendom of the sixteenth and nineteenth centuries reflected. I saw my face in that mirror, and I was a Monophysite.

Commenting on Newman's standing as a patristic scholar, F. L. Cross has noted: "There was perhaps no one in any country who, in the first half of the nineteenth century, had a greater knowledge of Athanasius than Newman." Thus it was as a scholar who had spent many years poring over Greek texts in the library that Newman came to his theological decisions. But that is no less true of his educational decisions, including the decisions that led to the composition of *The Idea of a University* and to the reflection that went into it. It was also as such a scholar that he could be justifiably proud of at least one of his concrete accomplishments as rector of the Catholic University of Ireland: not only did he create a fine school of medicine, but he was, as Culler puts it, "able to add to its facilities a distinguished medical library of five thousand volumes, acquired from Germany." Yet, scion of libraries that he was, he felt that he was, if anyone was, entitled to disparage the pedantry expressed in "the mere multiplication and dissemination of volumes" in the library, as "this most preposterous and pernicious of delusions" and as a part of "the error of distracting and enfeebling the mind by an unmeaning profusion of subjects" in the undergraduate curriculum (I.vi.8). For "the variety of useful or entertaining knowledge contained in . . . libraries . . . never can serve as a substitute for methodical and laborious teaching" in the university (II.ix.7).

In the present reexamination of the idea of the university as "the endowment of living genius," which is primarily devoted to expectation, it may appear out of place to be preoccupied with memory as "the embalming of dead genius." For a superficial impression might conclude that in coining a phrase like this Newman is in surprising agreement with, of all people, Thomas Huxley, who in a letter written on 30 May 1889, shortly before Newman's death, called him "the slipperiest sophist I have ever met." Huxley wrote three years later: "The mediaeval university looked backwards: it professed to be a storehouse of old knowledge. . . . The modern university looks forward, and is a factory of new knowledge: its professors have to be at the top of the wave of progress." But this is a misleading distinction. For it is only by "the embalming of dead genius" in its libraries, museums, and galleries that the university can become a repository for "the oracles of the world's wisdom," and only by "looking backwards" as "a storehouse of old knowledge" that it can become "a factory of new knowledge" and, as such, can "look forward." Recognizing as few others have that for the university, as perhaps for no other institution except the church, memory and expectation are inseparable, Newman pondered the implications of this for both institutions. As one of the most important of modern treatises on the idea of tradition has said, Newman's "hypothesis of a development, which he thought of as the opening out of the aspects of an 'idea' which retains its original meaning throughout its differing historical forms . . . became an inner dimension to that of tradition." A university that would, in its enthusiasm for "living genius" or in its eagerness for "development" and "looking forward," neglect its vocation as a repository for "the oracles of the world's wisdom" and for the tradition would lose not only the past but the present and the future as well. It would, moreover, do so not for itself alone, nor only for its students and its several other constituencies, but for the entire society and culture it is called to serve. Not only are the university and the church defined by their memory, but within Western culture at any rate they have been and still are in a special way the custodians of the common memory for everyone. Whenever, after an era of mass amnesia like the present, the search for cultural identity becomes, as it must again, a search for cultural and spiritual roots, a new generation will turn to these repositories to tell it about its lost grandparents—and thus about itself and about generations yet unborn. The epigram of Newman's contemporary, Thomas Carlyle, formulated in a lecture on 19 May 1840, "The true University of these days is a Collection of Books," was certainly an oversimplification, but it was an oversimplification in the right direction.

This vocation of preserving the common memory represents a moral obligation for the ethos and the curriculum of every school and department of the university, determined though some of them (such as literary criticism) have been from time to time to forget this obligation. There are, nevertheless, some departments and institutes for which the moral obligation assumes a primacy that sets them apart. Among these, the university library may lay claim to pride of place as the "scholar's workshop," because every university has a library and most research libraries are at research universities, while the museums and galleries of most nations tend in significantly larger proportion to be free-standing. What pertains to the university library, moreover, pertains as well to those galleries and museums that are based at universities. The dynamic interrelation of research with teaching, and of both with the acquisition, preservation, and circulation of documents and artifacts, applies to galleries, museums, and above all to libraries. It bears pointing out that some of the largest and in many respects the most important repositories for "the oracles of the world's wisdom" in the world are not based in universities at all: the Bibliotheca Apostolica at the Vatican, the British Library, the Bibliothèque Nationale, the Lenin Library, the Library of Congress, the New York Public Library, the Smithsonian Institution. By any definition of a university except the most narrowly institutional, however, it can be argued that all of these complex institutions are in fact universities without degrees, carrying out the vocations of research, teaching, and publication within their own programs and supporting these tasks in the life of "other" universities and of the national and international university community as a whole. In the future of the university and of the university library, moreover, the network of university and library can only become more intertwined. Therefore it is simply sober fact to say that no single institution in the contemporary world of scholarship has a greater bearing on the future of the university than the library, just as nothing in the history of the university has had a greater bearing on its scholarship.

It is a truism that the relation between scholars and libraries is a symbiosis, a truism documented in the life of the thinker with whose *Idea of a University* this book is in dialogue, John Henry Cardinal Newman, and in the life of his bête noire, with whom he in turn was in a lifelong dialogue, Edward Gibbon. Both of them were the grateful offspring of research libraries. Gibbon wasted much of his youth on desultory reading of scholarly tomes dealing with a random assortment of recondite subjects, with the result that, as he says in his autobiography, he "arrived at Oxford with a stock of erudition that might have puzzled a doctor and a degree of ignorance of which a schoolboy would have been ashamed." He describes how, after his disastrous fourteen months at Oxford, a series of other research libraries provided him with the immense learning that then shaped his great history. In that history, too, libraries play a significant part. Near the end of the work, with a sardonic turn of phrase that would identify this passage as Gibbon's even if it were anonymous, he observed in describing the fall of Constantinople in 1453, which is the Götterdämmerung of his *Decline and Fall*:

A philosopher . . . will . . . seriously deplore the loss of the Byzantine libraries, which were destroyed or scattered in the general confusion: one hundred and twenty thousand manuscripts are said to have disappeared; ten volumes might be purchased for a single ducat; and the same ignominious price, *too high perhaps for a shelf of theology,* included the whole works of Aristotle and Homer, the noblest productions of the science and literature of ancient Greece.

In the next chapter I shall speak about the obligation of the university and its scholars to "publish or perish," about scholarly writing, and in that connection also about the aesthetic dimension of scholarship. But first it is necessary to be concerned not with the processes of scholarly writing, but with its presuppositions and its productions, thus with the special mission of the library within the business of the university, specifically research and teaching. With a clarity that the secularist academic mind sometimes finds disturbing, Newman recognized that learning and scholarship must have a moral dimension or they can become demonic. Long before the moral crisis of the German universities in the 1930s and 1940s—which indelibly impressed that insight on some scholars of that generation and of those that have followed—he saw that the academic community is as liable to corruption as is the state or the marketplace or even the church.

Reversing the earlier order for the moment, we may begin with the most obvious expression of the mission of the university library, which upon closer examination proves to be not so obvious at all: the business of teaching. Beyond the practical obligations of the professor to prepare undergraduate reading lists that are checked for accuracy and are delivered on time, and the corresponding obligation of the librarian to subordinate the efficient operation of the shop to the educational purpose of the shop, the nature of the collegiality between library and faculty in undergraduate teaching calls for serious attention. For if it were the primary function of the undergraduate teacher, in Newman's phrase, to "[spend] his day in dispensing his existing knowledge to all comers" (I.pr.) and merely to communicate the so-called assured results of scholarship, it would be the correlative function of the library merely to see to it that the books containing those assured results are available. But today's "assured results" are the raw materials for tomorrow's history of scholarship. Therefore it must be the deeper function of undergraduate teaching to induct the young into the mysterious and ongoing process by which that will go on happening. In that case, even the undergraduate librarian at a university must be something of a research librarian, for it is the librarian's responsibility to build and maintain collections through which each successive generation will be inducted into that process. If, as I have argued earlier, it is indeed not only the What but the How of knowledge that is the crucial consideration—especially in fields that are changing fast, where the temptation of the university faculty is to present the results of their own research as the latest revelation, or even the final revelation—the university library must be there to provide context, balance, and correction. In graduate study that mission becomes all the more essential. I must confess here that I am, to an alarming extent, a bibliographical autodidact. I did not learn about many of the standard manuals in my fields from my professors in seminars or lectures or libraries but more or less had to stumble upon these reference works myself. And in some cases, to my acute embarrassment, I have learned about such guides only decades after completing graduate study, at least partly because the methodological (and theological) presuppositions of my professors had excluded them from view. That is a risk that we should not have to run with our graduate students; or, to put it more accurately if more brutally, that is a risk that our graduate students should not have to run with us, the risk that the prejudices and bibliographical blind spots of the professor can be visited on the student. As the volume of scholarly helps increases, the need for professional guidance in the use of such helps increases with it; and that professional guidance can come only from subject bibliographers who are sensitive and thoroughly trained and whom research scholars recognize as their peers and colleagues in the raising up of future scholars. Graduate students trained that way, incidentally, are also more likely, in their work as teachers of undergraduates, to recognize their colleagues in the library as genuine peers, and thus perhaps the cycle can be broken.

Consideration of graduate education inevitably leads to a consideration of the mission of the university library in scholarly research as such, as the modern university has developed into the research center that it is. To make a general point concrete, it is only necessary to examine one specific genre of scholarly research that is, in an era of continually exploding scholarly information, becoming increasingly central to the research enterprise, not only in the natural sciences and the social sciences, where it already holds a prominent place, but in the humanities: the bibliographical essay or survey of scholarly literature, whether it is a chapter in a book (as it is here) or written for separate publication as an article. Although most scholarly books come equipped with conventional bibliographies, it is clear that whatever such lists may do to help the reader identify the scholarship on which a book or article or lecture has drawn, they do not by themselves advance research. By contrast, the bibliographical essay, if prepared with just the right blend of thoroughness and imagination, can serve at least two major purposes simultaneously. It can be a necessary prolegomenon to research, by means of which scholars are enabled to locate their new discoveries or insights in the context of the total state of the art. Thus scholarly and scientific readers can, with a minimum of slippage, see where their new research has truly done something new, and can therefore begin to assess its significance. Conversely, the new research may also have achieved its results through a dangerous oversimplification of problems that earlier scholars had recognized in their full complexity, and the well-written bibliographical essay can provide a scholar with perspective also on that issue. Beyond that function, however, the bibliographical essay is an important chapter in intellectual history, especially when it deals with an aspect of one of those seminal issues that systems of human thought and belief use over and over to identify themselves. By this means the scholar's own research points beyond itself to the continuing tradition of study and debate. Few enterprises are more fundamental for the future of university research than this.

As anyone who has ever attempted it will testify, however, preparing a bibliographical essay of that kind is not for the faint of heart. For unless one is committed to some party line, be it political or philosophical or theological or literary, such a report on the state of the art has the moral obligation to report and summarize the historical development and current status of the research with the objectivity described (if not always achieved) by Tacitus in the *Annals:* "sine ira et studio." For a research scholar and speculative thinker who has now reached some fairly definite conclusions about an issue, such objectivity may seem tantamount to a betrayal of the truth, and it can therefore be sacrificed to polemics. That is where the collegiality between research scholars and research librarians becomes obligatory. The scholar's impatience to get on with the research will often brush aside important monuments of scholarship that merit abiding attention, and the research librarian is there to draw attention to those monuments. But the collegiality has a more profound mission. There is nothing so ecumenical as the library, as one of Newman's favorite poets (I.vi.10), George Crabbe, said:

> Calvin grows gentle in this silent coast,
> Nor finds a single heretic to roast;
> Here, their fierce rage subdued, and lost their pride,
> The pope and Luther slumber side by side.

That ecumenism stands as a curb on the tendency to subordinate the history of all hitherto existing scholarship to the party line. It also introduces into the presentation a range of sensibilities and an awareness of nuance that are all too easily lost. Only if the research scholar begins to have some of the qualities of the bibliographer and if the research librarian is a philologist of sorts can research in all fields begin to acquire literature surveys of the quality it ought to have for scholarship to thrive. This reexamination of the idea of the university is arguing that essentially the business of the university can be said to consist of three interrelated stages: the advancement of knowledge through scholarly investigation; the extension and interpretation of knowledge through teaching, including professional training; and the diffusion of knowledge through scholarly publication. At each stage, the vocation of the university depends absolutely on the library.

Such a dependence implies the need for the university library to be involved as a genuine and full partner of the other components of the university in both short-range decisions and long-range planning. One major example of that need is the opening of new fields for teaching and research. It is perhaps easier to discuss this issue now, because throughout most of the world universities happen to be in a position of retrenchment, or at best in a steady state, without the rapid and dramatic growth that characterized university life a few decades ago. A consequence of that retrenchment, and one with grave implications for the university, is great hesitation among university leaders everywhere (borrowing Newman's word) to "initiate" (I.ix.10), despite the urgency, whether intellectual or cultural, scientific or technological, political or economic, that attends certain fields. It was difficult enough to practice educational statesmanship when new programs, departments, and entire professional schools were opening up everywhere; it is infinitely more difficult in the present situation. There is all the more reason, therefore, to pay close attention to the processes that ought to precede the creation of a new program of study, even for undergraduates and especially for graduate and professional students. The area studies phenomenon of a generation ago ought to be an object lesson. It is one thing to recognize the demand for more attention to the contemporary Near East, but it is quite another to take the full measure of that demand. There must not be courses merely on the political struggles since the creation of the state of Israel. There must also be courses in Hebrew, in Arabic (or the several forms of Arabic), and in Farsi; yet, to stay with the last of those languages, Farsi was being studied recently by only two students in the Foreign Service Institute of the U.S. State Department, both of whom, according to a report published at that time, "have since graduated, and as of now no one is enrolled in the language at the institute." Courses merely in these languages, moreover, would not be sufficient without study in their literature, religion, and culture. All of this calls for the acquisition of library resources on a massive scale.

The converse, however, does not necessarily follow. For although the university must not undertake a field of study in its teaching and research for which it does not have logistical support in the library, it often may, and sometimes must, expand and deepen the holdings of the library in a field where, at least for the moment, it is not doing significant research or teaching at all. Some of us who have been denizens of the library stacks at many universities often amuse ourselves by trying to estimate the years of appointment and of retirement of a distinguished scholar by checking when the library began to acquire heavily in that field and when it discontinued doing so. Yet it is obvious how shortsighted such a policy is for the university, for collection-building must be independent of the current configuration of scholars on the university's faculty. This is partly because of the special problem of the rare book library, which must have the flexibility to acquire such books when they become available, so that when the need for them arises it is ready. Some mixture of antiquarian and pirate is called for in an aggressive and successful acquisitions librarian in this field, and it goes on being necessary, within the practicalities of the real world, to create and sustain the conditions for that mixture to appear. Even the availability of funding is no guarantee. There must also be rare book librarians with the scholarly intuition and the intellectual taste to choose from among existing opportunities. They should not be asked (or even permitted) to do this on their own. Such choices call for a collegial give-and-take between research librarian and research scholar, even if neither of them is a specialist in this particular field.

This area of the university library is, in a special sense, an "embalming of past genius" but also a "treasure trove of common memory." Special collections have a unique bearing on university scholarship in the humanities and in the natural sciences. By sheer bulk but also by their unique contents, the personal papers and other documents from the history of literature often dominate special collections in the university library, and without them scholarship in the humanities would be significantly impoverished. More broadly, however, special collections continue to be necessary for the study of literature and the humanities in their total context. It is possible to argue, without being trapped into a discussion of what Harold Bloom calls "the anxiety of influence," that the context of literary works must include an understanding of the works by which writers have been formed. For example, most of the great European writers even in the modern era did not, as we would put it in the present-day university, "major" in English or French or German, but in the Greek and Latin classics. It was not Shakespeare but Shakespeare's contemporary, George Chapman, who by his translation of Homer called forth from Keats the words:

Then felt I like some watcher of the skies
When a new planet swims into his ken.

Similarly, the most important thinker of the thirteenth century was not Thomas Aquinas but Augustine; and the various interpretations of Augustine by Aquinas, Bonaventure, Duns Scotus, Dante, and others are an essential key to the movements of thought in that exciting era. To trace these various interpretations, humanistic scholarship must have access to the way our past has used its past; and that requires the collection and identification, if possible, of the editions, translations, and compilations upon which these interpreters drew—a formidable assignment, as any editor of a substantial corpus of works, including me, can testify. Where but in the special collections of a university library can such scholarship hope to find these documents? Sometimes they may even have priceless marginal glosses and notes added, which can be a means of identifying this context more accurately.

Although this use of special collections by scholarship in the humanities is probably their most obvious contribution to research, it is becoming increasingly evident that they are fundamental to the proper study of the sciences as well. It is a significant mark of the development and maturation of the natural sciences within the university that in recent decades scientists have been deepening their own historical consciousness about their fields and, conversely, that social and intellectual historians have begun to acknowledge that they cannot begin to come to terms with the thought and life of an era, not only in the recent but also in the distant past, without studying its science. For example, the historian of medieval ideas who assumes as a matter of course the necessity of connecting theology with philosophy and metaphysics must go on to connect metaphysics with physics. Historical perspective is needed to dispel the mythology that has arisen—partly because of the naïveté of the lay public and partly, it must be admitted, because of the posturing of some scientists—about the processes of scientific discovery and creativity. In the study of science, the attention both of specialists and of laypeople is irresistibly drawn to the "flashes of insight" involved in the breakthrough into new data or new syntheses. Like other historical landmarks, the scientific breakthrough acquires an aura of inevitability, as though no other conclusion or perhaps no other procedure could have been conceived. But laboratory notebooks can illuminate the broader picture of scientific research in important ways. Novelists and scholars in various fields often discard trial outlines and first drafts after they have completed a work, and scientists have tended to find such obliteration of their footsteps even easier. Hence it is no longer possible to find out which steps—and which missteps—formed the path through the valley to the peak; and yet, like most mountain trails, such a path often moves down as well as up, sideways as well as forward. If the scientific heritage is to make intellectual sense, the university with its library has the obligation to make possible a sophisticated understanding of how scientific investigation works and of how its results come. Such an understanding is impossible without special collections.

Perhaps, then, it is necessary to reverse Huxley's distinction, that "the medieval university looked backwards; it professed to be a storehouse of old knowledge. . . . The modern university looks forward, and is a factory of new knowledge." For as Newman suggests, contradicting the simplistic identification of the Middle Ages as the age of faith, "the very age of Universities" in the Middle Ages "was a time when the intellect went wild, and had a licentious revel" (II.viii.5). Commenting on the twelfth and thirteenth centuries, he observes: "The medieval schools were the *arena* of as critical a struggle between truth and error as Christianity has ever endured. . . . Scarcely had Universities risen into popularity, when they were found to be infected with the most subtle and fatal forms of unbelief" (II.v.2). Thus in fact they were, in Huxley's phrase, trying to function as factories of new knowledge without functioning sufficiently also as storehouses of old knowledge. In the modern university, as eventually in the medieval university, the new knowledge has repeatedly come through confronting the old, in the process of which both old and new have been transformed. For the achievement of that transformation, in the modern university as in the Ptolemaic foundation at Alexandria that Newman correctly identified as its ancestor, it has been necessary to combine "two great conceptions . . . the embalming of dead genius [and] . . . the endowment of living [genius]." For the university—and, as the university needs to remind especially the society of the twentieth and twenty-first centuries, for all of human culture—these two conceptions, memory and expectation, are finally inseparable.

12

THE DIFFUSION
OF KNOWLEDGE
THROUGH PUBLISHING

When John Henry Newman, in his introductory definition of the university, declared "that its object is . . . *the diffusion . . . of knowledge*" (I.pr.), his conception of what was implied by the diffusion of knowledge, as distinct from its advancement through research, was largely confined to teaching, and "diffusion" through publishing was not an explicit part of the definition. Prolific author and consummate English stylist that he was, however, Newman did reckon with both the possibility and the expectation that publications would come out of his university. The possibility was formulated in a lecture of 1854 entitled "Catholic Literature in the English Tongue," where Newman, speaking about "indications that we have able scientific men in our [English Roman Catholic] communion," immediately added: "If we have such, they will be certain to write, and in proportion as they increase in number will there be the chance of really profound, original, and standard books issuing from our Lecture-rooms and Libraries" (II.iii.2.3). The expectation was expressed in his marginal note to the "Rules and Regulations for the Catholic University" of 1856, which reads, in Newman's own hand: "Professors to write books." This form of the diffusion of knowledge as an integral dimension of "the business of a University" (I.vii.1), which was called by one of the pioneers of university publishing in the United States "a real awakening on the part of the whole University to its opportunity to disseminate knowledge, to spread light and truth, far beyond its own walls," may be examined from three related but distinct angles: the vocation of professors in the university to publish the results of their scholarly research; the training of graduate students not only in research but in writing and scholarly publishing; and the mission of the university as a scholarly publisher.

On the basis of my earlier catalog of "The Imperial Intellect and Its Virtues" (a title I conflated from Newman and the *Nicomachean Ethics* of Aristotle), as these virtues pertain to the ordering of the common life of the university, it is possible also to describe some of the intellectual virtues that are expressed specifically in the vocation of the scholar to diffuse knowledge through scholarly publishing. Many have been itemized by Nathan M. Pusey. "The standards of the scholar," he wrote, "the mature scholar who . . . has also become a mature person, continue to impress us." Pusey's list included: "patience, honesty, industry, a sense of 'standard,' humility, a vision of something beyond the tawdry and the broken." When we speak about "the intellectual virtues," we sometimes tend to fall back on a distinction that comes to us, as does the concept of the intellectual virtues, from classical antiquity, and was then elaborated in medieval thought: the distinction between the active and the contemplative life. Near the end of the *Nicomachean Ethics* Aristotle suggests that "the activity [which is] perfect happiness is contemplative." Thus when Philosophy appears to Boethius in the prison cell, she has on her garment "in the lower part the Greek letter Pi, and in the upper Theta," standing for "philosophia praktikē, the philosophy of the active life," and "philosophia theōrētikē, the philosophy of the contemplative life." Although Boethius had been consul of Rome and was a prominent figure in the public life of the Latin West during the sixth century, his primary vocation was that of a scholar, probably the most eminent scholar of his time, and therefore it was "the philosophy of the contemplative life" that he needed in this vocation, as well as in his existential situation as a prisoner. This meant that one has to choose between becoming an Alexander the Great, who conquered the world, and becoming his teacher Aristotle, who understood the world; according to Plutarch, Alexander wrote to Aristotle: "For my part, I assure you, I had rather excel others in the knowledge of what is excellent, than in the extent of my power and dominion." Or one has to choose between Martha, who "was cumbered about much serving," and her sister, Mary, who had chosen "the one thing needful" and who gave first place to the contemplation of the truth. Or, to borrow a distinction from quite another source, one has to choose between "interpret[ing] the world" and "chang[ing] it."

Apologists sometimes make the vocation of scholarship sound like that of one of the contemplative orders of medieval monks. Thus Newman's exposition of the thesis that "knowledge is its own end" is, as he himself acknowledges, "summed up in a few characteristic words of the great Philosopher," Aristotle (I.v.4). He then quotes the *Rhetoric* on one of the basic corollaries of the distinction between the active and contemplative life. There was and remains a place for contemplatives both in the church and in the university; as the saying goes, some of my best friends in the church and in the university are just that. Nevertheless, as a key metaphor for the vocation of the scholar, the purely contemplative order is not quite appropriate. Rather, I would propose as a description for the virtue of the scholar the motto of the Dominican Order, the Order of Preachers (which has included scholars of the eminence of Albertus Magnus and Thomas Aquinas, as well as many others in more recent centuries): "contemplata aliis tradere," to communicate to others the fruit of one's contemplation. In the formula of Thomas Aquinas, "As it is better to enlighten than merely to shine, so it is better to give to others the fruits of one's contemplation than merely to contemplate." It must be remembered, as has been pointed out by one of his biographers, himself a Dominican, that "by 'contemplation' he meant not only the infused contemplation that comes from prayer, but also the acquired contemplation that comes from study." For the sacred vocation of the scholar, no less than for the sacred vocation of the Dominican friar, "contemplata aliis tradere," the readiness not only for contemplation but for communication, or, in Newman's phrase, for "the diffusion of knowledge," also belongs in the catalog of the virtues of "the imperial intellect."

This readiness "contemplata aliis tradere" moves simultaneously on several tracks. It includes, of course, the imperative to teach the results of research to students. When Newman argues that "to discover and to teach are distinct functions; they are also distinct gifts, and are not commonly found united in the same person," and therefore that "he who spends his day in dispensing his existing knowledge to all comers is unlikely to have either leisure or energy to acquire new" (I.pr.), he appears to be overlooking in theory something that he did not overlook in practice: that the most exciting form of teaching, also of undergraduate teaching, is the communication not of some other scholar's "existing knowledge" but of one's own "discovery" in the very process of its being carried on (and revised). But "contemplata aliis tradere" implies, perhaps above all, the obligation to share with one's colleagues in the discipline the outcome of the scholarly research in which one is engaged. "Publish or perish!" is not, as undergraduate newspapers often charge when a favorite teacher fails of promotion to tenure because of a lack of scholarly publications, an arbitrary rule invented by the network of established scholars to keep upstarts out of the university's faculty, or perhaps by the university press to stay in business. "Publish or perish!" is a fundamental psychological, indeed almost physiological, imperative that is rooted in the metabolism of scholarship as a sacred vocation. For that is how research remains honest, by exposing itself to the criticism and correction of other scholars and by inviting them—or daring them—to replicate its results if they can and, if possible, to carry those results further or to refute them by more careful or imaginative research. Only the diffusion of knowledge through some form of scholarly publishing can make this process possible.

Scholarly authors in the university, however, need to pay more attention than they have traditionally done to a corollary of this obligation, the duty to become themselves the communicators of the outcome of their research for a broader public, instead of leaving that task to the authors of text-books, magazine articles, and other works of popularization. They may well share Newman's rather patronizing attitude toward "reviews, maga-zines, newspapers, and other literature of the day, which, however able and valuable in itself, is not the instrument of intellectual education" (II.ix.7). But if they do, they have no right to complain about the works that fill the vacuum; for, in the words of a distinguished present-day paleontologist, it remains the case that "we can still have a genre of scientific books suitable for and accessible alike to professionals and interested laypeople." As George Parmly Day once said, "If our University Presses merely print meritorious works and find few readers for them, they are manifestly not accomplishing their purpose." He articulated that purpose in the formula: "That the University itself not only might but should serve, through pub-lications actively fostered and encouraged by it, the world at large as well as the world of scholarship and letters." Yet it is distressing to see how many scholarly books are still being written more with the reviewer than with the reader in mind. Because the economic realities both of graduate education and of scholarly publishing are making the traditional scholarly mono-graph (which is all too often still a euphemism for the slightly revised doctoral dissertation) increasingly difficult to produce without pricing it out of its already shrinking market, alternate methods of diffusing such knowledge, above all through microfilm, have been in place since the end of the Second World War. Therefore scholars must learn "contemplata aliis tradere" beyond the charmed circle of other professors. If scholars are to carry out this publishing responsibility, they have the obligation to give more attention than they now do to the question of how we are to publish lest we perish.

To shift to the autobiographical modality for a moment, let me identify an arbitrary rule to which I adhered throughout the five volumes (and two decades) of producing *The Christian Tradition:* to identify every proper name except that of Jesus Christ and to define every term that does not appear in *Webster's Collegiate Dictionary*. At one point I thought of preparing a glossary of technical terms, of which there certainly are a goodly number in the history of Christian dogmatic theology, but I eventually rejected that idea (although I have employed it elsewhere). Instead, I endeavored, either through a logical definition or through a cumulative description or through a judicious use of cross-references or through the index (or through all of the above), to provide such an identification, or at any rate as much as was necessary in the context, in the course of the book. That problem of how much to explain has been brought home to many readers, who had perhaps never thought about such problems before, by the portrayal in Umberto Eco's *Name of the Rose* of that enigmatic and complex figure, the fourteenth-century thinker and reformer Ubertino of Casale; and it is, I learned, no easier in handling the various medieval and Reformation doctrines of the real presence (or real absence) in the Eucharist, or the dogma of the Holy Trinity. But I discovered that this arbitrary rule repeatedly necessitated a clarification of things that may have seemed obvious to me but were in fact not obvious at all. My experience was analogous to the burden many émigré scholars have taken on upon coming to the United States and learning to speak English. Such problems are now becoming, if anything, even more difficult for university scholars in a global context.

But beyond the intellectual clarification made necessary by writing a book for one's readers rather than only for one's reviewers, there is the sheer task of writing it, and of writing it well. All too often, scholarly research that has been carried out conscientiously and thoroughly, even imaginatively, loses its effectiveness because the scholar does not take the time and trouble—or perhaps, does not have the ability and interest—to present its results with clarity and grace, but instead expects the results to speak for themselves. The time does seem to have come for thoughtful people, particularly scholars, to restore rhetoric to its honorable place among the skills of language, including the rhetorical skill of clothing high scholarship in language of sensitivity and taste. In the words of Newman quoted earlier, "Thought and speech are inseparable from each other. Matter and expression are parts of one: style is a thinking out into language" (II.ii.4). But if the university is to contribute to such a development, there needs to be a change in how graduate students are trained in research, writing, and publishing. It is unfortunately true that few undergraduate or graduate students give evidence in their papers of having taken this final step of testing their presentation for the power of its language; nor do their teachers always reserve their very highest grades only for those papers that have earned such grades simultaneously for their scholarly content and for their written form. That raises with new acuteness the problem of university scholarship, as that problem come to its most important focus in the preparation of scholars as writers, and therefore in the role of the senior adviser. The best published studies of that role have concentrated on the natural sciences, where the relation of the mentor's research to the student's research is particularly crucial, both because of the situation of apprenticeship in the laboratory and because of the way such research and teaching are funded. But these studies in the history of science bear also on other disciplines, and they indicate the usefulness of considering that role under a variety of metaphors that have been employed to describe it.

In his comparison of two eminent German chemists, Emil Fischer and Franz Hofmeister, Joseph S. Fruton has commented: "As one reads the doctoral dissertations of Fischer's students, one cannot but be struck by their limited scope and relatively modest contribution to chemical knowledge." He goes on to a "consideration of the question whether, in the description of a scientific discipline, priority should be given to the problems it seeks to solve or to the methods it uses to solve them." He concludes, on the basis of "the examination of their research groups," that "selective genealogical tables offer little insight into the relation of the fame of a group leader to the later renown of his scientific progeny." What Fruton's comparative study does clearly suggest is that there is often a discernible genealogy from a *Doktorvater* (or *Doktorgrossvater*) to the Ph.D.s learning to write in his or her laboratory or seminar, but that this is frequently a genealogy not of eminence but of method—or, as Fruton calls it, of "scientific style."

For the phenomenon that is often called, especially in contemporary literary debate, "the cult of theory" has as its counterpart the tyranny of method (which it seems to have become obligatory to call "methodology") in the genetic transmission of scholarship and in its diffusion. Thus no one today could afford to dismiss this question, as one eminent scholar from the nineteenth century used to do, with a brusque, "Method is mother wit!" One important task of the mentor as Doktorvater, therefore, is the definition and delimitation of the proper method both for carrying out an investigation and for publishing its results. Scholars in the humanities who turn to the works of their colleagues in political science or sociology, and now increasingly also in history, are often dismayed to discover that a reliance not only on a quantitative method but on "modeling" has made many such works increasingly inaccessible to them. Deeper investigation of such changes, whatever their direction might be, will often identify as the source of the methodology one or another Doktorvater whose recruitment and training of doctoral candidates set the procedures of scholarly research and fixed the perspectives of scholarly writing that introduced new standards (and often new metaphors or "paradigms") into the discipline and its scholarly literature. It is intriguing to observe the paths by which these standards and metaphors have sometimes been carried over from another discipline in which the Doktorvater was originally trained. For example, Irving Fisher, one of the most influential of twentieth-century economists, came to economics with a Ph.D. in mathematics, and it appears to have been Fisher who introduced into economic theory a concept from mathematical physics, "equilibrium," together with the methods that his followers found appropriate for studying it. Whether or not Thomas Carlyle was right in calling it "the dismal science," such economics could claim to be real science.

By contrast, there is no such metaphor as *Doktormutter*, nor even *Doktortochter*. Instead, the Socratic metaphor of "midwife" springs easily to mind in a consideration of the mentor's function in the process through which a publishing scholar comes into the world. Recalling that his mother had been a midwife, Socrates suggested that midwifery was practiced by women who had once given birth to children of their own but had now passed childbearing age, since Artemis, the goddess of childbirth, "could not allow the barren to be midwives, because human nature cannot know the mystery of an art without experience." It was his assignment, Socrates declared, to "attend men and not women, and to look after their souls when they are in labor, and not after their bodies." "And the triumph of my art," he said, "is in thoroughly examining whether the thought which the mind of the young man brings forth is a false idol or a noble and true birth." To practice that art, he had to have become "barren": "I ask questions of others," he said in paraphrasing the widespread criticism of him, "and have not the wit to answer them myself." Søren Kierkegaard, having written his dissertation on the concept of irony in Socrates, made this maieutic metaphor part of his attack on the writings of Hegel and the Hegelians. For Kierkegaard, all teaching and all serious writing had to be "indirect."

Applied to the Ph.D. mentor, the Socratic metaphor of the midwife can have a variety of implications. These would not include, presumably, an absolute insistence on the Socratic requirement that the mentor as midwife be "barren" and past the age (or stage) of productive research and publishing. But they do include the presupposition that the student, not the professor, is the one who is fertile and, in the language of Socrates, pregnant with thought. Commenting on the widespread influence of such a scholarly "midwife," the German chemist Adolf von Baeyer, Joseph Fruton notes that "with some exceptions . . . all the major pre-1914 German universities had, at one time or another, full professors of chemistry who had been members of the Baeyer research school." Fruton observes at the same time that "Baeyer was rather more generous than most other leading German professors of chemistry in allowing his Dr.phil. students and the postdoctoral guests who worked with him to publish their results alone." Meanwhile, Baeyer himself "published somewhat over 300 papers bearing his name from his laboratories in Berlin, Strassburg, and Munich." It does not seem presumptuous to suggest that these three circumstances of Baeyer's scholarship and mentorship bear some causal relation to one another. In addition, there have always been scholars whose own published scholarly output has been rather modest in scope but who directed a series of elegant dissertations that became important books, none of which reflected a party line but each of which represented an expression of the student's scholarly integrity. The Ph.D.s of such a mentor tend to manifest a bewildering heterogeneity; and at least in some instances, it does appear necessary to ask whether the mentor as midwife, in the effort not to interfere with the natural processes, has exercised a sufficiently critical function in the gestation and birth of the newborn scholar-author. Socrates the "midwife," after all, did busy himself with distinguishing between a "false idol" and "a noble and true birth," and with seeing to it that the former did not come to full term.

Quite another metaphor for the mentor is the character of Dr. Victor Frankenstein in Mary Wollstonecraft Shelley's youthful work of 1818. As its subtitle, *The Modern Prometheus,* indicates, the book was inspired by classical mythology; its plot is familiar enough, albeit more from motion picture versions than from the book itself. Having discovered the secret of life while doing research as a student at the University of Ingolstadt, Victor Frankenstein fashioned dead men's bones into a quasi-human being, "tremendous and abhorred" but very strong, which turned on its maker and murdered Frankenstein's bride and brother. The theme of the work, some passages of which sound almost as though the author had anticipated Freud's *Moses and Monotheism,* was the bitter hatred and rebellion of the monster against the scientist, which could only end with the death of both in an Arctic wasteland. The tragic hybris of Mary Shelley's Dr. Frankenstein, which belongs in some respects to the topos of the mad scientist and seems to have contributed significantly to the rise of modern science fiction, has received an additional ironic twist: present-day usage regularly attaches the name "Frankenstein" to the creature rather than to the creator, whose identity has thus disappeared in the reputation of the Adam on whom he conferred the gift of life.

The applicability of the metaphor of Dr. Frankenstein to the experience of some Ph.D. mentors becomes dramatically visible in the careers of those nineteenth-century academics whose own books are now largely forgotten but who played the part of Doktorvater to the "God-slayers" coming out of that century: Marx, Nietzsche, and Freud. Nietzsche is in many ways the most interesting of the three. His Doktorvater was the renowned philologist and Plautus scholar, the editor of the *Priscae Latinitatis Monumenta Epigraphica* and thereby the founder of the Berlin *Corpus Inscriptionum Latinarum,* Friedrich Wilhelm Ritschl. The roster of the scholars and books that came out of Ritschl's seminar at Bonn and then at Leipzig is awe-inspiring: Georg Curtius, Ihne, Schleicher, Bernays, Ribbeck, Lorenz, Vahlen, Hübner, Bücheler, Helbig, Benndorf, Riese, Windisch—and Friedrich Wilhelm Nietzsche, who studied under him both at Bonn and at Leipzig. When Nietzsche was only twenty-four, Ritschl wrote of him: "However many young talents I have seen develop under my eyes for thirty-nine years now, never yet have I known a young man . . . who was so mature as early and as young as this Nietzsche. . . . He is the first from whom I have ever accepted any contribution at all [for publication in the journal *Museum*] while he was still a student." Of Ritschl's students, Nietzsche was almost certainly the only one to receive his Ph.D. sans dissertation and to earn his professorship (at Basel when he was twenty-five) without the customary second book, the *Habilitationsschrift.* What he wrote instead was *The Birth of Tragedy from the Spirit of Music,* which he published in 1872, three years after becoming professor at Basel. Already in 1868, Nietzsche had described philological scholarship as (speaking of metaphors) "the whole molish business, the full cheek pouches and blind eyes, the delight at having caught a worm, and indifference toward the true and urgent problems of life." *Die Geburt der Tragödie* could not be accused of that kind of philological scholarship, for its real Doktorvater was not Ritschl at all but Wagner. The philologists, speaking through the young Ulrich Wilamowitz-Moellendorf in a treatise sarcastically entitled *The Philology of the Future,* proceeded to excommunicate Nietzsche. Ritschl still rates a brief article in the *Micropaedia* of the new *Encyclopaedia Britannica* (contrasting with the substantial article on him by James Smith Reid in the eleventh edition, which observes that "to the world in general Ritschl was best known as a classical scholar" and which does not so much as mention Nietzsche); but the first of the two cross-references to the *Macropaedia* reads "Nietzsche as protégé," and there is no cross-reference to Plautus.

If the real Doktorvater of the young Nietzsche was Richard Wagner, Wagner's own development had provided an ideal metaphor for the mentor of publishing scholars and for the very idea of the university, in the central character of *Die Meistersinger von Nürnberg*, Hans Sachs, a historical person who assumed in the opera the position of sponsor to the young nobleman Walther von Stolzing. As such, he had the task of channeling the raw talent of the young Walther without destroying it. Walther's talent without discipline was anarchy: "I learned to sing in the forest, there where the birds are," he declared. Beckmesser's discipline without talent was academic pedantry, with his eagerness to "write down on this tablet every mistake, great or small." But Sachs, responding to Walther's exclamation that he could "be saved without earning a master's degree," declared in his closing monologue: "Do not, I say, despise the masters, but honor their art!" For only by the creative application of their discipline to native ability, what Peter Medawar once called "imaginativeness and critical temper," would enduring art (or enduring scholarly publication) emerge.

Yet neither the individual publishing activity of the university faculty nor their training of scholar-authors is a sufficient vehicle for the university's publishing responsibility to diffuse knowledge. The university itself has an obligation "contemplata aliis tradere," to diffuse the results of research, both that of its own professors and graduates and that of the international scholarly community in general. Although much needs to be said about the university press as an institution in its own right, as I have sought to show elsewhere, I wish to concentrate here on the relation between the mission of the university press and the mission of the university, a relation that goes back to the beginnings of the printed book. "The University Press," William Rainey Harper, the first president of the University of Chicago, declared upon the founding of the university (and the simultaneous founding of its press), "constitutes an organic division of the University." Conversely, as the fiftieth-anniversary history of that press by Gordon J. Laing suggested in 1941, "Perhaps there is no better index of the real character of any University than the catalogue of its Press." That definition has gradually spread to other universities, so that, to quote again from George Parmly Day of Yale University Press, "the most interesting development in their brief career has been the growth of the idea throughout the university that [the productions of the press] are as essential a part of Yale today as the departments of student instruction, and as indispensable to the institution."

The university press is one of the most effective of the devices by which the university can simultaneously address two constant dangers: the danger of the university's becoming a museum or even a mausoleum, a final resting place for the wrong ideas of dead men, or, in the phrase quoted earlier from Newman himself, a place for "the embalming of dead genius"; but also the danger on the opposite side, that the research and writing of the learned may become as faddish as clothing fashions, if both scholarship and teaching succumb to what Newman calls "viewiness" (I.pr.). The university must have devices for immunizing itself not only against the dead hand of the past but against the dead hand of the present. What Lord Acton once said of the study of history applies with even greater force to the university as a whole (including, of course, its research, teaching, and publishing in history): "History must be our deliverer not only from the undue influence of other times, but from the undue influence of our own, from the tyranny of environment and the pressure of the air we breathe." Yet at the same time the university needs to teach its members how to participate responsibly in the only period of history in which any of them will ever live.

The catalog of the university press bears evidence that "lost causes" and "unpopular names" often find their Valhalla in books, and the need to take such risks in the name of scholarship on behalf of the university as a whole is one of the reasons that the university and the university press must reckon with "the impossibility of it doing its work except at a financial loss." For a much smaller investment, the university can sometimes make a greater contribution to scholarship by subsidizing a series of books than by appointing a professor or even supporting a graduate student. For example, even a university that does not have a divinity school or a department of religious studies, perhaps especially such a university, can accord the scholarly study of religion its just due through its press, whose publications can thus substantiate the dictum that religion is too important to be left to the theologians. Science publishing is the obvious instance of how the university can often accomplish things through its press that it could not afford even to attempt through its laboratories, just as, conversely, science publishing can sometimes illustrate the problems incurred by the university press when it ventures into fields of research that are not adequately represented in its own faculty and laboratories. The press may also serve as the university's instrument for a tentative probe into an area of thought and study that it is not yet ready to include in its academic activities. It publishes a book without granting it tenure, and if it has guessed wrong, it can bury its mistakes—or remainder them. In both these ways, the university continues to rely on its press to help define its mission and its proper "business."

That mission is becoming increasingly global, as the university everywhere seeks to come to terms with its international responsibilities. Yet the study and the knowledge of other languages continue to be on the decline throughout American education, including the American university. The reform of foreign language study and the stimulation of a sense of urgency about the monolingual illiteracy of the educated classes, including some professional scholars, are matters of vital importance for schools, colleges, and universities as they review their standards of admission and graduation. On the most pragmatic and at the same time on the most idealistic of grounds, the society must require of its educational system that it guide and assist the members of the next generation to transcend the particularities of their own culture in the name of humanity. This is what is valid about the emotional calls for "cultural diversity," which would, I must admit, sound vastly more persuasive to me if more of those who have made this such a cause took the trouble to learn several languages besides their own. For the university, the need for language study continues to create serious complications. For if it is committed to the principle that the advancement of knowledge through research and the extension of knowledge through teaching belong together, the university will find it difficult to mount large-scale undergraduate teaching programs for which it does not have a graduate counterpart and in which therefore it cannot appoint distinguished scholars as professors. Yet teaching based on scholarship cannot be confined to the fields in which the university happens to have a Ph.D. program and a research faculty.

Helping to bridge that gap is a major contribution that the university press can make to the university. In a much more systematic and thorough manner than has ever been done before, university publishing needs to canvass the scholarly literature that is available for undergraduate instruction on the various cultures and subcultures of the globe, and to identify the research scholars who can be commissioned to fill the lacunae in that literature. Through books, and increasingly through less traditional means, the university press must make the results of that research available to students and colleagues on other campuses. The idea of the university according to which teaching and research belong together is correct; but it does not necessarily imply that they must always go on at the same place, only that the teaching needs to be grounded in research. A special area of concern must be the business of translation, where the university press has both the opportunity and the obligation to take the lead for the entire publishing community. Translation and the diffusion of the results of research through scholarly publication are, taken together, fundamental to the vocation of the university, but the university cannot fulfill that vocation without the university press. In that sense, and not only in that sense, it is valid to say that just as, in the words of Gordon J. Laing quoted earlier, "there is no better index of the real character of any University than the catalogue of its Press," so too "the idea of the university" depends also on the "idea" of the university press; and "the business of a university" depends on the diffusion of knowledge through scholarly publishing.

III

13

DUTIES TO SOCIETY

One of the most besetting vices of the university, and yet at the same time one of its most charming characteristics, has always been its quaint tendency to look inward and ignore the context of the society within which it lives and without which it could not exist. There is a story—no doubt apocryphal—that at the outbreak of the First World War a group of patriotic Englishwomen who were going about the countryside recruiting soldiers swept into Oxford. On the High Street one of them confronted a don in his Oxonian master's gown who was reading the Greek text of Thucydides. "And what are *you* doing to save Western civilization, young man?" she demanded. Bringing himself up to his full height, the don looked down his nose and replied, "Madam, I *am* Western civilization!" The story does not say so, but the Oxford don might well have tried to buttress his case by quoting another Oxford man, John Henry Newman, who had died a quarter-century earlier. For the fundamental social and political presupposition of Newman's educational philosophy, and the one with which many of his present-day critics are the most uncomfortable, was the thesis that "that training of the intellect, which is best for the individual himself, best enables him to discharge his *duties to society*." On the basis of that presupposition, he felt able, later in the paragraph, to affirm: "If then a practical end must be assigned to a University course, I say it is that of training good members of society. Its art is the art of the social life, and its end is fitness for the world" (I.vii.10). In speaking about these "duties to society" in relation to the university, therefore, he was primarily concentrating on the contribution that the university makes to society through the subsequent lives and careers of individual students, rather than on the university's own institutional "duties to society."

Yet the tenor of Newman's nine discourses and ten occasional lectures and essays, directed as they are to the creation and justification of a university for Ireland, makes it obvious that a purely individualistic explanation of the duties to society would fall far short of Newman's own vision. From the serious attention he paid to the details of the university's position within the complex situation of mid-nineteenth-century Ireland and to its relation with the city of Dublin it is abundantly clear that he had more than the individual in mind. "It is impossible," he wrote, "to doubt that a future is in store for Ireland," economically and politically but above all intellectually and culturally; and, he continued, "the seat of this intellectual progress must necessarily be the great towns of Ireland," especially Dublin, Cork, and Belfast, which was why an Irish University was envisaged for Dublin (II.ix.2–3). Ireland, in turn, had an international contribution to make, as Newman suggested eloquently in a visionary description of "the island I am gazing on" and its "flourishing University" a century in the future. Within the total framework of what he calls "the business of a University" (I.vii.1), then, the duties of the university to its several societies—the local, the national, and the international—all have a significant part to play, according to Newman. But Newman soon learned what successive generations of those who assume responsibility for a university anywhere have had to learn, that these several societies are frequently perceived as competing with one another, and that sometimes—though perhaps less frequently—they indeed do compete, although in different ways within different areas of the university's mission of research, teaching, and publication.

What the university does as one institution and corporation of society among others is an important component of that "business of a university." The university as institution, employer, wage-payer, and property-owner contributes to its local society and in turn depends upon it: if either of these partners is sick, the other suffers as well. But as is graphically demonstrated by one biographer's use of a phrase like "not [a time] of great intellectual fervor for undergraduates on campus" to describe one of the most exciting experiments in the history of university education during the twentieth century, those who advocate greater and more direct economic, social, and political involvement by the university as a duty to its several societies—and especially, it would seem, those advocates who are chiefly concerned with the university's duties to local society—may all too easily overlook or oversimplify the relation of such involvement to the primary mission of the university, and thus also the relation of the university to its total context. As the president of the University of Chicago said in a talk on "Unrest and the Universities" delivered in the fateful year of 1968, there were at that turbulent time some who believed "that it is good that disruption and unrest have found their way to colleges and universities because, after all, it is a problem for education." His view was considerably more sober: "And yet," he continued, "for this very reason it is a peculiarly difficult problem for education to deal with. The movements tend to reject reason, which is the way of education. They buttress this rejection by replacing reason with personal qualities thought to be more than adequate substitutes." As he sadly concluded, in a wide-ranging indictment of much that passes for university education, "the corruptions of thought come home to roost." In historical perspective it does seem that it has usually been the more immediate societies of the university that have tended, for obvious reasons, to lay the more demanding claims upon it. Therefore the societies that are less immediately visible, lacking vocal advocacy and political clout, have had to depend for their defense on the university itself.

Yet the university is, with the church, especially charged with a responsibility not alone for its immediate society but for its larger societies, with all of which it has something of a moral contract. As Edmund Burke said in a classic formulation that could have been spoken specifically about the university, "It is a partnership in all science; a partnership in all art; a partnership in every virtue, and in all perfection. As the ends of such a partnership cannot be obtained in many generations, it becomes a partnership not only between those who are living, but between those who are living, those who are dead, and those who are to be born." That comprehensive definition is the ultimate context within which to consider the several contexts of the university's duties to society, including the context that requires the members of the university, in another formula from Edmund Burke, "to be attached to the subdivision, to love the little platoon we belong to in society, [as] the first principle (the germ as it were) of public affections. It is the first link in the series by which we proceed towards a love to our country and to mankind." I want to relate what Newman calls the university's "duties to society" to what Burke calls "the little platoon we belong to," to "our country," and to "mankind," each in turn; and I shall do so by relating research (including publication) and teaching, the two principal components of "the business of a University" as rehearsed earlier, to each of these three contexts.

All three have legitimate claims upon the universities as "the greatest and most important centers in modern times for cultural and national life," and as, in most cultures, the primary staging area for scientific research and scholarly publishing. For almost every university in the world, "the little platoon we belong to" is in fact a modern city. Those who live in the academy should not forget that such a field of research as the study of its own society and city can provide the university with a unique opportunity to examine firsthand many of the forces and trends with which its scholars deal chiefly in a macroeconomic mode and to make the results of such study available through scholarly publications. Ever since Jacob Burckhardt, the historians of the Italian Renaissance of the Quattrocento and Cinquecento have known that the Renaissance was primarily an urban phenomenon, and that it was the interaction of "civic humanism" and "classicism" in a city like Florence that created the political, economic, and intellectual matrix within which the Renaissance emerged. The research methodology of the social sciences, broadly conceived but rigorously applied, can examine those same dynamic forces in a contemporary setting, specifically in the university's urban setting, with results that are significant theoretically but relevant practically as well. But as is the case in the study of the Italian Renaissance, so also in the study of contemporary urban issues, university research and publication on such questions must not be confined to the social sciences but must look at the interaction between those disciplines and the arts, the humanities, and the sciences of human biology; for it has been and will be in that total interaction that "renaissances" as well as social tragedies are generated.

For a variety of reasons, including the methods followed almost everywhere for funding research, the predominant "duties to society" in the research enterprise of universities and in their scholarly publishing have been the duties of the university to its national society, in preference to either its local or its international society. One direct consequence of modern nationalism, largely unnoticed because it seems so obvious, has been its impact on how scholars study. There have, for example, been two working assumptions for most scholars in the humanities at the university, and thus also for the university press, about the proper methodology for the study of literature. They have been identified by René Wellek, in comments about Johann Gottfried von Herder, as "theoretical historicism" and "practical patriotism": first, the assumption that such study should be carried on historically; and second, the assumption that it should follow the history of literature in a national context. Neither assumption is at all obvious, nor for that matter have they always been in force. The first, though not without important precedents going back to "Aristotle's picture of the development of philosophy in the first book of the *Metaphysics*," which set many of "the conventions of the history of philosophy," is largely the product of nineteenth-century historicism, which dictated that the history of literature—together with, for example, the history of law, the history of philosophy, and the history of theology—should be the prolegomenon to the study of each of those disciplines, and which thus established those fields and methods in the university curricula and scholarly bibliographies. In part, the second assumption, about the history of national literatures, finds its warrant in the circumstance described by Newman in his observation that "a Literature, when it is formed, is a national and historical fact" (II.iii.3.2), thus among other things in the intractable reality of linguistic provenance, which seems to require that works produced at one time be studied in relation not to similar works elsewhere but principally in relation to works produced at another time that happen to have been written in the same language. Because it is increasingly the case that the venue for the study of literature "now is largely an academic setting, in the universities and their departments of literature," which are therefore being "asked to define literature," their understanding of literature tends to become normative. But it is also the case that for the study of literature the predominance of the university's duties to its national society has frequently been modified and qualified, not only in research and teaching but especially also in scholarly publishing, in one direction by attention to regionalism and in the other direction by the growth of comparative literature as a distinct scholarly discipline.

The disciplines of the university vary widely in their awareness of this duty to the international society. The leadership position that American scientific research has taken in the decades since the Second World War is reflected in the footnotes, bibliographies, and citation indexes of the biological and physical sciences from every nation, whatever the future outlook for that leadership may be. As a result, the ability to read English is, as was the ability to read German two generations ago, an absolute prerequisite for work on most fields of natural science today in most countries of the world. The obverse side of this hegemony of English in the sciences is a linguistic situation that is both more troubling and more complex; for it has tended to confirm American university students, as well as all too often even their teachers and their university presses, in their traditional resistance to working with any language other than their own. By contrast, the translation into English of scholarly works and especially of research papers and reports also seems to move faster in the sciences than in any other field (except perhaps military intelligence or industrial espionage, about which we are, by definition, less well informed). Because of the language barrier, it sometimes seems that in other fields than the sciences research in various countries can often get by with practically ignoring the international dimension. Most graduate professors who have conducted language examinations for Ph.D. candidates have had the experience of being "shocked at the number of mature men and women who suppose that foreign prose is basically nonsense. They must suppose this, or they would not put down English nonsense as its equivalent." As part of its duties to society, the university and its faculty need to press in every possible way for the recognition and implementation of the international context of research and publication.

But perhaps the most striking point of conjunction, and sometimes of competition, between the duties of the university to society becomes evident in its mission to teach. How it relates its teaching to each of the societies to which it has duties—repeating Burke's phraseology, to "the little platoon we belong to," to "our country," and to "mankind"—and therefore how it relates those duties to one another can decisively affect its entire mission. Especially is this true if under the rubric of teaching we include, as we must, not only undergraduate and graduate teaching in the arts and sciences but professional training and lifelong education. In the most rudimentary (and perhaps most important) sense, the university's duties to society for its teaching mission within its three contexts imply that the university must see to it that all three contexts are adequately represented in those whom it teaches and in what it teaches them.

The system of governance of most universities throughout the world is designed to guarantee majority representation of local or national groups in the student bodies of universities, which by their fee structure and admissions policies are explicitly pointed toward students from the area or the nation; that orientation will and should continue. Even the most provincial of universities, however, will need to resist the pressures to make admission to the university for foreign or out-of-state students still more difficult than it now is. Conversely, the policy of admitting to the local or state university anyone who has obtained a diploma from a state high school is based on the effort to provide education for all. Yet it is potentially as hazardous to the students whom it is intended to benefit as it is to the university, for it can run the danger of debasing the educational currency in the very process of redistributing it. Behind this policy, nevertheless, is a valid intuition, which has been well articulated by Henry Rosovsky: "We believe that education, particularly in selective schools, is one path leading to upward social and economic mobility, and are anxious to make available these advantages to segments of the population that have been, and in many cases still are, victims of discrimination and exclusion." But that very belief requires that admission to the university not be drained of its meaning and standards, and, conversely, that secondary schools in various countries, probably in cooperation with their national universities, undertake locally the kinds of programs of enrichment and deepening that have, often with spectacular success, taken woefully unprepared secondary school graduates and fitted them for meaningful participation in the university and in society at large. Although the process is all too easily and all too frequently corrupted, this has been the educational justification for the recruitment of disadvantaged students to the university by means of inter-collegiate athletics. Such programs of enrichment, within the local context of any university, are, however, only one part of the university's responsibil-ity to devise ways of bringing its educational benefits to an ever enlarging and broader constituency, to which I shall be turning again.

Yet this must not happen at the cost of the increasingly urgent need for the university to recognize and carry out its duties to society in an interna-tional context. A study published by Philip H. Coombs a quarter-century ago examined the vital importance of that international context of univer-sity education, especially as it pertains to the movement of students (and of senior scholars) across national boundaries. Such movement there has always been in the universities going back to the Middle Ages, as the peregrinations of Thomas Aquinas between Italy and Paris or of Duns Scotus between Paris and Oxford attest. Sad to say, some of the most influential of these peregrinations also in our own time have been involun-tary, as senior and junior scholars have fled tyranny and in the process have invigorated university life in their new land. But Coombs and others are primarily concerned with the invigorating power that can come from plan-ning and policy in the international exchange of students and professors. It seems difficult to imagine any future for the university in which this dimen-sion will not play an increasing role. But if that is the case, the university has before it a major task of educational reform. The obvious barriers are those constructed by regimes—totalitarian and authoritarian regimes, but not only those—that fear the intellectual viruses students who study abroad may bring back into the cultural bloodstream. In that fear they are, to be utterly candid, quite justified, as for example the later influence of the foreign students who had studied at the University of Wittenberg and at Geneva in the era of the Reformation, or at Moscow in the 1920s, amply demonstrates. But efforts to repress such foreign influence by barring inter-national exchange often stimulate the very revolt they try to prevent.

The training specifically of professionals through international ex-change deserves separate attention in this consideration of the interna-tional context of the university's teaching mission. For despite Newman's oft-repeated thesis that "knowledge is its own end," it was, as I have pointed out, for professional training as physicians and lawyers that many Irish students were going to the English universities in the nineteenth cen-tury, thereby provoking the agitation that led to the creation of Newman's Irish University; and it was in the area of professional training, specifically in medicine, that Newman's university was most successful. That professional dimension of international exchange will certainly become even more important than it is now. Studies of development economics all emphasize that a prime need—perhaps the prime need—for the development of countries in what we have come to call the Third World is the preparation of cadres of trained professionals in everything from architecture and ecology to public health and traffic control. As far into the future as anyone cares or dares to look, the universities of the developed world will be charged with the educational and political responsibility, which is ultimately a moral responsibility, of recruiting and equipping such professionals.

There is, however, more than a little basis for the doubt whether university-based professional education in the developed countries, including the United States, will be properly equipped to handle that formidable assignment, which moves the issue from the question of who is taught to the question of what is taught. That question in turn is also closely related to—though by no means identical with—the question of what the university preserves in its libraries, museums, and galleries. To begin with a problem that is at once the most obvious and the most complex, the kind of professional training a university in the developed world provides for its students—including, at least in this respect, the graduate education leading to the Ph.D., which is and yet is not "professional training" in this sense—is often poorly designed for the needs of a student from a developing country, for it presupposes access to resources that may simply not be available there. Thus when a Ph.D. mentor in the humanities (following one or another of the metaphors examined in chapter 12) seeks by both example and precept to inculcate in such a student strict standards of research into primary sources in the original languages and careful attention to the state of the art on the basis of an extensive survey of the scholarly literature in all languages, the professor could well be preparing the student for a life of utter frustration back in the home country, where there may not be in the entire nation or region the fundamental bibliographical materials needed to adhere to such standards. It deserves to be added that modern library technology and new techniques of publishing do hold forth the promise of "cooperative enterprise" that is beginning to close that gap. Yet the gap remains and will remain for a long time. This situation is duplicated in many of the scholarly and scientific disciplines and professional skills that top the list of prime needs in the developing world. Although in some areas of the world parasites cause more deaths than cancer, research and training at university-based medical centers in the developed world have all too often set priorities on the basis of the incidence of disease and the statistics of mortality in the industrial West and thus have contributed less to Third World needs than might appear. The same problem applies to engineering in all its branches, to market economics, and to law. So acute has the awareness of it become, in both the developing and the developed worlds, that the establishment of international universities is being planned at various strategic locations, where senior scholars from both worlds and perhaps even students from both worlds can work together to address these unique challenges.

It will be a deplorable by-product of this bold and hopeful experimentation, however, if the universities of the West take it as an excuse to lower their attention to their duties to society in the international context of their curriculum. Yet every survey, whether of university curricula or of knowledge and attitudes among students, reinforces the impression that universities everywhere have an endemic tendency to "miss the boat" and to slip back into ethnocentric habits. An international crisis or a trade deficit may temporarily reverse that tendency, as the perception grows that for the university the intellectual trade deficit is a crisis even more grave, which will have to be addressed if anything is to be done about the larger international context. There has been valid criticism of "area studies" as the methodology for research or the curriculum to provide an international context at universities. Similar criticism has greeted the growth, at a number of universities in various countries, of programs in international studies, in peace studies, or for that matter in war studies; and the objection to them is sometimes, though not always, scoring a correct point when it deplores what it sees as their tendency toward ideological bias or sentimentality or lack of intellectual rigor. But that criticism does not mitigate the urgency to review the international context of the university curriculum—as well as of the curricula of secondary and elementary schools—with a view to identifying the university's duties to its several societies. Of course it remains to be seen whether the university can mount the resources and summon the will to redefine itself in all three contexts: in the words of Edmund Burke, "the little platoon we belong to, our country, and mankind." This issue has repeatedly stood out from all the others, as the one without which, in a real sense, the other issues of the business of the university cannot be addressed, nor its duties to society properly identified.

14

THE UNIVERSITY
AS GROUND OF PROMISE
IN THE FUTURE

The superficial initial impression that Newman's distinction between the two kinds of education, which is based on the thesis that "the end of the one is to be philosophical, of the other to be mechanical" (I.v.6), is in fact nothing more than a poorly disguised distinction of class stands corrected by his recognition of "a great movement in behalf of the extension of knowledge among those classes in society" who had remained largely out of reach of the university but whom the Catholic University of Ireland was now intended to address (II.ix.4). For he saw "one remarkable *ground of promise in the future* of Ireland, that that large and important class, members of which I am now addressing,—that the middle classes in its cities, which will be the depositaries of its increasing political power," could be simultaneously "so sound in faith" and yet so true to the best of "the ancient fame of Ireland as regards its intellectual endowments" as to be able to participate in the intellectual and spiritual renaissance that would be represented by the Catholic University (II.ix.3).

Thus it was with the national aspirations of Ireland in mind that Newman spoke so lyrically about the future of the university—of what at that time could be called "his" university, since to such a large extent it still existed only in the mind of its maker:

I am turning my eyes toward a hundred years to come, and I dimly see the island I am gazing on, become the road of passage and union between two hemispheres, and the centre of the world. . . . The capital of that prosperous and hopeful land is situate in a beautiful bay and near a romantic region; and in it I see a flourishing University, which for a while had to struggle with fortune, but which, when its first founders and servants were dead and gone, had successes far exceeding their anxieties. Thither, as to a sacred soil, the home of their fathers, and the fountain-head of their Christianity, students are flocking from East, West, and South, from America and Australia and India, from Egypt and Asia Minor, with the ease and rapidity of a locomotion not yet discovered, and last, though not least, from England,—all speaking one tongue, all owning one faith, all eager for one large true wisdom; and thence, when their stay is over, going back again to carry over all the earth "peace to men of good will."

Elsewhere he justified the selection of Ireland as the "proper seat" for a Catholic University by his firm belief that "a future is in store for Ireland." "In the times now opening upon us," he continued, "nationalities are waking into life," and "the wrongs of the oppressed . . . are brought under the public opinion of Europe." Thus, he concluded, "retribution is demanded and exacted for past crimes in proportion to their heinousness and their duration." What was called for was a university that would help make reparations for those crimes, on behalf not only of the Irish but of all the oppressed and underdeveloped "nationalities" and peoples of the earth (II.ix.2).

Newman's emphasis on "the wrongs of the oppressed" and of the underdeveloped "nationalities" of the earth, and on the exacting of "retribution," shows how essential it is to be reminded that the university is uniquely "the ground of promise in the future." On 15 August 1914, Andrej Sheptycky, Metropolitan of the Ukrainian Catholic church, addressed a memorandum to the Austrian Parliament about the needs of the Western Ukrainians, who were then living under the Habsburg crown. Among many other demands, he appealed for "the creation of an independent university" for them, because, he insisted, universities were "the greatest and most important centers in modern times for cultural and national life." More than fifty years later and more than a thousand kilometers to the West, his exiled successor, Metropolitan Josyf Slipyj, after his liberation from eighteen years of Soviet imprisonment, strove to carry out in Rome that vision of the Ukrainian University. For universities still are "the greatest and most important centers in modern times for cultural and national life," as the three-fourths of a century since Sheptycky's memorandum have demonstrated, not only for the hopes of Ukrainians but for the national aspirations and the personal ambitions of peoples everywhere. This became evident, to mention only one example, in the contribution of the University of Strasbourg to the development of Alsace-Lorraine between the Franco-Prussian War and the Second World War. The university is a place in which the past asserts itself with a special claim upon the present, and properly so. Nevertheless, even the most ardent traditionalist must never forget that the university is a staging area for the future, devoted not only to "the embalming of dead genius" but to "the endowment of living [genius]." The concept of opportunity is therefore essential to the definition of the idea of the university. When the university has neglected the imperative of opportunity and has permitted itself to degenerate into a private club, it is not only those who are excluded who have suffered; it is the university itself that has been impoverished, both as institution and as idea. The processes by which universities have learned that lesson have frequently been painful for all concerned, but the outcome of the process has been a deeper affirmation of the true nature of university education and of the university as a free and responsible community. Whether as a ladder or as a door, the university remains in many ways the unique channel of opportunity.

The university is, moreover, seen as the channel of opportunity around the world, as even a sampling, almost at random, of current publications by and about universities in various lands will indicate. "University education," one such publication affirms and in doing so speaks for all of them, "aims, through studies and scientific research, to aid in the development of the mental capacities of individuals." "Service through excellence in teaching and research" is defined as the goal of another such university, which declares that "it is opposed to discrimination on grounds of race, colour, nationality, religion or sex, and regards merit as the only acceptable criterion for determining student admissions and staff appointments." Another has formulated its credo about the future in these words: "On the threshold of its fourth half-century, the University, fully aware of the problems, difficulties and contradictions inside it, around it and before it, desires to continue its endeavours in the field of Science and also in the Letters and Arts. . . . It wishes, maintaining its autonomy but in co-operation with its social setting, to aim at a dialectical blend of the search for truth and the service of society, the co-existence of democratic dialogue and quality in its educational and research work." A university, according to yet another publication, is entrusted "with two missions: to seek knowledge and to impart knowledge. Both are geared to one purpose—to enrich the human life." Those four statements have come from, respectively, Egyptian, South African, Greek, and Philippine sources.

Yet as becomes clear both from the contexts and from the explicit statements of these definitions of the university as the ground of promise in the future and as the door to opportunity, it is to the professional and vocational training offered by the university, and not to what Newman calls "liberal learning," that these nations and their students are chiefly looking. Thus (observing the same order in which they have just been quoted), the Egyptian university has defined it as the purpose of education to "help solve the problems of society [and] increase production." South Africa is proud of MEDUNSA, the Medical University of South Africa, "a university that, until this year, consisted only of faculties devoted to health care—medicine, dentistry and veterinary science." (It has a parallel in, among other institutions in various lands, the Oregon Health Sciences University, established in 1974.) The National and Capodistrian University of Athens strives "to combine more successfully theory and practice, teaching and research, vocational training and the provision of higher education." The University of the Philippines defines its aim as the enrichment of life, "whether such enrichment be the joy of knowing what used to be unknown, or contemplating what was hitherto hidden or non-existent, or in the more mundane but essential physical creations that ultimately enable humanity to live better, longer, and to accomplish more." In spite of the formalized, almost stilted academic language of these declarations, it is evident that the Four Horsemen of the Apocalypse remain far too grim a reality to permit these nations or their universities to indulge in the luxury of deferring such professional and vocational training by any longer than is absolutely necessary.

At the same time, the tone in which these universities and ministries of education formulate this case for professional education indicates their awareness of the potential danger of a utilitarian outlook that would define "opportunity" in excessively vocational and therefore short-range terms. This could lead to the neglect of what Newman calls the "process of training, by which the intellect, instead of being formed or sacrificed to some particular or accidental purpose, some specific trade or profession, or study or science, is disciplined for its own sake, for the perception of its own proper object, and for its own highest culture," which, he adds, "is called Liberal Education" (I.vii.1). Moreover, when he defined "formation of mind" as "a habit of order and system, a habit of referring every accession of knowledge to what we already know, and of adjusting the one with the other; and, moreover, as such a habit implies, the actual acceptance and use of certain principles as centres of thought, around which our knowledge grows and is located" (II.ix.7), he was speaking not to Oxford aristocrats but to the Irish urban middle class. Simply put, the argument of my reexamination of the idea of the university implies that it is no less a denial of opportunity—and, ultimately, a denial of opportunity even more grave—if, in the interests of vocational and professional preparation, students are deprived of the obligation to address the content of such a "liberal education," to acquire such a "formation of mind," and in the process to come to terms with the intellectual traditions out of which they have sprung. The government of India acknowledged this when it recognized that there exists a "schism between the formal system of education and the country's rich and varied cultural traditions," and expressed the hope that through the university "education can and must bring about the fine synthesis between change-oriented technologies and the country's continuity of cultural tradition." In part this problem is related to the interaction between general education, concentration on an academic subject major, and technical professional training; for there are analogies to that interrelation in many kinds of professional education, and the clarification of this issue is a central demand on the university everywhere, no less in developed than in developing countries.

To be "opposed to discrimination on grounds of race, colour, nationality, religion or sex" and at the same time to regard "merit as the only acceptable criterion for determining student admissions and staff appointments," as the multiracial University of Natal in South Africa puts it on the basis of the complex history and bitter struggles of that country, is to juxtapose and seek to balance two principles that are often labeled, philosophically but also sometimes politically, as egalitarian and as elitist, the principle of equality and the principle of quality. Though used rhetorically, both principles—and the profound tensions between them—come from the democratic and Enlightenment tradition, as articulated not only for the United States of America but for all of humanity by Thomas Jefferson: the axiomatic doctrine of the American Declaration of Independence that all have been "created equal"; and the no less "self-evident" truth "that there is a natural aristocracy," one that is based not on birth or wealth, as earlier aristocracies were, but on "virtue and talents." From the first of these principles comes the egalitarian drive toward equal opportunity for all, and therefore toward the elimination of artificial barriers to the full development of the natural talents of each. From the second comes the elitist recognition that these natural talents are not evenly distributed among the populace and that therefore equal opportunity for all implies as well— paradoxical though this may appear—special opportunity for the talented few. Not everyone can run a four-minute mile, or master the oboe, or understand the intricacies of high energy physics. "Equal rights" cannot be taken to mean that everyone should be able to do these things; nor does it mean that if not everyone can do them, no one should be allowed, or indeed encouraged, to do them. What it does mean is that those who can do them should not on any extraneous grounds be denied the opportunity to develop their talents. Despite its appeal, the polarity between egalitarianism and elitism is, therefore, basically a spurious antithesis, at least for the university.

Newman's portrait of a "gentleman" as "the creation, not of Christianity, but of civilization," together with his admission there that "the school of the world seems to send out living copies of this typical excellence with greater success than the Church" (I.viii.8), has come to be identified— although, as Culler has said, "Newman did not like it"—with his definition of the mission of the university. Indeed, that portrait of the gentleman has sometimes even been taken to mean that elitism can become an end in itself, to the exclusion of the doctrine of fairness that is implied by the egalitarian ideal. If pressed to some ultimatum, such an understanding of elitism could even become a deterministic theory of social Darwinism, which is hardly what Newman had in mind. On the contrary, however, the philosophical perspective being argued in this book would look upon "elitism"—be it in Olympic competition or in an academic pursuit—as the consequence of a process in which everyone ought to be equal at the starting line. This is, to be sure, a principle whose definition and implications also raise serious questions. As one vigorous statement of the problem has put it, "schooling for all" comes into conflict with the grim realities of class and race, bringing on nothing less than "the decline of the democratic ideal." For if, because of historic injustice or social prejudice, not everyone is equal at the starting line, the society and the university must do what they can to achieve such equality. But having once done so, they must also be prepared to accept the outcome of the competition. Otherwise, the polarity of elitism and egalitarianism comes to be seen as a part of the natural order of creation or of the social structure, and therefore presumably unchangeable, except through the illusory promises of class revolution.

Perhaps nowhere is the need to transcend the polarity by coming to terms simultaneously with both Jeffersonian principles more self-evident in principle, and yet more complicated in execution, than it is in the university. As on so many other challenges to the democratic society, not only in America but everywhere, Alexis de Tocqueville saw clearly what was at stake here. "The more closely I consider the effects of quality upon the mind," he wrote, "the more I am convinced that the intellectual anarchy which we see around us is not, as some suppose, the natural state for democracies." Nevertheless, he also had to acknowledge, as he had said earlier, that "in America the purely practical side of science is cultivated admirably, and trouble is taken about the theoretical side immediately necessary to application. On this side the Americans always display a clear, free, original, and creative turn of mind. But hardly anyone in the United States devotes himself to the essentially theoretical and abstract side of human knowledge." He added that "in this the Americans carry to excess a trend which can, I think, be noticed, though in less degree, among all democratic nations."

Tocqueville recognized in "the provisions for public education" the forces "which, from the very first, throw into clearest relief the originality of American civilization." But he went on to explain that he was referring only to primary education, since "higher education is hardly available to anybody." When applied to education, the democratic doctrine of the equality of all implied for him that "though mental endowments remain unequal as the Creator intended, the means of exercising them are equal." But as the twentieth century closes—when it quite obviously can no longer be said to be true, either in the United States or in all the various countries to whose university systems we have been referring here, that "higher education is hardly available to anybody"—it follows necessarily that the university must exercise a major share of leadership in redeeming the pledge of equality, by insisting that what Tocqueville called "the means of exercising mental endowments" truly become equally available, even while recognizing that "mental endowments remain unequal." In doing so, the university must go on striving to eliminate from its own programs of student admissions and faculty appointments as well as from its curriculum the vestiges of discrimination and prejudice against race, class, or gender that still remain, and in societies as divergent as those of the United States, South Africa, and Eastern Europe that is what the university has been doing. But at the same time the university must go on being able to identify, and then to attract and hold, those relatively few individuals, regardless of race or class or gender, whose "virtue and talents" give promise of advancing the boundaries of knowledge through research and development. If the university, in the name of universal opportunity for all, were to renege on this latter duty, for fear of appearing elitist, that would be a caricature of authentic egalitarianism; for it would deprive the "all" of the intellectual and moral capital in which, finally, they have begun to gain the chance of having their just share. Indeed, in view of the critical shortage of such virtue and talent, it is self-defeating as well as unjust to exclude anyone on other grounds.

What is at risk in this critical situation for both quality and equality in every country where there is a university is, ultimately, the centrality of the power of the trained mind as both an intellectual and a social force. "Such a power," according to Newman, "is the result of a scientific formation of mind; it is an acquired faculty of judgment, of clearsightedness, of sagacity, of wisdom, of philosophical reach of mind, and of intellectual self-possession and repose," acquired by "discipline and habit" (I.vii.1). For the most valuable of all natural resources, particularly at a time when all natural resources are under threat, is critical intelligence; and the most important of all national products, particularly at a time when all production has become problematical, is trained intelligence. This is also, ultimately, the resource on whose presence the development and the conservation of all the other resources depend. It is as well the opportunity that provides the intellectual and social context for the other opportunities. And thus it is, in the fullest sense, "the ground of promise in the future." It would, of course, be fallacious to claim, in a century that has produced as many technological advances as the twentieth century has, that the ingenuity needed for the application of critical intelligence is unattainable outside the university. But to deal with the concerns of societies and the needs of environments that have been as fundamentally transformed as they have by those technological advances does require a pooling of the insights and the discipline of the natural sciences, the social sciences, and the humanities, as these coexist in the research and teaching of the university—and, practically speaking, nowhere else. Considerations of technological efficiency, of social utility, and of human value—all three of these bear upon such questions. Any proposed solutions that, like many of those being most strongly advocated in many countries, ignore any of these three sets of considerations—especially those that ignore the third—or that treat them in a shallow way, are bound to fail. To find solutions for the issues of the day, including the issues of quality and equality, any society must draw upon the knowledge and basic research received from the past. But if its successors—"those who are to be born," as Burke calls them—confronting similar issues whose contours are not yet even discernible, are to have at their disposal some similar intellectual drawing accounts, those will have to be deposited now, and the university is, in every nation and in the international community as a whole, the central bank for such deposits.

For it has long been recognized that although the university, in Newman's words, "does not promise a generation of Aristotles or Newtons, of Napoleons or Washingtons, of Raphaels or Shakespeares" (I.vii.10), only the university can be relied upon to develop a pool of investigators, scholars, and thinkers who will contribute to basic knowledge. Unless the critics of university research are prepared to assert that all the important basic research in all the arts and sciences and in all the professions has been completed and that in this generation and in the several to follow we need only apply these assured results to a series of practical considerations, it is impossible to justify an abandonment of basic study. Without a continuation of such study, practical application faces the constant threat of being premature and thoughtless, and eventually of becoming intellectually sterile. Therefore the assurance of continuing recruitment of new talent into the research, teaching, and publication of the university is a primary need. To concentrate for the moment on the university in America, it is dismaying to note that the United States has, from time to time in recent years, declined in the percentage of its gross national product being devoted to basic research and development. Because industry has sometimes been more sensitive to this need than either the academy or the government, scholarship and science could face the prospect (already a reality for some fields in some countries) that basic research would move out of the university into other centers of research that are only tenuously connected to the university. Those who are to carry out the industrial application of the basic sciences, moreover, must themselves be the products of a university system in which basic science continues to play a strong and independent role.

Ultimately, however, the x factor in all of these equations is service. Several of the statements of purpose for the university quoted earlier include this factor. Thus the Greek university speaks of "aim[ing] at a dialectical blend of the search for truth and the service of society." Similarly, the University of Natal seeks to instill "service through excellence in teaching and research." One of the most eloquent formulations ever of this principle came in two lines from Newman's disciple, the British poet Gerard Manley Hopkins:

> This pride of prime's enjoyment
> Take as for tool, not toy meant.

Yet the formulation of a rational case for such service as a primary goal and first principle of the university—a case that would be based, as Newman insisted, on "natural" grounds (I.iii.10)—is less obvious than it might first appear. Charging that there is a "disregard for truly substantive questions," one observer has put the problem this way: "Just as the modern university has no time for the most important human subjects, it has, ironically, no place on its faculty for the brightest people." Nor can it be said with assurance that the conduct of university graduates all over the world consistently conveys the impression that the correlation between opportunity and service, or between privilege and responsibility, is in any decisive way central to their understanding of what comes with a university education, and therefore to an understanding of this correlation that has been communicated to them, through precept or example, by the university. Yet it is the question of such a correlation that springs into public view whenever one or another field of activity for which the university is a preparation faces public notoriety. The complicity of Japanese businessmen in the Lockheed scandal, the implicating of a Vatican official in bank manipulation, the involvement of physicians in Medicaid fraud, the participation of American lawyers in Watergate—these and similar scandals in various of the learned professions (including in these cases business, theology, medicine, and law) all over the world have reverberated on university campuses. They have prodded reluctant faculties in professional schools and in the arts and sciences into scrambling to address the moral dimension of university education and even into putting together courses or entire institutes on ethics, despite the endemic fear of "the menace of metaphysics" and the consequent reluctance and embarrassment with which the modern university is accustomed to treat that moral dimension of its higher education.

When Newman speaks about "the singular example of an heterogeneous and an independent body of men, setting about a work of self-reformation, not from any pressure of public opinion, but because it was fitting and right to undertake it" (I.i.1), he indicates by the phrase "singular example" that ordinarily it is not realistic to expect the university, or any other entrenched institution, to address the moral dimension of its programs and structures without the external "pressure of public opinion." Yet it is fundamental to any reexamination of the idea of the university to recognize that the pressure of public opinion is already raising fundamental questions not only about opportunity, quality, and equality, as each of these social goods finds its special locus within the university, but specifically about the dedication of the university to the goal of service. It continues to be true that the university cannot ultimately meet this crisis of confidence and this call for moral and educational self-reformation unless it is able to show that it has done so also "because it was fitting and right to undertake it." But the record of higher education in finally moving during this century toward equality of opportunity for the deprived, which was "fitting and right to undertake" if anything in academic morality ever was, is not altogether reassuring to the case of those who maintain that the university and other educational institutions, if left completely alone, can be trusted to address the crisis of confidence and of self-confidence. Therefore it continues to be necessary to justify the ideal of public service in the program of the university also on pragmatic and political grounds, although not only on such grounds.

The members of the university have traditionally resisted, as anti-intellectualism or know-nothingism, the demands for accountability, whether they have come (as they did in the Middle Ages, and even since) from ecclesiastical officials or (as they have in all periods of university history) from wealthy private patrons or (as they have under all political and economic systems) from government. Somewhat cynically one might observe that the universities seem to have been considerably less reticent about social benefits and social service when they have been soliciting support from any or all of these sources of funding, to each of which they have been willing to describe, before the fact, what blessings would accrue from the support. Just as the stockholders of corporations, the readers of newspapers and viewers of television news, the voters in countries all over the world, the clients of health care, and the faithful in the pews of religious bodies have all become increasingly demanding in their insistence that these agencies see themselves as rendering a public service and as being accountable for that service, so the university must become far more imaginative and resourceful than it is in response to a similar insistence. This is true in relation, first, to its students, in what David Riesman has called "the academic enterprise in an era of rising student consumerism," when students have learned to voice their expectations about the product that they or their parents or the taxpayers are receiving. Therefore the service of the university to its students, and the service of the university to society through its students, must be the first line of defense against the accusations of "profscam" or the charge that "higher education has failed democracy and impoverished the souls of today's students." But such a defense will only be tactical rather than substantive unless the university, both in its academic curriculum and in its extracurricular program for faculty and for students, has become far more creative in finding ways to define service as an essential element of its mission, "not from any pressure of public opinion, but because it was fitting and right to undertake it" (I.i.1).

15

THE UNIVERSITY
AND THE SPREAD OF
REVOLUTIONARY
DOCTRINES

During a period of revolutionary social change such as the present, when revolutions are being overthrown by revolutions, the position of the university is inevitably dialectical; for both as institution and as idea, it is at one and the same time a seedbed of revolution and an object of attack by the revolution. Newman identified the intellectual ground of that dialectic when he observed that "the Classics, which in England are the means of refining the taste, have in France subserved *the spread of revolutionary . . . doctrines*" (I.v.1), becoming in the first case a pillar to hold up the Establishment and in the second a tunnel to undermine the ancien régime. An acknowledged master both of dialectic and of revolution, Newman's contemporary Karl Marx, wrote in the last of his *Theses on Feuerbach* in the very year of Newman's conversion, the spring of 1845 (although the *Theses* were not published until 1888, shortly after Marx had died): "The philosophers have only *interpreted* the world, in various ways. Nevertheless, the point is to *change* it."

In the twentieth century this axiom has become the common property not only of Marxist philosophers—indeed not only of Marxists or of philosophers—but of many critical and thoughtful intellectuals in societies all over the world, and it is often repeated without being ascribed to Marx. The distinction between those who "merely" interpret the world and those who change it has come to carry special persuasive power for those who, while living and working in the university during times of momentous social upheaval, criticize the university for being an ivory tower. It is, they charge, the scholars as a total class, and not just the philosophers, who "have only interpreted the world, in various ways" instead of recognizing that "the point is to change it"; thus historians are content to write history instead of making history, and economists are able to make a comfortable living by carrying on their research into the causes of poverty. As an oasis of privilege amid a desert of social and economic deprivation, the university has therefore sometimes become the object of the rage directed against the Establishment—a word that used to refer to the Anglican church as, in the familiar slogan, the Tory party at prayer, but that has come to be used, especially since the 1960s, for virtually any prevailing culture and its structures. At the same time, it is not necessary to be a historian of the university, but only a reader of the daily newspaper, to know that all over the world the university has become an agent of social change and of violent protest against the Establishment.

The ambivalence of the position of the university in relation to radical social change is well illustrated by the case of one self-professed rebel, the author of *Reveille for Radicals,* Saul Alinsky. He was the product of the college of the University of Chicago, at a time which was, in the judgment of his biographer, Sanford D. Horwitt, "not one of great intellectual fervor for undergraduates on campus," which, it is clear from his following sentence, should be taken to mean that there was "little serious political activity, little interest in making waves on social issues." Yet in various complicated ways, Alinsky's years at the university did help to nurture his radicalism, through the influence of fellow students, of several individual teachers of sociology, and of his own reading and thinking. Three decades later, therefore, there was "something of a political tug" when Alinsky's political agitation had put him into the position of being a leader in the "assault against his alma mater." For he had come to believe that the University of Chicago, as landlord and employer, was not, as it ought to be, the agent of social reform but the major instrument of economic and social oppression in the Hyde Park-Kenwood neighborhood of Chicago's South Side. So he went to war against the University of Chicago, an educational institution from which nevertheless he "was proud that he had graduated"; indeed, *Reveille for Radicals* was published by the University of Chicago Press. Forty years later a young Jessica Siegel would have a parallel experience on the same university campus. The ambivalence of universities toward social change persisted—and persists.

It bears noting at the outset that in the dynamics of revolution and social change the university is still, sometimes to its great embarrassment, an elite institution. As the preceding chapter has argued, it may be and it should be an elitism based on what Thomas Jefferson called a natural aristocracy of virtue and talents rather than an aristocracy of birth or wealth, but the place of the university in the achievement of social change is nonetheless defined by its elite position. Ever since Marx and Lenin, it has been a truism about revolutions that despite their egalitarian and populist rhetoric they are usually led by elites—a paradox that Hannah Arendt has examined in the keen and critical analysis of the concept of "elites" with which she closes her book *On Revolution,* quoting the concept from Maurice Duverger of a "government of the people *by an élite sprung from the people.*" The recent historiography of revolution, on the other hand, has striven to go beyond that paradox. In the words of a leading historian of the French Revolution who is not completely convinced by this historiography, "these writers look at the Revolution 'from below.' They explore the popular militancy and mass action of the anonymous (but in 1793 hardly inarticulate) common people." His own approach, he continues, "by design sees the Revolution 'from above.' It deals with the twelve strangely assorted men who were set up as a committee of the National Convention—the Committee of Public Safety—and who attempted to govern France in the turmoil of revolution, war, civil war, and invasion." In the twelve, as he points out a little later, there was "not an inkling of the peasantry, who constituted four-fifths of the population"; and all but one "had received a good deal of formal schooling." They were, then, the classic example of the well-educated elite who have traditionally led the spread of revolutionary doctrines and become the agents of social change, all in the name of the common people.

But that leaves unanswered the question that must be of primary concern to this reexamination of the idea of the university: What part, if any, will the institutions of learning, which produce the leaders of revolutions, play—or what part should they play, or can they play, or should they be conscious of playing—in the process of revolutionary social change? There should be, I hope, no controversy about at least one aspect of the answer to this question. The process of revolutionary social change is one of the most important and most fascinating historical phenomena to which the research and teaching of the university can be addressed. Although Edward Gibbon, the author of perhaps the most brilliant (if massively prejudiced) historical study of political and social change ever written, at least in English, was not a university professor, it seems safe to assume that *The Decline and Fall of the Roman Empire* will continue to be read more often in the setting of the university than anywhere else. It is even safer to assume that research and speculation about the central theme of his book—as he himself calls it in his preface, "the memorable series of revolutions which, in the course of about thirteen centuries, gradually undermined, and at length destroyed, the fabric of human greatness"—will be primarily the business of university professors. At the same time, the worldwide response to various considerations of the theme of revolution by university scholars is an indication that interest in the question is by no means confined to the university. The lessons about social change to be derived from the history of revolution are neither obvious nor trivial. But those lessons, whatever they may be, will come also in the future from the kind of care in research and freedom in interpretation that only the university is able to provide on a continuing basis.

While it is somewhat unusual for a physician who is a coroner to function also as a diagnostician, there is a direct line from this historical study of revolution to the consideration of the causes of revolution in the past and thus in turn to the examination of contemporary social unrest and social change. As the social sciences refine still further their instruments and methods for measuring the indices both of social unrest and of social change, the universities, together with think tanks and foundations allied to them, will be the primary agency combining the linguistic, historical, statistical, and comparative scholarship for the scientific mapping of this phenomenon worldwide. For neither governments nor intergovernmental bodies can undertake the task by themselves, and when they do carry on such research it needs to be reviewed and verified by university scholarship. Here again the communities of scholarship beyond the borders of individual campuses or even of individual nations are increasingly essential to the university, as the only practical means of assembling and interpreting the pertinent data and, invoking a distinction drawn earlier, of turning this information into knowledge (if not also into wisdom). So easily, however, can diagnosis turn into advocacy, and so subtly can a center of research on social change transform itself—or allow itself to be transformed—into a cell for galvanizing a society into action to accomplish such change, that the university urgently needs to find new ways of protecting the freedom of inquiry without allowing itself to become the tool of the polarities of nation, race, class, and gender that will continue to shape the ideological climate both outside and inside the academy.

If it is true that this problem acutely affects the scholarship of the university in its diagnostic activity, it is an even graver issue to confront when scholars at the university undertake, as they must, to construct and propose models of the good society as alternatives to the present, or at any rate as improvements upon the present. The legitimacy of their doing so should not be in question (although in some societies it is), but the limitations on their doing so certainly are in the present climate, as the experience of earlier scholars with the discussion of "democracy and leadership" attests. Predictably, any definition of the limitations often reflects a judgment about the political or moral adequacy of the particular model in question, and the propensity to apply such judgments not only to the intellectual validity of the proposal but even to its permissibility has sometimes come from political ideologies that are otherwise diametrically opposed to one another. Yet the classic "revolutionary doctrines" and prescriptions for social change and the good society, from the *Republic* of Plato (whatever ways of reading it a scholar may adopt) to *The Federalist* and *Das Kapital* of Karl Marx, often are, and should be even more often, a mainstay of the university curriculum. Repeatedly, as the biographies and autobiographies of social activists attest, an exposure, usually at the university, to such classics has stimulated someone both to reflection and to eventual action to change society, presumably for the better. The question of limitations on the use of the university classroom for advocacy, perhaps even for recruitment, is an especially sensitive instance of the definition of the university as a free and responsible community. But at the very least it would appear to be a necessary corollary of that definition to insist that at a university the professor's evaluation of students or colleagues must not be based on their acceptance or rejection of the professor's ideological position: critical understanding, not adherence or discipleship, whether uncritical or critical, is the criterion.

On the basis both of history and of principle, it seems evident that the chief contribution of the university to social change and to "the spread of revolutionary doctrines" continues to come through its students, also through what they do beyond the classroom and library. The university makes that contribution most effectively when it concentrates on its primary vocation to be a center of research, teaching, and publication. History and principle both imply, moreover, that such teaching and research at the university usually affect social change most profoundly in ways that are often implicit and indirect, rather than through a course bearing the label "Revolutionary Change 101a" (with laboratory sections meeting in the streets). To cite the most notable example of all, Karl Marx during the 1850s and 1860s stayed with his historical researches at the British Museum, instead of aligning himself with the German workers' movement in 1862. This was after the Communist Manifesto of 1848, for even then Marx went on believing that it would be through his research into the history and economics of the British coal industry that he as a scholar would have his principal effect on the revolution. As Hannah Arendt has said quite critically, "Karl Marx, the greatest theorist the revolutions ever had, was so much more interested in history than in politics and therefore neglected, almost entirely, the original intentions of the men of the revolutions, the foundation of freedom, and concentrated his attention, almost exclusively, on the seemingly objective course of revolutionary events." For although Marx had said in 1845, "The philosophers have only *interpreted* the world, in various ways. Nevertheless, the point is to *change* it," he believed that change, even revolutionary change, would be mindless unless it were based on understanding, which was the depth dimension that scholars and intellectuals could bring to it. A view of this scholarly process like the one being presented here, which diverges fundamentally from the Marxist view, would have to express a profound and continuing suspicion about any such research or teaching that has as clear and specified an outcome as did his investigations of the history and economics of the British coal industry. This suspicion holds whether one happens to agree or disagree with that outcome, philosophically and politically. It is cheating to play the scholarly game with marked cards even if one can win that way: complete objectivity may be impossible, but scholarly honesty is not.

A related divergence lies in a philosophical and moral difference, the place of *idealism*. The opposition of Marx to German Idealism as a metaphysical doctrine about the reality of *Geist* and his espousal of materialism in its place demarcated a line between him and the Hegelian tradition out of which he had come, but it also affected his attitude toward idealism in its other (though related) meaning of a moral outlook that formulates standards and normative principles of the good life that are to guide ethical and social action, therefore also to social change. His conviction that he by contrast had found a view of society that was "scientific [*wissenschaftlich*]" documents his ambivalent but unbroken continuity, despite all the attacks in both directions, with the cultivation of *Wissenschaft* at the German university of the nineteenth century, as that goal had been formulated especially by the founding fathers of the University of Berlin. But it also became his way of setting his brand of socialism apart from all the others, which he could brand as utopian, precritical, naive, and, above all, as idealistic and unscientific. Yet if the question is to be, as the title of this chapter puts it borrowing a phrase from Newman, "the university and the spread of revolutionary doctrines," and if the emphasis is to be on the students of the university, both while they are students and after they finish their studies, as agents of social change, then there must be a prominent place for idealism, at least in this second sense. For corresponding to the roles of university scholarship as the coroner-*cum*-diagnostician and as the source of models for the new social order is, on the receiving end of that scholarship, the role of university students in identifying social injustice and in calling for the realization of social ideals. Conversely, the experience of many nations confirms again that any society in which the capacity of university students for moral outrage and social idealism has been suppressed should not and will not long endure.

As has been suggested, then, the university's responsibility in relation to the spread of revolutionary doctrines is dialectical: to provide intellectual and philosophical nurture for the moral outrage and social idealism of its students, by exposing them to a wide range of serious reflection about the nature of the good life and the good society and by aiding them to develop rational methods of analysis for relating such reflection to social and political reality; but at the same time to provide them with the instrumentalities by which reason can continue to stand guard through moderating the visions and expectations of unthinking revolutionaries, in order, as Edmund Burke said in anticipation of the revolutions that have followed during the two hundred years since he published his *Reflections on the Revolution in France,* "to make the Revolution a parent of settlement, and not a nursery of future revolutions." Conversely, it would seem to follow necessarily that the university is rendering a grave disservice to its students when it serves only one pole of this dialectic, either by becoming itself an apologist for an unjust society or even an accomplice in the politics of repression, or by surrendering its scholarly and rational mission by being swept away in the tide of revolutionary doctrine and social change. It has been the grim experience of universities that selling out to either pole of the dialectic brings on the revenge of the other pole, because, to quote yet again from Burke's *Reflections on the Revolution in France,* "kings will be tyrants from policy when subjects are rebels from principle."

This analysis of "the university and the spread of revolutionary doctrines" has, for fairly obvious reasons, been defining the university chiefly as the faculty of arts and sciences in its dual function of teaching and research, and defining social change chiefly as revolutionary doctrine. Much of this analysis applies to every kind of social change and to the university as a whole. Nevertheless, for social change of every kind, but perhaps especially for social change through evolution rather than through revolution, the professional schools in the university play a decisive part, as did the laboratories of medical schools when they permanently changed human society by revising such basic components of the social equation as infant mortality and life expectancy. As I am suggesting in several chapters, there is need to examine the intellectual and the administrative connections between what is investigated and taught in the professional schools and the corresponding disciplines in the graduate school of arts and sciences—to wit, genetics in biology and in the medical school, the Constitution of the United States in the law school and in history or political science, Shakespeare on the page and on the stage, market economics in the economics department and in the business school. But what is it about the professional schools of the university taken together that makes them especially qualified to be and to equip agents of social change?

To begin with an obvious characteristic that is in fact not always so obvious, most of the professional schools of the university are charged with direct responsibility for training professionals in social change. Thus in the modern state one of the principal mechanisms of social change is legislation, and therefore, consciously or unconsciously, the preparation of lawyers in the law school will, by placing its studies into the context of "the whole field of man as a social being," recognize that it will be the task of a significant number of the school's graduates not only to practice within (or "under") the existing laws, but to change them, either through legislation or through interpretation. As the history of schools of law at various universities demonstrates, the presence on the faculty of scholars and social philosophers with a specific agenda for social change can have a profound and direct influence on the public careers of their students, but also upon the judiciary. Similarly, during the heyday of the Social Gospel at various university-related divinity schools as well at some independent seminaries, candidates for the Christian ministry learned to see their future profession as one of active involvement not only in ministering to people within the social structures but in challenging and changing the structures themselves. In schools of social work, similarly, there is the recognition, in the words of Ernest DeWitt Burton, that "the promotion of the humanitarian interests of society in an efficient and scientific way" calls for such a school to do its work "in a University setting where the cooperation of the basic social sciences may be secured"; therefore the preparation of students for the healing responsibilities of the profession has led to the recognition that the social context of human ills implies a responsibility for doing something about the society as a whole, not only about its victims one at a time. It bears mentioning, moreover, that one of the most influential books of the most influential philosopher of the progressive movement in education, John Dewey, bears the title *School and Society*, first published in 1899. Dewey as an educational philosopher sought to organize the school as a "miniature community," through which, Dewey believed as a social philosopher, the broader community of the total society would be reformed.

As becomes evident in a bizarre way from its distortion in the career of Albert Speer, who became chief architect for Adolf Hitler's Third Reich in 1934, architectural education in the twentieth century increasingly defines itself on the basis of the social responsibility of the future architect as agent of social change, and the establishment of departments of urban studies and social planning within such schools has been an attempt to address this perceived need.

Each of the professional schools, moreover, in a form and to an extent that is not characteristic of the academic departments in the faculty of arts and sciences of the university, has a relation to the specific constituency of its profession. In a professional school of the university, therefore, the dialectic I have been describing throughout this chapter takes the special form of being obliged to train students for membership in the profession as that profession is understood by its practitioners and their accrediting associations, and at the same time of equipping them for critical and innovative participation in the profession; that is the meaning behind the epigram quoted earlier from Edward H. Levi, that "the professional school which sets its course by the current practice of the profession is, in an important sense, a failure." Because the same dialectic would in turn accurately describe also the relation between each of the professional constituencies and the society as a whole, a professional school runs the danger either of affirming an ambiguous status quo in the profession and in the society or of losing touch with the profession and with the society at large by treating the concerns and structures of the profession with contempt and alienation. Although some professional schools in some universities have sometimes managed to get by with doing the latter for decades, as was true of the Protestant schools of theology at many German universities in the nineteenth century, pressure from the constituency or from the university or from both will eventually compel that the alienation give way to a more constructive engagement with the profession. Within that dialectic, the school's awareness that it serves a constituency into which its graduates will have to find their way gives the professional school of the university a unique opportunity to make a concrete difference in the profession, and through it in the society.

If this dialectic characterizes the university's professional schools, it also provides the school with what are called, perhaps a bit patronizingly, "real world issues" for its teaching and research, so that through these the professional school can address the dynamics of social evolution with a directness that is usually denied the faculty of arts and sciences. It was in recognition of this opportunity that the Harvard Business School developed its case study method of teaching. Whatever the pedagogical advantages of that method may be, it turns out, ironically, that this consideration of practical strategies by these future managers of capitalism has become one of the most successful application to university education anywhere of Marx's maxim that while "the philosophers have only interpreted the world, . . . the point is to change it." Critics of the business school as a concept, particularly those critics who are also critics of the capitalistic system, have described this method of instruction as a subtle means of co-opting willing recruits who will reinforce the present inequities of property and income distribution instead of doing something about changing them. That criticism has been directed even more sharply against the research into real world issues carried out by the faculty of such schools, often as consultants. It is, nevertheless, not necessary for the moment to take sides in the consideration of that criticism to recognize that, to a degree usually unavailable even to those scholars in the arts and sciences who are in the same discipline, scholars in the professional schools are able in their research to gain access, through their more direct involvement in the profession, to the structures of business, finance, and government, and to the institutions of the nonprofit sector of society, such as schools and churches. Conversely, they are able to see the results of their research become instruments of social change, as is already becoming increasingly evident in the direct influence of university-based research upon public and private social policy in the environmental area.

Yet the professional schools of the university, also for their contribution to social change, need to be in constructive interchange with the faculty of arts and sciences. For if a substantial part of the critical idealism leading to social change is the fruit of the general education that is in a special way the vocation of the college, the administrative and intellectual barriers between the college of the university and its professional schools require drastic reevaluation. The professional schools in the university must not look upon social change—or as it is sometimes described, social engineering—as primarily a technical assignment, though it certainly has important technical dimensions, but must be in a position to address to it as well the philosophical and moral questions that arise in the context of general education. To address those questions to their curriculum and their profession, the faculty and the students of the professional schools need easier access to the undergraduate community and to those who teach in that community. In the research of the graduate school, the distinction between basic research and applied research, which always has a certain validity, may lead to the mistake of ignoring the close connection between the two throughout the history of research and the history of the university. Particularly as it affects the contribution of the university to social change, that distinction needs to be seen in light of the way some discoveries of basic research have in fact come from the issues that have been raised in the consideration of concrete structures and social practice. For that very reason, the relation between the idea of the university and the spread of revolutionary doctrine depends for its validity and effectiveness on the invention of new ways to bring together the disparate elements of the university's research activity, as well as of its teaching and publishing.

16

THE TASK OF
INITIATING A WORK
OF SELF-REFORMATION

The title of this chapter represents the combination of two phrases from opposite ends of Newman's nine original discourses. At the beginning of his first discourse Newman speaks of the changes that had taken place at Oxford at the beginning of the nineteenth century, characterizing this as "the singular example of an heterogeneous and an independent body of men, setting about *a work of self-reformation,* not from any pressure of public opinion, but because it was fitting and right to undertake it" (I.i.1). In the last paragraph of the last discourse he issues a disclaimer that any administrator (or quondam administrator) of a university in the closing decade of the twentieth century who has managed to study Newman's book through to the end will probably greet with empathy: "Neither by my habits of life, nor by vigour of age, am I fitted for *the task of* authority, or of rule, or of *initiation*" (I.ix.10).

Of the university's "duties to society," perhaps the most fundamental is the need and the possibility to initiate educational reform, including "the work of self-reformation" in the university itself. Such reform, moreover, must address also the responsibility of the university for educational reform at all levels. If it is accurate to speak, as I have earlier, about "the university in crisis," and if, moreover, that is a crisis both of confidence and of self-confidence, the entire body academic must bestir itself to address it. As is evident from the example of Oxford around 1800, or rather of what Newman calls the "century of inactivity" before 1800, however, the reform of the university will require a combination of intellectual, organizational, and moral commitment. A reexamination of "the idea of the university" like this one should, I trust, make some contribution; but the public constituencies of the university, including alumni, philanthropy, government, and the press, will need, despite what Newman says about "a work of self-reformation not [coming] from any pressure of public opinion," to assist the university by monitoring it without interfering in it, a high art and subtle distinction that they have not always practiced. Those who are at the university, however, continue to be the primary agents for such reform. Students, especially undergraduates, have often supplied almost instant response to conditions within the university that require reform; they have, somewhat less often, been willing to take on their share of the effort and commitment required to carry out the needed reform. Both traditionally and constitutionally, the members of the university faculty— "these thousand-odd kings"—are charged with primary responsibility for the welfare of the university enterprise, and Newman's "heterogeneous and . . . independent body of men, setting about a work of self-reformation . . . because it was fitting and right to undertake it" is proof that it can be done. But the administrative leader of the university continues to bear a primary responsibility, if not "for the task of authority, or of rule," then at any rate "for the task of initiation," especially in the area of educational reform—so long as the president remembers, as one of them has put it, that the chief executive officer of a university is the conductor of an orchestra made up entirely of composers. It is arguable, for example, that a breakdown in university governance has helped to precipitate the crisis in athletics on the campus. Although in the eyes of many it may well be too little and too late, the report of the Knight Commission, *Keeping Faith with the Student-Athlete,* is a serious effort to address that crisis. The report is based on the recognition that "as our nation approaches a new century, the demand for reform of intercollegiate athletics has increased dramatically"; but the report concludes by insisting that university presidents ought to be "the linchpin of the reform movement."

Perhaps nowhere in this reexamination is it more highly desirable than here in a consideration of educational reform to relate the philosophical idea to the concrete situation. One of the most illuminating examinations of Newman's ideas about university education, that of Fergal McGrath, has therefore proceeded on the basis of just such an analysis of the concrete situation of the Irish Catholic University. As Newman recognized, "Necessity has no law, and expedience is often one form of necessity. It is no principle with sensible men, of whatever cast of opinion, to do always what is abstractedly best. Where no direct duty forbids, we may be obliged to do, as being best under circumstances, what we murmur and rise against, while we do it" (I.i.3). Only occasionally did Newman pay direct attention to the reform of education leading up to the university (I.vi.3), which makes it all the more important in this area to discuss the relation between the idea of the university and educational reform by looking at specifics. A highly specific, deeply touching, and profoundly unsettling recent vignette of secondary education in action is Samuel G. Freedman's *Small Victories*. As is evident from its subtitle, "The Real World of a Teacher, Her Students, and Their High School," it deals with the crisis in American public education. Despite the comment from Hannah Arendt quoted earlier, that "it is somewhat difficult to take a crisis in education as seriously as it deserves, [because] it is tempting indeed to regard it as a local phenomenon, unconnected with the larger issues of the century," this book manages to bring the crisis home in graphic terms.

For instead of being a comprehensive statistical study or a broad overview, like other widely debated books, Freedman's book presents an examination of the educational crisis as seen through the prism of one high school teacher, Jessica Siegel at Seward Park High School in Manhattan, during the academic year 1987–88, thus interpreting the local phenomenon as an epitome of the larger issues by observing the classic Aristotelian unities of place and time. Sometimes chilling and sometimes comic, *Small Victories* follows master teacher Siegel and her students through personal challenges, academic successes and failures, and complex social situations. There are pictures of gang struggles (white, black, Hispanic, Asian) and accounts of the politics of academic appointment and promotion, teen-age pregnancies, and bleak prospects for the future—all of this interwoven with the life story and career development of the courageous and confused young woman who is the protagonist. Yet for all its grimness and realism, this is in a curious way a story of hope and, as its title says, a story of "small victories," for the plucky Jessica Siegel, self-styled "Tough Cookie," for her students, even for the public school system. But *Small Victories* can also be read as a series of reflections on the initiative that the university has brought—and, no less important, on the initiative that the university has *not* brought—to reforming the educational system as a whole, which is its relevance here. For the idea of the university is a kind of subsidiary leitmotif of Freedman's book, both in the glimpses he gives us into Jessica Siegel's background and development and in the place that the university occupies in the hopes and plans of her students.

Perhaps most striking is the impression of the overwhelmingly deep chasm between the world of Seward Park High School and the world of the university. In an early chapter, the teacher has put on the blackboard for her students the assignment of writing an autobiography, "Journal Topic: Who Am I? Describe Yourself." This is intended partly as an ice-breaker and an exercise in self-expression, but also partly as a preparation for the personal essay that would accompany a college application. As Freedman explains, "The more immediate benefit is college admissions. Jessica constantly stresses college to her classes, yet she does not teach advanced sections and she harbors a particular fondness for underachievers, for fine minds trailing Cs and Ds like tin cans from a mutt's tail. She has seen a moving autobiography pry open the gates of academe." In an attempt at role-playing, she says to the class: "I want you to imagine you're an admissions counselor at Harvard. You're evaluating two hundred students for admission. Here are three. Which one would you pick?" But despite her assurance to the class that in fact "all these people could get into Harvard," it all seems more than a bit remote, and the response is nervous laughter. "The students joke about college," Freedman explains, "because humor disguises doubt. College is too much to ask. Harvard is a sweatshirt you buy if you want to dress like a preppy. Harvard is those guys on the subway carrying briefcases and the *Wall Street Journal*." Yet if the university is to continue to be the "ground of promise in the future" (II.ix.3), the path to opportunity and service and thus to both equality and quality, not only in the United States but in other developed countries and even more in the developing countries of the Third World, there will have to be more imaginative ways of bridging this chasm, and from both directions.

For despite the chasm, admission to the university does stand, both in symbolism and in substance, for aspiration and achievement. Samuel Freedman waits until the final page of *Small Victories* to inform us that since his completion of the book the teachers at Seward Park are "continuing to defy all expectations by sending 90 percent of each graduating class on to further education, carrying with them more than $100,000 worth of scholarships and grants"—which certainly seems to be no "small victory." Each time a college recognizes what it has taken for one of Jessica Siegel's students "to have graduated, to have stayed sane, to have stayed alive," and therefore grants admission to such a student, she sees this as another victory. Yet at times she tells herself, "In this moment, she can assume the impossible, that they will reach college, all of them. Without believing so, she could not have served any of them," still all the while regarding it as an impossible dream. In words of one student, "I want to get more skills in the english field, so that when and if I go to College I will be able to hold my owne," and thus the university becomes a standard of performance not only for the individual student but for the teacher and for the school as a whole. It is, however, not merely that admission to the university is a standard of performance and a recognition of achievement; the idea of the university itself also defines the intellectual and academic ambience of the high school in many particular ways.

The idea of the university, moreover, defines the intellectual and academic ambience of the high school no less substantially for those students who lack either the opportunity or the will or the ability to enter the university, much less to graduate from it. These are the ones whom the report of a "Commission on Work, Family and Citizenship" has identified as "The Forgotten Half: Non-College Bound Youth in America." Obviously, if admission to the university were the only measure of a student's success in high school, not achieving such admission would be tantamount to failure. In that sense, "the forgotten half" can be the victims of a pressure to get students into the university and, on account of the track they are following in secondary school, can be degraded into second-class citizens. Yet that is not the entire picture. More deeply, the university can significantly define and enrich the curriculum and the academic life of the high school system as a whole and for all its students, setting it free from the short-sighted vocationalism that so often afflicts those institutions of secondary education that have been specifically designed with that forgotten half in mind. There would seem to be a stronger case to be made in support of the demand for useful knowledge in the secondary school than in the university, for those who need vocational and technical preparation; but the outcome shows that "the results of vocational education are largely disappointing." What is called for is a secondary schooling that can be carried on in combination with apprenticeship under the auspices of industry or government or both. In meeting that demand, however, those who design the curriculum of secondary education have often been tempted to overlook the responsibility of such a curriculum, especially in a democratic society, to prepare its students for a life, not only for a living. This includes equipping students for intelligent participation in the decisions and votes that will affect the direction of their government and society. It includes introducing them to the resources of the human mind and spirit in literature and the arts, in the natural sciences and the social sciences, that can remain with them as a source of enlightenment, criticism, and inspiration throughout their adult lives. Now if the implication of the first principle, "Knowledge Its Own End," is sound, it will help to define the undergraduate curriculum of the university, also for those who go on to the graduate and professional study of the university, and will therefore raise questions about any premature specialization. But if it is taken seriously by the university, it should, in the opposite direction, become a presupposition for the secondary school, also for those who do not go on to the university, by drawing them on toward further and deeper knowledge.

In addition to what the university represents for the students and for the high school, however, its meaning for the recruitment and training of teachers is undoubtedly one of the most decisive contributions that the university can make to the task of initiating educational reform, and therefore any program for participation by the university in educational reform must make this a major issue. If, as most readers of *Small Victories* would agree, the system of primary and secondary education needs more Jessica Siegels if it is to be reformed, there must be critical attention to the question of how to increase the chances that such master teachers can be produced. It may be true, as the Latin proverb had it concerning poets, that "they are born, not made," but it is a counsel of total despair to draw from such proverbial wisdom the conclusion that the education of future teachers can contribute nothing to their careers. This issue is a recurring and in many ways troubling theme in Freedman's portrait of Jessica Siegel. Indeed, one of the most disturbing subsections of the book is the account of Siegel's experience as an undergraduate at the University of Chicago. Her mother had "attended the University of Chicago because some novel she had been reading had extolled it," although she did not finish college until many years later, when she earned a bachelor's and then a master's degree at Columbia University at age forty-eight. When Jessica went to Chicago, it was because "the University of Chicago was her mother's school; the University of Chicago had a reputation."

But Freedman introduces the narrative of Jessica's undergraduate years at the University of Chicago four-fifths of the way through the book, quite out of synchronization with the sequence of his account. His description of her mood and attitude on arriving at the University of Chicago campus is revealing: "Buffered on the outside by a demilitarized zone of abandoned tenements, defined on the inside by a rebus of cul-de-sacs, the campus was a hard place either to enter or to escape. Having managed the first, Jessica craved the second, for nothing had ever so overwhelmed her, academically or socially." By the time she was in her final year in the college, her attitude had changed considerably. For in the meantime she had discovered that "never, perhaps, was there a more exhilarating time and place for the undergraduate journalist than Chicago in the late 1960s." That transforming discovery, however, did not come through her university studies at all, but only when "she sought pleasure and fulfillment outside the lecture hall and library." It was the radical politics of the 1960s that made this such an exhilarating time and place, and student journalism joined with student activism to provide the exhilaration. Much of the time, there appeared to be little correlation between this heady atmosphere and "the lecture hall and library." Because the university did not define intellectual fervor that way, as Freedman observes, "Jessica would leave Chicago with a profound ambivalence about both her university and college itself," and she carried that ambivalence with her into her professional career as a secondary school teacher.

Of special interest in considering the initiative of the university in educational reform, however, must be precisely what did take place inside "the lecture hall and library," and what Jessica Siegel, who was to become a high school English teacher though she did not yet know it, studied as an undergraduate at the University of Chicago. "She was," as Freedman describes it, "deposited as if by parachute into a curriculum of Thucydides and Herodotus and Plato, Hobbes and Hume and Burke," authors from "The Great Books of the Western World," which formed the core of the curriculum. That Chicago vignette as a whole, and the specific reference to the Great Books curriculum, raises dramatically the basic question of the place occupied in the preparation of a teacher by general education at the university (howsoever this ambiguous term *general education* may be defined). The undergraduate curriculum of the college of the University of Chicago is, of course, not specifically designed to prepare a teacher—nor, for that matter, to prepare anyone for any vocation or profession, be it law or medicine or scientific research. But its educational philosophy of "knowledge its own end" takes it as a first principle that the general education achieved through the reading of "Thucydides and Herodotus and Plato, Hobbes and Hume and Burke" and their ilk represents the best possible foundation for law or medicine or scientific research—and, at least as much as for any of these, for teaching the young.

In spite of the hostility to this curriculum that Freedman does not even try to conceal, reflecting in his words Jessica Siegel's own feelings—for is it not also "as if by parachute" that most undergraduates at most colleges are "deposited" into a curriculum of quantum mechanics, monetary theory, adolescent psychology, or deconstructionism?—it does bear asking just how in fact she was prepared for the humanistic sensitivity she brings to her teaching in such a moving and effective fashion. It does not seem farfetched to suggest that what expresses itself in her teaching is the consequence not only of the sparkling personal qualities that come through in Freedman's portrait of her, nor only of the exhilarating political causes and the journalistic campaigns that she discovered in her extracurricular activities while at the University of Chicago, but at least in some measure of what she studied in all those classes. Throughout what she says to her students, and how she says it, are resonances from her reading. Even her political radicalism, moreover, goes beyond the emotionalism of the 1960s, because it appears to owe more than a little to the breadth and depth of a reading list that included not only the six classical authors whom Freedman lists but Marx and Freud. Teachers, including the graduate teachers of Ph.D.s, have frequently testified that the quality of teaching, as well as the quality of research, often depends not upon being better informed about the subject matter of one's special field, or at any rate not only upon that, but upon the quality of the general knowledge of the arts and sciences that has been provided, if at all, by secondary school and college. To communicate with their students, teachers repeatedly discover that they need to draw analogies and contrasts from across a range of subjects and books. If that is a sound judgment, a major initiative of the university in educational reform through teacher training will come from what it does for prospective teachers in providing them with general education rather than only from what it does for them specifically through teacher training.

Conversely, Jessica Siegel's experience with postbaccalaureate teacher training raises an entire set of questions on the other side. While working as a paraprofessional at Seward Park High School, she was urged by the teachers there to become a teacher herself. The teachers, for their part, were convinced that "there were only two ways anyone really learned how to teach, by teaching and by watching others teach. Learning how to teach was not an academic process as much as a tribal rite, a secret passed from elder to child, atavistic as charting the stars or planting the maize." But Jessica went ahead anyway and entered Teachers College of Columbia University to work for a master's degree, because "Teachers College, with its international reputation, seemed the place to learn" how to teach. But once again she was deeply disappointed by university education: "If only Jessica had been able to stay awake during her reading-education classes at Teachers College!" The reason for her boredom was in part that "so little in her courses struck her as practical. The professors could not be bothered with subjects as pedestrian as writing a lesson plan." In fact, in her entire course of study toward the master's degree, it was only in "her final, frantic semester [that] she took *the single memorable class of graduate school,* 'Arts and American Education.'" It was in that course that, apparently for the first time, "she learned the way she would teach [her students], by 'showing the connections between things.'" I must admit that I do find it difficult to comprehend why "showing the connections between things" should never have emerged as a theme of her undergraduate reading of the Great Books at the University of Chicago, in which this consideration has always been central. As its guiding spirit, Robert Maynard Hutchins, put it at the beginning of *The Great Conversation,* "The substance of liberal education appears to consist in the recognition of basic problems, in knowledge of distinctions and interrelations in subject matter, and in the comprehension of ideas." In addition, Siegel's experience at Teachers College of Columbia University raises another question, the place of the professional training of teachers within the constellation of the schools of professional training at the university, as well the question of the relation between the research orientation of the university and the realities of most primary and secondary schools.

There have been repeated efforts to relate the training of teachers to the liberal studies associated with the faculty of arts and sciences in the university, rather than chiefly to professional studies in education and pedagogy. In his pioneering study, *High School,* Ernest L. Boyer, opening with the simple declarative sentence, "The schooling of teachers must improve," has recommended the following program:

> 1. During the first two years of college, all prospective teachers should complete a core of common learning.
>
> 2. All teacher candidates should be carefully selected. Formal admission to teacher education should occur at the beginning of the junior year when students begin a three-year teacher preparation sequence.
>
> 3. Once admitted to the program, the teacher candidate should devote the junior and senior years primarily to the completion of a major in an academic discipline and classroom observation.
>
> 4. After grounding in the core curriculum and a solid academic major, every prospective teacher should have a "fifth year" of instructional and apprenticeship experience. This year would include a core of courses to meet the special needs of teachers.

"Simply stated," Boyer declares, "prospective teachers should major in an academic subject, not in education."

That program poses fundamental challenges to what used to be called "normal schools" and then were called "teachers colleges," for at least as they were traditionally conceived they were too isolated and too committed to early professional specialization to be able to carry out such a program in its total context. Many of them seem to have recognized this when they abandoned that earlier nomenclature and moved to transform themselves into "universities," though sometimes with fewer substantive changes than that shift in terminology might suggest. The proper context of teacher training and of educational reform is the university as a whole, in its undergraduate offerings but also in the graduate school of arts and sciences and in its programs of research. For if the university is to initiate a work of self-reformation as the key to educational reform, all three of these elements—undergraduate teaching, graduate teaching, and research and publication—will have to make their contribution. Having now considered the first two, let me turn to the third, and once again by considering specifics. In doing so, I shall concentrate on subjects that are heavily involved in what Whitehead, in his provocative essay on the "rhythms" of learning, calls the stage of "precision," following the stage of "romance" and preceding the stage of "generalization." Newman, too, concentrated on this dimension of the education leading up to the university (I.vi.3).

One of the most hopeful experiments in relating university research to educational reform in many lands today is the cooperation developing between university scientists and the teachers of science in secondary schools. Situated at some of the great scientific research centers of the world, these cooperative programs have been engaged in the task of developing curriculum and teaching materials for science instruction in both elementary and secondary schools. For this task, they can draw on colleagues in the departments and laboratories of the university. In spite of the misgivings that have sometimes been expressed about some of them, such programs arose out of the recognition that the science being carried out in the major laboratories and observatories was separated by a wide gap from the science being taught to students in elementary school and high school. That gap, moreover, has been widening, at least partly as a function of the growth in scientific research throughout the world during the past several decades. The conventional science textbook supplemented by a laboratory manual, even if it could be revised at periodic (and increasingly brief) intervals, has proved to be severely handicapped as a format for science education in the face of this new information. One stratagem developed by these centers in response to this is to move toward the creation of educational networks, through which university laboratories for research and school laboratories for teaching can be connected interactively through computers and other new technologies of communication. Another technique, which will eventually have to be organized on a national or even an international scale to be truly effective, is for the university to establish internships, workshops, and institutes of continuing education for teachers of science.

As recent studies and surveys have shown, the teaching of history is likewise in a parlous condition. In part this seems to be the consequence of the substitution of "social studies" for history in the high school curriculum, as a consequence of which it is not always possible to presuppose in the students produced by such a curriculum even the most elementary historical knowledge. Unlike instruction in the laboratory sciences, the teaching of history does continue to be text-oriented; but "text-oriented" means in this context both that the students need to have a narrative textbook in hand to hold the course together and that they need, just as early as possible, to learn how to work with texts, documents, and other primary sources. For a reform of the teaching of history that can take advantage of the educational use of "texts" in both these senses of the word, the university must become an indispensable partner. For although textbooks for college courses in history continue to be prepared by eminent scholars, relatively few university historians have taken on the even more daunting responsibility of writing materials aimed at a secondary school audience. In part this is due to the politicization of the process by which such textbooks are selected by state boards of education, where even the criterion of "readability" has frequently been defined in political terms. But seen in an international context, as it already must be seen and as it will need to be seen far more during coming decades, the problem is rooted at least as much, in most countries that have university scholars, in the absence of adequate channels of communication between those scholars and their colleagues who teach history in the *Gymnasium, lycée,* or high school. As instruction in history moves ever more toward a method in which all students use collections of primary sources, moreover, a greater participation of the university and its scholars in preparing such collections will assure that the most discriminating historical scholarship will be brought to bear on the selecting and editing of the documents.

An additional dimension is introduced into the university connection of secondary school teaching in such a field as language teaching. Throughout the world, the tumultuous political events of the final quarter of the twentieth century are underlining the desperate need for more and better foreign language instruction. There is probably enough blame to go around for this state of affairs, but the university is an important link in the chain, and that in at least two ways. One is related to the aforementioned function of the university and of college admission as a goal and standard for high schools and their students. When a university drops its foreign language requirements, that sends a signal to secondary schools that the ability to make significant use of a language other than one's own does not rank high in the list of specifications for an educated person. But it has also been through the university that the positive side of this question has received a new impetus, through the work of university professors concerned with language pedagogy. For example, the highly effective series *French in Action: A Beginning Course in Language and Culture,* prepared by Pierre J. Capretz and published in 1987, may be said without exaggeration to represent a genuine breakthrough, making use not only of textbooks, but of audio programs and video cassettes, to establish a working relation between the research of university scholars into learning theory and the classroom and language laboratory. Application of "the Capretz method" to the study of other foreign languages by speakers of English—perhaps even to the study of English by speakers of English?—will further confirm the pedagogical contributions of the university as a center of both research and teaching.

Even those who would reject as excessively narrow Newman's assumption about the student preparing for university, that "for some years his intellect is little more than an instrument for taking in facts, or a receptacle for storing them" (I.vi.3), should welcome such developments, which could have important implications for students in secondary schools, including "the forgotten half" of "non-college bound youth in America" and other countries, who will also have increasing need to know more, for both cultural and vocational purposes. For if the university can, by "setting about a work of self-reformation," put its hand to "the task of initiation" in the area of educational reform, it will be undertaking a "duty to society" that no other agency is in a position to perform.

17

ALMA MATER:
A LIFE OF LEARNING

Despite accents of hope, a sharp note of poignancy runs throughout Newman's *Idea of a University,* for it is as much an account of an Oxford lost as
of a Dublin envisioned. It is Oxford rather than Dublin that he has in mind
when he says that "a University is, according to the usual designation, an
Alma Mater, knowing her children one by one, not a foundry, or a mint, or
a treadmill" (I.vi.8). Therefore one of the deepest moments of pathos in all
of his writings appears in the *Apologia pro Vita Sua,* as he describes his last
days at Oxford and the separation from it that had been made necessary by
his conversion from Anglicanism to Roman Catholicism in 1845:

> I left Oxford for good on Monday, February 23, 1846. . . . Various
> friends came to see the last of me; . . . and I called on Dr. Ogle, one of
> my very oldest friends, for he was my private Tutor, when I was an
> Undergraduate. In him I took leave of my first College, Trinity, which
> was so dear to me, and which held on its foundation so many who
> had been kind to me both when I was a boy, and all through my
> Oxford life. Trinity had never been unkind to me. There used to be
> much snap-dragon growing on the walls opposite my freshman's
> rooms there, and I had for years taken it as the emblem of my own
> perpetual residence even unto death in my University.
>
> On the morning of the 23rd I left the Observatory. I have never
> seen Oxford since, excepting its spires, as they are seen from the
> railway.

Although, as the "Additional Note" taken from the London *Times* explains, he did return to Oxford on 26 February 1878 and "dined in Trinity
College Hall at the high table, attired in his academical dress," the expectation of "personal residence even unto death in my University"—as he said
elsewhere, "he never wished any thing better or higher than . . . 'to live and
die a fellow of Oriel'"—was now replaced by what Newman in his roman à

clef, *Loss and Gain,* describes as the sense of an Oxford University "suddenly recovered—recovered to be lost for ever!" For now "all had passed as a dream, and he was a stranger where he had hoped to have had a home."

In a familiar apostrophe to "the University of Oxford, for which I feel, and always must feel, the fondest, the most reverential attachment," Matthew Arnold (who counted Newman, together with Wordsworth, Goethe, and Sainte-Beuve as "one of the four persons . . . from whom he had really learned"), spoke about how Oxford—"steeped in sentiment as she lies, spreading her gardens to the moonlight, whispering from her towers the last enchantments of the Middle Age" and the "home of lost causes, and forsaken beliefs, and unpopular names, and impossible loyalties!"—had a way of affecting its graduates that way. This did not by any means apply to all of its former students. Edward Gibbon was at his bitterest and at his most eloquent when he spoke of Oxford, at which he matriculated as an undergraduate on 3 April 1752: "To the University of Oxford I acknowledge no obligation; and she will as cheerfully renounce me for a son, as I am willing to disclaim her as a mother. I spent fourteen months at Magdalen College: they proved the fourteen months the most idle and unprofitable of my whole life." Nor was there substantial disagreement between Gibbon and Newman about this (though there was about almost everything else); for Newman acknowledged that "about fifty years since" and "after a century of inactivity," a century that included the time when Gibbon had been an undergraduate there, Oxford had finally been bestirred to move away from "a time when (as I may say) it was giving no education at all to the youth committed to its keeping" and had regained "a sense of the responsibilities which its profession and its station involved" (I.i.1).

It is a metaphor but it is not a hyperbole when Gibbon speaks of having disclaimed a mother, or when Newman speaks of having lost a mother, an Alma Mater. Nor is it a hyperbole to say that the university is Alma Mater in a manner that is distinct even from the manner in which the college is Alma Mater, in a unique sense of that metaphor, despite the special affection that can often grow up between the college and its students past and present. For if the vocation of the university is not only the one it shares with the college, the extension of knowledge to undergraduates through teaching, but the preparation of professionals through training, the advancement of knowledge through research, and the diffusion of knowledge through publication, together with the creation of a free and responsible community in which such advancement and diffusion of knowledge are an ongoing and unending process, then it functions much as we may, if we have been blessed, remember our parents functioning—and as perhaps we also may, if we have been twice blessed, function as parents ourselves, at least from time to time. Because the university is where, in Newman's phrase, "a habit of mind is formed which lasts through life" (I.v.1), the university is Alma Mater for life, with whom her children have, in Newman's language, perpetual residence, intellectually and spiritually if not always physically, even unto death.

Moreover, because, as Newman also says, "there is no one in whom [Liberal Education] is carried as far as is conceivable" (I.vii.1), such perpetual involvement, even apart from perpetual residence, seems a necessary consequence of the very definition of the university. Since the university first came into being in the Middle Ages and even since the university came of age in the nineteenth and twentieth centuries, there have been many social and demographic changes, but none with consequences as portentous for the idea of the university and of its mission as the dramatic increase in life expectancy and in leisure time, together with the accompanying development, especially during the twentieth century, of patterns of retirement and second calling. Therefore it is difficult to believe that this role of the university as Alma Mater will not continue to grow. Of all the predictions about the future of the university that it seems possible to make, none would seem to be safer on the basis of what is already going on than the expectation that the university will never again be defined exclusively as an institution for educating young people but will increasingly go on taking upon itself a major responsibility for a complete life of learning as an integral part of its central educational mission. If that is a safe prediction throughout most of the world, the future of the university—intellectually and educationally, as well as for that matter financially and administratively—will be closely tied to how it performs in cultivating this lifelong bond and in carrying out this lifelong mission for each of its several overlapping constituencies.

Although it has been my repeated contention here that in many significant respects the intellectual and academic leadership of the university must come chiefly from the faculty of arts and sciences, whose basic research is also reshaping the curriculum and training offered by all the professional schools of the university, the program of lifelong education is one in which the members of the faculty of arts and sciences are learning to follow an example that has already been set by their colleagues in the professional schools. For it is the professional schools that have mounted by far the most impressive and, when it is done right, the most intellectually significant effort to involve the university in the deepening of the life of the mind for mature adults. This is due in part to the unique configuration of university-based professional schools, as distinct from independent training schools for the professions. When they are performing at their full potential, the professional schools of the university are positioned in a delicate balance between the university and the society, and specifically between the university and the professional constituencies for which the professional schools are responsible. The university protects them from becoming the vassals of the constituency or shaping their course to what the constituency believes at any particular moment to be needed for a true professional in the field, which may be, and usually is, significantly different from what such a professional will need some years down the line. But the constituency, in turn, protects them from becoming mere satellites of the graduate school of arts and sciences, where the subject matter of graduate research and teaching would be recycled for professional students.

That delicate balance puts the professional schools into their leadership position in the lifelong education that is reshaping the mission of the university as a whole. As one report on "Physicians for the Twenty-first Century" has put it, describing in the process the other learned professions as well,

> Most physicians are keenly aware of the need for continued learning, and they participate in programs of continuing medical education. Lifelong learning and adaptation of medical practice to new knowledge and new techniques will be even more important in the future. Students whose general professional education has provided them with the learning skills, values, and attitudes to continue learning throughout their careers will need easy access to information to pursue learning on their own.

Not only through institutes, conferences, seminar programs, and traveling exhibits but through "information management systems" that are "commensurate with the needs of physicians whose education has prepared them to be independent, lifelong learners," professional schools can bring to practitioners in the field a critical review of recent research and speculation about the profession and can receive from mature professionals the kind of critical reaction on the basis of practical experience that will form the basis for curricular revision and for new research. At the same time it must be pointed out that when the professional schools of the university have carried out this assignment imaginatively and effectively, it has often been in close collaboration with colleagues from the faculty of arts and sciences.

For what mature professionals need most from such schools are not the newest tricks of the trade, but the implications of research and reflection for the practice of the profession. Thus the law school renders them its best service when, for example, it provides a forum for airing current debates about the relation between "original intent" and "extended application" in the interpretation of the Constitution. This is an intellectual and scholarly issue on which not only professors from the law school but historians and political scientists from the faculty of arts and sciences—and perhaps even theorists of literary criticism, students of musical performance, and scholars in biblical exegesis, in all three of which "original intent" is also an issue—can all illumine a complex and fascinating problem. Academic medicine can and should, perhaps in collaboration with a hospital, help health care professionals "in the development, diffusion, and use of medical technology and pharmaceuticals." But its most basic contribution to their professional improvement will come from the laboratories of molecular biology, genetics, and immunology, which the school of medicine shares with the (other) biological sciences. The business school will always help to provide professionals with "updating" as, for example, tax laws change, but the business school that is at the university will be rendering a more substantial service if it puts such issues as tax law into their larger economic, political, historical, and international contexts. As Alfred North Whitehead said in 1928, early in the history of business schools, "We need not flinch from the assertion that the main function of such a school is to produce men with a greater zest for business," but "in the complex organizations of modern business the intellectual adventure of analysis, and of imaginative reconstruction, must precede any successful reorganization" of business. In the course of serving their professional constituencies in this more comprehensive manner, moreover, professional schools will be addressing the intellectual needs, if not at the same time the professional needs, of a far broader constituency and will thus be contributing to the overall development of lifelong education at the university.

The realization of such a definition of the idea and mission of the university faces significant obstacles, however, and at least in this instance a consideration of the obstacles may well be as useful a technique as any for considering the issue itself. To begin with the obstacles within the university, it will call for some rather massive readjustments on the part of each subcommunity in the university community. Undergraduates have always been tempted to suppose that the entire university exists for their benefit and that nothing may be permitted to interfere with this—neither faculty research nor scholarly publishing nor the needs of graduate and professional students nor alumni concerns nor legislative surveillance. There seems to be little statistical evidence regarding undergraduate attitudes toward the presence of continuing education students on their campuses, perhaps even in their classes; but anecdotal evidence (some of it from films, novels, and short stories) suggests that this presence often appears intrusive to them. Nor is that, as their elders often all too readily conclude, simply one more indication of adolescent selfishness. The questions with which older students will approach an experiment or a lecture or a text do reflect a significantly different mixture of book learning and experience, and one that must not automatically be equated with greater wisdom. Especially is this the case because it is often informed by a book learning that has surely been overtaken, but not necessarily overhauled, several times over through the advancement of knowledge over a period of decades. It is informed as well by a "wisdom" that may sometimes be little more than ingrained prejudice.

At least partly for that reason, professors have a considerable amount of residual resistance to taking on, in addition to their present duties or even in place of some of them, the task of reintroducing members of their parents' generation to materials that have traditionally been reserved for the members of their children's generation. It is often difficult enough to convince a scholar that undergraduate teaching itself is not a waste of time or a hindrance to scholarship, without having to make the additional case that the teaching of adults should also be included among the tasks of the university professor. If, as Newman says, "the common sense of mankind has associated the search after truth with seclusion and quiet" (I.pr.), the threat to such seclusion and quiet would in some respects seem to become even more profound when it comes from mature students. Behind that resistance, however, lies a deeper presupposition, which it will be useful to raise to explicit discussion. That is the assumption that school is for the young, whom the university prepares for an adulthood in which they should be able to carry on their continuing education for themselves. Even those who would not subscribe to the principle that as professors they stand "in loco parentis" do often define their teaching role in generational metaphors; and those of us who had the privilege of teaching the returning veterans of the Second World War under the G.I. Bill of Rights, many of whom were older than the newly minted Ph.D.s who were their instructors, can recall how confusing it was to have the generations scrambled as they were. Although that was treated as an unusual situation, which it was at the time, it was actually a dress rehearsal for a significant portion of the future of university teaching.

This style of teaching, nevertheless, can bring compensatory benefits both to professors and to undergraduates. For professors who are publishing scholars, there is much to be gained from preparing material for presentation to an audience who in certain respects may be even closer to the potential readership of some of their books than a group of undergraduates. I make it a practice at the beginning of an undergraduate history course to try to determine which public event the students might be able to remember as something contemporary to them rather than as something their parents described to them after the fact. As the perspective of undergraduates has moved forward year by year, this makes the teaching of ancient or medieval history a special challenge, because to these students nearly everything seems to be ancient or medieval. It is almost a cliché to add, moreover, that the young lack the experience and knowledge—especially if their precollegiate studies have followed the disastrous trend of substituting "social studies" for history—to draw even elementary parallels and contrasts between the historical period under study and some other period, including their own. Parallels and analogies may be deceptive or even dangerous, as the debate of the 1960s over "the Munich analogy" or more recent debates over "the Vietnam analogy" demonstrate, but when handled with some sophistication and perhaps a bit of learning they can be highly instructive. The clash over their relevance to the historical situation or to the contemporary situation is another benefit that can come from teaching different generations at the same time. Professors of English would find it far more rewarding in many respects to teach *King Lear* to a class that includes people who have known suffering and bitter disappointment—in their children, their jobs, their world, and themselves—than to one made up completely of students in early adolescence, many of whose greatest tragedies, deeply felt though these undoubtedly have been, will eventually appear trivial even to them. But those professors will grant that they would rather teach *Romeo and Juliet* to the adolescents, who will weep with the young lovers rather than merely over them. From this it would seem to follow that the study and teaching of both plays would be enriched by the sharing across generations and by the conflict between generations.

Another serious obstacle within the university that must somehow be overcome is an almost Luddite hostility to the introduction and adaptation of new technologies to the teaching process. For decades, educators have been suggesting that the adaptation of television to college and university teaching was long overdue, but such adaptation has not been able to move as fast or as far as many might have hoped. Such achievements as the new technologies for the teaching of foreign languages through television and video or the television accomplishments of BBC and PBS have begun to probe the vast potential of this medium, but it is noteworthy that the prime movers in much of this development have been creative television professionals rather than innovative academics, whose role has been principally that of consultants. Like much computer hardware and software, television and video equipment has often been designed for business or entertainment and has had to be adapted, more or less successfully, to the needs of the university. But the rate at which the computer has found acceptance among senior scholars in the humanities suggests that the habits of scholarship established over a lifetime or over several are not easily changed. Whenever I see a tape recorder at a lecture where a student ought to be, it is almost irresistible to suggest caustically that everyone including the professor should stay in the library and let the tape recorders deliver lectures to one another. Nor can professors be expected to show an automatic enthusiasm over some new system of mortmain that would permit their predecessors to lord it over succeeding generations with their televised lectures and master classes, lectures that are increasingly out of touch with the current research but that are nevertheless—or therefore?—especially appealing to certain mature audiences. It does seem likely, however, that a repository of the great lectures of the past will take its place alongside the libraries, galleries, museums, and other "embalmments of dead genius," and that this will be especially useful to the university in its mission of lifelong education.

At least as important as the changes that will be necessary within the university if it is to address this new opportunity are the changes that will have to be wrought in the potential audience. There is a natural audience to be found in the alumni body of every university—natural because of the ties, both personal and intellectual, that already exist to "a University [that] is, according to the usual designation, an Alma Mater, knowing her children one by one, not a foundry, or a mint, or a treadmill" (I.vi.8), and because of the educational programs to which, in greater or lesser measure, many alumni associations now devote attention. By themselves, these activities are not an adequate response by the university to its mission of lifelong education, but they are a significant beginning in that direction. Yet portraits of student life as varied as *The Student Prince at Heidelberg* and *Dink Stover at Yale* are documentation for the almost endemic anti-intellectualism of some alumni, who resent the intrusion of the university's educational mission on their retelling of war stories from their undergraduate days and on their athletic enthusiasms. It does seem, nevertheless, that a generational shift is taking place in this respect, too. Perhaps it reflects an earlier shift in university admissions, but those who have come out of the modern research university (and who elected to go there in the first place) seem to manifest a far greater eagerness than did earlier generations to be introduced to the methods and results of the ongoing research at the university, both while they are there and after they have graduated. On the other hand, lifelong education at the university does not have to be quite as grim as it sometimes sounds, and the university will need to devise as rich a combination of the classroom and the hidden curriculum for this activity as it has developed within the traditional forms of university education.

Quite another obstacle to the university's ability to innovate in the field of lifelong education is the competition of education in this or any other form with the other diverting activities that beckon university graduates and everyone else. In the first century B.C.E., the Latin satirist Juvenal complained about the Roman citizens of his day that there were only two things about which they cared, "bread and circuses," an entertainment diet that seems by modern standards, at least in the West, to be rather quaint or downright ascetic. When one begins to contemplate how many different kinds of bread and how many variations of circuses the world of the future will undoubtedly hold out to its citizens, the question is: Will the university with its program of lifelong education be able to compete in such an atmosphere? The question will have to be answered in several settings at once. In the most basic sense, the question is addressed not only to the university but to all of formal education; and the university will have to learn to be far more inventive, and far less condescending, in its collaboration with the elementary and secondary school and with the college, both in the traditional work that these institutions do and in this common task. It will have to learn as well how to tell the difference between education and schooling, and thus to cultivate a collaborative relation also with the many educational institutions that are not schools—museums, libraries, galleries, journals, media, and churches—to which it can contribute a great deal and from which it can learn at least as much.

When it has done all that, however, the university will also have to learn to live with the reality of still being what it is. For although the polarity between egalitarianism and elitism may ultimately be a spurious distinction, the university will have to be prepared to live with the polarity, also in determining what kind of lifelong education it is in a position to provide. In *The Great Conversation* Robert Maynard Hutchins gave eloquent voice to the educational dream of his life:

As the business of earning a living has become easier and simpler, it has also become less interesting and significant, and all personal problems have become more perplexing. This fact, plus the fact of the disappearance of any education adequate to deal with it, has led to the development of all kinds of cults, through which the baffled worker seeks some meaning for his life, and to the extension on an unprecedented scale of the most trivial recreations, through which he may hope to forget that his human problems are unsolved . . . .

Yet the substitution of machines for slaves gives us an opportunity to build a civilization as glorious as that of the Greeks, and far more lasting because far more just. I do not concede that torpor of mind is the natural and normal condition of the mass of mankind, or that these people are necessarily incapable of relishing or bearing a part in any rational conversation, or of conceiving generous, noble, and tender sentiments, or of forming just judgments concerning the affairs of private and public life. If they are so, and if they are so as a result of the division of labor, then industrialization and democracy are fundamentally opposed; for people in this condition are not qualified to govern themselves. I do not believe that industrialization and democracy are inherently opposed. But they are in actual practice opposed unless the gap between them is bridged by liberal education for all.

Hutchins wrote those words during the Second World War, twenty years or so before going on to write *The University of Utopia.* Yet his words continue to present a challenge not only to the University of Utopia but to Alma Mater, and they compel a continuing and critical reexamination not only of the university as institution but of the idea of the university as well.

18

THE IDEA OF THE
UNIVERSITY IN
SCHOLARLY LITERATURE

Newman's *Idea of a University* is in many ways a book about books, and therefore it is fitting that this reexamination of the idea of the university also include a chapter about books. The bibliography of "Works Cited and Consulted" is an accounting of the many intellectual and scholarly debts I have incurred in writing this book, and in the notes to individual chapters I have specified these even more precisely. But having put myself on record in chapter 11 as recommending the bibliographical essay, I feel obliged to undertake one in this final chapter. I have contravened my own recommendations (and predilections), as expressed in several chapters, by largely confining myself, both here and in the bibliography, to titles in English, except where resort to other languages seemed unavoidable.

John Henry Newman. As the most influential English-speaking theologian who ever lived (and in many respects the fountainhead of the Second Vatican Council) and as the author of the most important book ever written about the university, John Henry Newman has received wide attention from scholars, especially from British and American Roman Catholics but also from many others. The year 1990 was the centenary of his death, providing the occasion for a spate of new books, as well as for the reissue of others. The massive biography by Ian Turnbull Ker, *John Henry Newman: A Biography* (Oxford: Clarendon, 1988), supersedes its predecessors for sheer comprehensiveness and detail. Several of these nevertheless remain important: Maisie Ward, *Young Mr. Newman* (New York: Sheed and Ward, 1948), examines his intellectual and personal development in the early years, while Louis Bouyer, *Newman: His Life and Spirituality*, translated by J. Lewis May (reprint ed.; New York: Meridian Books, 1960), traces his religious development as though "from within." My favorite among the biographies of Newman remains C. D. Dessain, *John Henry Newman* (London: Thomas Nelson and Sons, 1966), by a scholar who spent a lifetime studying and editing Newman's writings and who was helpful to me personally in my study of Newman. Henry Tristram's edition, *John Henry Newman: Autobiographical Writings* (New York: Sheed and Ward, 1957), pulls together in convenient form many of Newman's own reflections about himself. For *The Idea of a University* itself, it is once again I. T. Ker, in his edition, *The Idea of a University Defined and Illustrated* (Oxford: Clarendon, 1976), who provides the definitive text, with valuable introductory material and notes; Fergal McGrath, *Newman's University: Idea and Reality* (London: Longmans, 1951), relates idea and institution, and Dwight Culler, *The Imperial Intellect: A Study of Newman's Educational Ideal* (New Haven: Yale University Press, 1955), illumines every aspect of the book. As a scholar who works on the history of Christian doctrine, I have a particular interest in Newman's pioneering *Essay on the Development of Christian Doctrine* of 1845, for which two modern studies are especially important: Owen Chadwick, *From Bossuet to Newman: The Idea of Doctrinal Development* (Cambridge: Cambridge University Press, 1957); and J.-H. Walgrave, *Newman the Theologian: The Nature of Belief and Doctrine as Exemplified in His Life and Works*, translated by A. V. Littledale (New York: Sheed and Ward, 1960).

The University in Crisis. As I have suggested, diagnosis of the university seems to have become a favorite indoor sport and a cottage industry, as any reader of any magazine of opinion has ample opportunity to discover; a recent example, far more thoughtful than many, is "The Changing Culture of the University," a special issue of *Partisan Review* for 1991. In addition to the magazine articles, the problems are also the subject of a small, but constantly growing, library of books. Allan Bloom, *The Closing of the American Mind: How Higher Education Has Failed Democracy and Impoverished the Souls of Today's Students* (New York: Simon and Schuster, 1987), has provoked an unexpected response from a wide readership, thus showing how deeply felt the problems and issues are. Charles J. Sykes, *Profscam: Professors and the Demise of Higher Education* (Washington, D.C.: Regnery Gateway, 1988), concentrated on allegations of corruption, both financial and ethical, in professorial ranks. On the other hand, Roger Kimball, *Tenured Radicals: How Politics Has Corrupted Our Higher Education* (New York: Harper and Row, 1990), is especially concerned about the establishment of a new political orthodoxy of the Left, above all in university departments of literature and the humanities. Dinesh D'Souza, *Illiberal Education: The Politics of Race and Sex on Campus* (New York:

Free Press, 1991), approaches some of the same phenomena, but with special attention to the implications of such issues as "affirmative action" for the intellectual and scholarly life of the university. Page Smith, *Killing the Spirit: Higher Education in America* (Penguin Books edition. New York: Penguin Books, 1991), puts his sense of betrayal into the context of the history of higher education in America. Martin Kenney, *Biotechnology: The University-Industrial Complex* (New Haven: Yale University Press, 1986), examines the beginnings of a scientific entrepeneurship that can have pervasive long-range significance for the university; and Bruce Wilshire, *The Moral Collapse of the University* (Albany: State University of New York Press, 1990), probes the ability—and the inability—of the university to form and to express a sense of conscience in relation to this trend and others.

The University as Institution and Idea. The subject of this book is the university as *idea,* not the university as *institution.* But because so many of the studies devoted to the university have concentrated on its institutional forms and functions, they should also be a useful place to look for reflections on the idea of the university, although in such studies it is often only implicit and sometimes seems largely absent. In his Godkin Lectures, *The Uses of the University* (Cambridge: Harvard University Press, 1963), one of the most influential of modern observers of the university, Clark Kerr, articulated his own "idea of the university," and in a volume he edited under the title *Twelve Systems of Higher Education: Six Decisive Issues* (New York: International Council for Educational Development, 1978), he put this into a comparative context. Jacques Barzun, *The American University: How It Runs; Where It Is Going* (New York: Harper and Row, 1968), is a genial series of observations and reflections. In a series of books over the years, my sometime colleague, David Riesman, has consistently addressed his thoughtful inquiries to the basic issues in American higher education. The volume he produced with Christopher Jencks, *The Academic Revolution* (Garden City, N.Y.: Doubleday, 1968), retains its freshness after more than two decades; and in his joint volume with Gerald Grant, *The Perpetual Dream: Reform and Experiment in the American College* (Chicago: University of Chicago Press, 1978), the tradition has found a voice. The warnings sounded already in his *Constraint and Variety in American Education* (Lincoln: University of Nebraska Press, 1956), and then nearly a quarter-century later in *On Higher Education: The Academic Enterprise in an Era of Rising Student Consumerism* (San Francisco: Jossey-Bass, 1980), have, unfortunately, proved to be accurate. Henry Rosovsky, in *The University: An Owner's Manual* (New York: W. W.

Norton, 1990), pulls together a dean's occasional pieces into a coherent and instructive essay. For reasons both of substance and of sentiment, let me add the collections of such occasional pieces by my late colleague and friend, A. Bartlett Giamatti, especially *The University and the Public Interest* (New York: Atheneum, 1981) and *A Free and Ordered Space: The Real World of the University* (New York: W. W. Norton, 1988).

The Business of a University. Of the three American university presidents from the end of the nineteenth century whom I have singled out as deserving of special mention and as having decisively shaped the modern American university, as well as the thought and study going into this book, Daniel Coit Gilman is the subject of Fabian Franklin's The *Life of Daniel Coit Gilman* (New York: Dodd, Mead, 1910), and is the central figure in the narrative of Hugh Hawkins, *Pioneer: A History of the Johns Hopkins University, 1874–1889* (Ithaca: Cornell University Press, 1960). The many-faceted career of Andrew Dickson White has been recounted in Glenn C. Altschuler, *Andrew Dickson White: Educator, Historian, Diplomat* (Ithaca: Cornell University Press, 1979). The intellectual and spiritual wellsprings of the thought of William Rainey Harper are dealt with in James P. Wind, *The Bible and the University: The Messianic Vision of William Rainey Harper* (Atlanta: Scholars Press, 1987), and his achievements as an educator in Richard J. Storr, *Harper's University: The Beginnings* (Chicago: University of Chicago Press, 1966); a wealth of quotations from Harper appear in William Michael Murphy and D. J. R. Bruckner, *The Idea of the University of Chicago: Selections from the Papers of the First Eight Chief Executives of the University of Chicago from 1891 to 1975* (Chicago: University of Chicago Press, 1976). Even more evident here is my debt to Robert Maynard Hutchins, president and chancellor of the University of Chicago while I was a graduate student there. Among others, I note especially two of his statements of purpose for the university: *Education for Freedom* (New York: Grove Press, 1963) and *The University of Utopia* (Phoenix ed.; Chicago: University of Chicago Press, 1964). There is a biography of him by Harry S. Ashmore, *Unseasonable Truths: The Life of Robert Maynard Hutchins* (Boston: Little, Brown, 1989), and a deeply moving essay from a unique blending of personal and scholarly perspectives by William H. McNeill, *Hutchins' University: A Memoir of the University of Chicago, 1929–1950* (Chicago: University of Chicago Press, 1991).

Research and Teaching. If, as this book argues, "the advancement of knowledge through research" and "the extension of knowledge through teaching" are inseparable in the definition of the university—such is also the contention of Ernest Boyer in *Scholarship Reconsidered: Priorities of the Professoriate* (Princeton: Carnegie Foundation for the Advancement of Teaching, 1990)—they should probably not be separated here either. The most important source for my argument in this book—and, second only to Newman's classic, the most important for my own reflection about the idea of the university—is the seminal thought that went into the establishment of the University of Berlin. Wilhelm von Humboldt was its founding genius, the great philosopher of German Idealism, Johann Gottlieb Fichte, its first rector, and the great theologian of German Idealism, Friedrich Daniel Ernst Schleiermacher, one of its earliest interpreters, together with the philosopher of religion, Friedrich Wilhelm Schelling—a constellation that would have been remarkable anywhere. Their treatises on the place of research and teaching in the university are collected in a book which—like that of Karl Jaspers's *Idea of the University,* translated by H. A. T. Reiche and H. F. Vanderschmidt (Boston: Beacon Press, 1959)—shows Newman's influence in its very title: *Die Idee der deutschen Universität: Die fünf Grundschriften aus der Zeit ihrer Neubegründung durch klassischen Idealismus und romantischen Realismus* (Darmstadt: H. Gentner, 1956). Joseph S. Fruton's *Contrasts in Scientific Style: Research Groups in the Chemical and Biochemical Sciences* (Philadelphia: American Philosophical Society, 1990), describes the research atmosphere created there in nineteenth-century Germany, which is, in its political dimension, also the subject of L. Burchardt's *Wissenschaftspolitik im Wilhelminischen Deutschland* (Göttingen: Vandenhoeck und Ruprecht, 1975), and of K. H. Jarausch, *Students, Society, and Politics in Imperial Germany* (Princeton: Princeton University Press, 1982). Throughout this century, there have been vigorous protests against the importation of this German atmosphere into the American university, ranging from William James, "The Ph.D. Octopus," *Harvard Monthly* 36 (1903): 1–9, to Lynne V. Cheney, *Tyrannical Machines: A Report on Educational Practices Gone Wrong and Our Best Hopes for Setting Them Right* (Washington, D.C.: National Endowment for the Humanities, 1990). And, as this book both suggests and documents, the debate goes on.

Professional Education. At least in North America, serious reflection about professional education and its place in the university, as it pertains not only to the preparation of physicians but to training for all the learned professions, must take its start from Abraham Flexner, *Medical Education in the United States and Canada* (New York: Carnegie Foundation for the Advancement of Teaching, 1910), which, rather than tinkering with the development of a practicum, put its recommendations on the basis of scientific research as it should shape the training of doctors; twenty years later Flexner wrote *Universities, American, English, German* (New York: Oxford University Press, 1930), which bears not only on this chapter but on this entire book. For the origins of professional education, again as it pertains to medicine, I have learned from Vern L. Ballough, *The Development of Medicine as a Profession: The Contribution of the Medieval University to Modern Medicine* (New York: Hafner, 1966). The history of professional theological education in the modern period, and in the New World, is the subject of a comprehensive study edited by William Adams Brown, *The Education of American Ministers*, 4 vols. (New York: Institute of Social and Religious Research, 1934), but it has also been told, with his characteristically affable mixture of anecdote and erudition, by Roland H. Bainton, *Yale and the Ministry: A History of Education for the Christian Ministry at Yale from the Founding in 1701* (New York: Harper and Brothers, 1957). Roland Bainton's colleague (and mine), H. Richard Niebuhr, joined with Daniel Day Williams and James M. Gustafson to produce *The Advancement of Theological Education* (New York: Harper and Brothers, 1957). For the medieval origins of legal education, G. de. Vergottini, *Lo studio di Bologna, l'impero, il papato* (Bologna: Studi e memorie per la storia dell'Università di Bologna, 1956), puts the educational history into the stormy context of medieval church-state relations; a volume edited by Göran Hasselberg, *Juridiska Fakulteten vid Uppsala Universitet* (Stockholm: Almqvist and Wiksell, 1976), relates the history from the other end of Europe; and Frank L. Ellsworth, *Law on the Midway: The Founding of the University of Chicago Law School* (Chicago: Law School of the University of Chicago, 1977), shows that the tradition still lives. Of the other professions with which the modern university deals, the most significant—and in some respects the most problematical—is probably business, and Jeffrey L. Cruikshank, *A Delicate Experiment: The Harvard Business School, 1908–1945* (Boston: Harvard Business School Press, 1987), has documented both the significant and the problematical aspects of the place of the business school in the university context. The preparation of teachers is in many ways the stepchild of the modern university, as Ernest L. Boyer suggests in *High School: A Report on Secondary Education in America* (New York: Harper and Row, 1983); and even those who do not accept the programmatic recommendations of Bernard R. Gifford, *The Good School of Education: Linking Knowledge, Teaching, and Learning* (Berkeley: Graduate School of Education, University of California, 1984), will benefit from his clear recognition of the issues. My analysis has been deepened by the scholarship and thought of Diane

Ravitch, *The Schools We Deserve: Reflections on the Educational Crisis of Our Times* (New York: Basic Books, 1985).

Books and the University. The epigram quoted from Thomas Carlyle, "The true University of these days is a Collection of Books," draws attention to the special place of books—the collecting of books, but also the producing of books—in the very definition of the university. Indeed, it would be possible to write the history of university scholarship on the basis of the history of libraries, as becomes evident in such a work as Kenneth J. Brough, *Scholar's Workshop: Evolving Conceptions of Library Service* (Urbana: University of Illinois Press, 1953). A number of scholars have illumined that relation in the essays edited by Edward C. Lathem, *American Libraries as Centers of Scholarship* (Hanover, N.H.: Dartmouth College, 1978). William Bentinck-Smith's *Building a Great Library: The Coolidge Years at Harvard* (Cambridge: Harvard University Press, 1976), recounts with loving care an outstanding example of how this has worked at a private university, and Wayne S. Yenawine, "The Influence of Scholars on Research Library Development at the University of Illinois" (Ph.D. diss., University of Illinois, 1955), documents the symbiosis at a public university. The proliferation of knowledge and of the means for communicating it must draw new interest to the criteria and the techniques of library collecting, about which J. P. Danton has written in *Book Selection and Collections: A Comparison of German and American University Libraries* (New York: Columbia University Press, 1963). The several chapters of Arthur T. Hamlin, *The University Library in the United States: Its Origins and Development* (Philadelphia: University of Pennsylvania Press, 1981), approach the relation between the university and its library from a number of angles. One of these angles that is often overlooked is the contribution that a research library makes also to undergraduate teaching and learning, as I. A. Braden suggests in *The Undergraduate Library* (Chicago: American Library Association, 1970). All of this, in turn, should call attention to the professional status of research librarians within the university, about which there is much to be learned from the chapters in Jerrold Orne, ed., *Research Librarianship: Essays in Honor of Robert B. Downs* (New York: Bowker, 1971). The implications of this professionalism for the definition of the relation between research librarian and research scholar have engaged the Association of College and Research Libraries (ACRL) in the volume *Faculty Status for Academic Librarians: A History and Policy Statements* (Chicago: American Library Association, 1975). But the university defines itself by its output of books as well as by its input of them. Continuing and deepening the early work of his predecessor, George Parmly Day, *The Function and Organization of University Presses* (New Haven: Yale University Press, 1915), Chester Kerr's *Report on American University Presses* (Chapel Hill: Association of American University Presses, 1949) surveyed the state of university publishing and made far-reaching proposals, many of which are, if anything, even more cogent four decades later. The university press in America locates itself in the tradition especially of the Oxford University Press, whose ways have been delightfully described in K. M. Elisabeth Murray, *Caught in the Web of Words: James Murray and the "Oxford English Dictionary"* (New Haven: Yale University Press, 1977), and of the Cambridge University Press, whose history is the subject of Michael Black, *Cambridge University Press, 1584–1984* (Cambridge: Cambridge University Press, 1984). Three historical records of American presses (and thus of their universities) are, in strictly chronological order: George Parmly Day, *The Yale University Press* (New Haven: Yale University Press, 1920); Gordon J. Laing, *The University of Chicago Press, 1891–1941* (Chicago: University of Chicago Press, 1941); and Max Hall, *Harvard University Press: A History* (Cambridge: Harvard University Press, 1986).

Educational Reform. It is not only the criticism of the university that has become widespread; so has the passion for the reform of education at all levels. *Reforms and Restraints in Modern French Education,* by W. R. Fraser (London: Routledge and Kegan Paul, 1971), describes the process in France; the British situation is treated historically in Brian Simon, *The Politics of Educational Reform, 1920–1940* (London: Lawrence and Wishart, 1974), while the materials assembled in Rolf Neuhaus, ed., *Dokumente zur Hochschulreform, 1945–59* (Wiesbaden: F. Steiner, 1961), and the proposals in Kreis Hofgeismar, *Gedanken zur Hochschulreform* (Göttingen: Verlag der Deutschen Universitäten, 1956), show the reformatory ferment among the educators of Germany. Two university-related areas of special interest to educational reformers are: medical education, discussed by Robert H. Ebert and Eli Ginzberg in "The Reform of Medical Education," *Health Affairs,* suppl. (1988): 5–38, and by Steven A. Schroeder, Jane S. Zones, and Jonathan A. Showstack, "Academic Medicine as a Public Trust," *Journal of the American Medical Association,* 11 August 1989, 803–12; and teacher training, analyzed in Timothy Weaver, *America's Teacher Quality Problem: Alternatives for Reform* (New York: Praeger, 1987).

NOTES

Page
and
Line

Chapter 1: In Dialogue with John Henry Newman

3:6   Eliot 1871–72 (Hornback 1977); see Haight 1968, 420–55.
3:12   Showalter 1990, 72–75.
3:16   Eliot 1871–72, III.29 (Hornback 1977, 193).
3:20   Ellmann 1973, 19.
3:28   Eliot 1871–72, II.20 (Hornback 1977, 136–37).
4:1   Eliot 1871–72, I.8, III.28 (Hornback 1977, 4, 192).
4:6   Eliot 1871–72, II.21 (Hornback 1977, 144).
4:11   Haight 1968, 52–59.
4:16   George Eliot to Sophia Hennell, 13 July 1864, Haight 1954–78, 4:159.
4:23   Letter of 21 January 1820, quoted in Culler 1955, 18.
5:9   Quoted in Tristram 1957, 259.
5:16   Newman 1864, IV (Svaglic 1967, 213).
5:22   McGrath 1951 and Culler 1955, 156–70.
5:25   Bouyer 1960, 300.
5:37   Quoted in Ker 1976, xxvii.
6:29   Pater 1913, 18.
6:32   Quoted in Svaglic 1960, vii.
6:34   Cameron 1956, 24–25.
6:36   Brubacher and Rudy, 1958; Jaspers 1959.
6:39   Barzun 1968, 210; but see 76–77.
7:1   Smith 1991, 199.
7:5   Dealy 1990, 232.
7:8   Shuster 1959, 21.
7:13   Svaglic 1960, vii.
7:23   Quoted in Ker 1976, lxxv, and the final words quoted also in Svaglic 1960, xxvii.
7:28   Sayers 1935, II (Gollancz 1958, 26); see the quotation from Matthew Arnold in chapter 17, below.
7:33   Giamatti 1988, 166–67, 118–26.
9:11   Svaglic 1960, vii; italics added.
9:14   Gilson 1955, 18.

Chapter 2: The Storm Breaking upon the University

11:3   Quoted in Tristram 1957, 49.

12:2   Muller 1984, 2; see also, e.g., Oakley 1991, 1.

12:11   Giamatti 1988.

12:20   Giles 1991; DePalma 1991.

12:36   Phillips 1990, 59–66, 71.

13:5   Matthews 1990, 447.

13:8   Kenney 1986.

13:18   Lindroth 1976, 243–44.

13:29   Arendt 1958 (1961, 174).

14:8   Quoted in Pelikan 1959, 46–47; italics added.

14:14   See Pelikan 1964, 157–58.

14:20   *Hamlet,* act I, sc. 2.

14:29   Stybe 1979, 33–34.

14:33   Pečujlić 1987, 63–72.

15:9   Brooks 1991, 24.

15:10   Oakley 1991, 1.

15:16   Rev. 6:8.

15:21   Blum 1976, 141–45, summarizes some of the chief effects of the Second World War on American colleges and universities.

15:28   Steiner 1971, 88. Evariste Galois, the young mathematical genius whose name is still associated with "Galois groups," was killed in a duel before his twenty-first birthday.

16:3   Tuchman 1963, 347–62, "The Flames of Louvain," is a moving account of these events.

16:7   It becomes more poignant still as a result of the division of the University of Louvain into Louvain-La-Neuve (French) and Leuven (Flemish). "The division of the books upon the partition of the university in 1968," according J. Herbert Altschull, "was a complicated affair. The Solomon-like compromise adopted whenever negotiation could not resolve specific disputes, sent books with serial numbers in an even digit to Louvain-La-Neuve while those with an odd ending remained at Leuven" (1981, 42).

16:10   F. Fischer 1967, 155–73.

16:18   Kellermann 1915, and, now far more critically, Schwabe 1969.

16:35   On the "utopian" educational philosophy of Comenius, see Prévot 1981.

17:10   Pross 1955; Grubel 1977.

17:29   Karim 1986.

18:32   Quoted by Don Wyclif, *New York Times,* 12 September 1990.

19:9   Flexner 1910.

19:15   Ebert and Ginzberg 1988.

19:39   Gen. 1:28.

20:21   Fruton 1990, 158–60.

20:24   The documents have been conveniently assembled in Stoff 1991.

20:27   See Kenney 1986.

Chapter 3: Pushing Things up to Their First Principles

23:10 China [1988], 19.
23:17 India 1986, 14, 20–21.
23:21 Mexico 1987, 47.
23:27 Saudi Arabia 1402/1982, 2.
23:35 Dogramaci 1989, 19–20, 24.
24:19 Berlin 1991, 1.
24:35 Davis 1990, 90, n. 4.
25:4   Mann 1933 (1985, 92).
25:39 Newman 1864, II (Svaglic 1967, 54); also Svaglic's notes, 519–20.
26:3   Newman 1864, note A (Svaglic 1967, 260–62).
26:11 Newman 1864, IV (Svaglic 1967, 179).
26:17 Newman 1864, I (Svaglic 1967, 46).
26:22 Walgrave 1960, 59–60.
26:32 Newman 1870, X (Ker 1985, 266).
26:40 Hutchins 1963, 22.
27:7   Steel 1980, 47.
27:16 Steel 1980, 262–63.
27:29 The brief chapter "A Private Philosophy," in Steel 1980, 491–501, summarizes the book and the reactions to it.
28:6   In *Oxford English Dictionary*, 8–II:170; italics added.
28:11 Moore and Fine 1990, 160; it should be noted that the word *reasonable* appears in quotation marks in the original.
28:33 Milton, *Paradise Lost*, II, 113–14.
28:39 Ellsworth 1977, 92–110.
29:5   Nore 1983 has carefully charted Beard's development.
29:10 J. E. Smith 1963, 38–79.
29:37 Quoted in Young-Bruehl 1982, 190.
30:1   Maritain 1960, 2, 39.
30:5   Maritain 1960, 72.
30:22 The landmark work on the subject remains Murray 1960.
30:27 Newman 1864, II (Svaglic 1967, 54).

Chapter 4: Knowledge Its Own End?

32:9   Cicero, *On Duties* I.4.
32:14 Culler 1955, 213.
32:17 Aristotle, *Metaphysics* I.1.980a.
33:24 Quoted by Ward 1948, 69–70.
33:34 Quoted in Fruton 1990, 159.
34:14 *Encyclopaedia Britannica*, 11th/12th ed., 7:958–62, 27:788.
34:23 *Encyclopaedia Britannica*, 11th/12th ed., 32:261–67.
35:6   *Webster's New Dictionary of Synonyms* 1968, 481.
36:12 Goethe, *Faust*, I, 354–65.

37:37   Pascal, *Pensées,* IV, 277.

38:2   Fleming and Bailyn 1969.

38:18   Wilson 1978, 28–49.

38:22   Shepherd 1983, 580–83.

38:40   Gay 1989, xx, note 6.

42:1   A. N. Whitehead 1942, 21.

42:4   Aristotle, *Metaphysics* I.1.980a.

42:7   Aristotle, *Politics* I.2.1252a.

42:12   Newman 1864, I (Svaglic 1967, 28).

42:33   Hutchins 1942, 22–23.

43:13   Aristotle, *Nicomachean Ethics* I.1–2.1094a.

43:19   On the "Nazi doctors," see Katz 1973, 292–306.

Chapter 5: The Imperial Intellect and Its Virtues

44:8   Aristotle, *Nicomachean Ethics* VI.1.1139a; italics added.

44:22   Quoted in Culler 1955, 163.

45:6   Newman 1870, IX (Ker 1985, 228–29).

45:25   Rashdall 1936 is an extensive treatment of the subject, and Daly 1961 a concise one.

46:6   J. S. Whitehead 1973.

47:28   A. N. Whitehead 1948, 49–50.

48:10   Aristotle, *Nicomachean Ethics* VI.1.1139a.

48:24   Newman 1870, IX (Ker 1985, 228–29).

49:11   Quoted and interpreted in Bickel 1975, 63–64.

49:23   See the brief but helpful comments of Broad 1981, 137–41.

50:5   Sayers 1935 (Gollancz 1958, 336).

50:26   Gould 1989, 53–239, 257–58.

50:31   Eliot 1871–72, I.8 (Hornback 1977, 47).

50:33   *On Dreams* (1911), in Gay 1989, 142.

51:1   A. N. Whitehead 1948, 4.

52:3   Merton 1965.

52:12   Fruton 1990.

52:22   On the relation of Galileo with Robert Bellarmine, see now Blackwell 1991.

52:26   On that tradition, see Weisheipl 1959.

52:40   On the reinterpretation of Galileo, see Gay 1966, 527, and the essays collected in Wallace 1986.

53:24   DeVane 1957, 26.

54:21   "Statement from Chancellor Chang-Lin Tien of the University of California at Berkeley," 27 September 1990.

55:6   Beyerchen 1977; Ericksen 1985.

55:27   Quoted in Von Zahn-Harnack 1951, 388.

Chapter 6: The Mansion-House of the Goodly Family of the Sciences

57:8   "A word, invented as the name of a bazaar of all kinds of artistic work, which has (through the fortune of the building) come to be applied to a large warehouse for storing furniture" (*Oxford English Dictionary*, 7:429).

58:21	Taylor 1975, 26.
58:25	Jaeger 1943–45, 2:27–76.
59:1	Plato, *Meno* 81d.
59:5	Plato, *Theaetetus* 150; see also chapter 12, below.
59:31	This dynamic is charted in Fruton 1990.
60:10	Boyer 1987, 138.
61:5	Kockelmans 1979.
61:15	Kant 1798, I (Cassirer 1921, 7:380).
62:6	Chickering 1974, 53–68.
63:1	Fruton 1990, 231.
63:4	Andrews 1979 is a fine example of such comparative study.
63:14	Linehan 1982, 468.
63:19	K. M. E. Murray 1977, esp. 314–41.
64:28	See chapter 9, below.
65:4	Emerson 1838 (Spiller 1971, 1:99–116).
65:29	Burke 1790 (O'Brien 1969, 194–95).
65:39	Giamatti 1988, 110.
66:31	Ker 1976, lxxiii–lxxv.

Chapter 7: The Business of a University

72:20	Much of the pertinent information is collected in F. Franklin 1910; see also Hawkins 1960, 316–26.
72:24	Altschuler 1979.
72:27	Storr 1966. On Harper's vision of the university and of the world, see Wind 1987.
73:2	Despite the quality of their rhetoric, Dealy 1990, 144–67, and Sperber 1990 do present damaging figures on the finances of intercollegiate athletics.
73:13	Griswold 1959, 107–13, voiced this warning at a crucial juncture in the history of the university.
73:21	Cruikshank 1987 is a "case study."
73:31	DeVane 1943, 35.
74:8	Annarelli 1987.
74:14	Veblen 1918 remains the most eloquent denunciation of such interference.
75:11	See the thoughtful comparative comments in Gerhard 1977, 154–74.
77:1	Boyer 1987 is a landmark in that task of defining the college.
77:8	Pelikan 1983, 5–14.
77:15	Boyer 1990, 2.

Chapter 8: The Advancement of Knowledge through Research

78:19	Ker 1976, 575.
79:17	Newman 1845 (Image 1960, 63).

80:14   See the polemical but provocative expression of these concerns in Sykes 1988.
81:27   P. Smith 1991, esp. 177–98.
82:37   Newman 1870, VII.2 (Ker 1985, 163).
83:34   Quoted in Culler 1955, 47, and 289, n. 4.
83:39   Chadwick 1957, 111–13.
84:3   Newman 1864, II (Svaglic 1967, 45).
84:14   The foundational documents have been conveniently collected and edited in Schelling et al. 1956.
84:17   Furniss 1965, 18.
84:20   See the provocative discussion in Flexner 1930.
84:25   Gerhard 1977, 175–98: "The Educational Reforms in Germany and the United States at the End of the Nineteenth Century: A Comparison," by a scholar and historian well acquainted with both systems.
85:3   Harnack 1930, 251; italics in original.
85:14   See the debates reprinted in Neuhaus 1961.
85:33   In Sutherland 1975, 253.
85:38   Aristotle, *Metaphysics* I.1.980a.
86:7   See the summary, "The Organization of Research," in Jaeger 1948, 324–41.
86:28   See Segert and Beránek 1967, on the history of the study of Semitic philology at Prague.
88:2   *Oxford English Dictionary,* 9:221–22.
88:5   Dilthey 1927, 79–120.
88:12   Furner 1975.
88:15   On their development, see now the study of Ross 1991.

Chapter 9: The Extension of Knowledge through Teaching

90:10   On the definition and development of the docentship, see Busch 1963, summarizing in English some of the material in the full-length German study, Busch 1959; also Bock 1972, on assistantships.
90:14   Lindroth 1976, 156.
90:23   See the repeated anecdotes recorded in Breasted 1977.
90:30   For examples, see Kenney 1986, 41–49.
90:31   Lederman 1991, 10.
91:3   The highly informative volumes of its journal, *Courier,* document the comings and goings of physicists from all over the world, as well as their joint work.
91:28   J. H. Fischer 1965.
91:30   Cheney 1990.
91:39   See the moving account of Cousins 1979.
92:8   See the thoughful and witty comments of Rosovsky 1990, 75–98: "Making Choices."
92:21   For a comparison of Swarthmore College with Princeton College (as well as two other institutions), see Leslie 1971.
93:26   Boyer 1990, 16; italics in original.

93:37   Boyer 1990, 9–11.
94:2   Boyer 1990, 2.
95:5   Boyer 1990, 16.
95:30   Kockelmans 1979.
96:18   Gay 1988, 442.
96:27   Boyer and Levine 1981.
96:32   Kagan 1991, 48.
97:39   Giamatti 1981, 145.
98:4   Especially charming is the account of an education at Cambridge University by Hutchinson 1979, 74–136.
98:13   Quoted in Boyer 1990, 24.
98:27   Harnack 1930, 251.

Chapter 10: Knowledge Viewed in Relation to Professional Skill

99:1   Ziolkowski 1989.
99:5   Goethe, *Faust*, I, 354–56.
99:9   Schelling et al. 1956.
100:16 Huber 1843, 1:34, also quoted in Ker 1976, 626–27; italics in original.
100:27 Fruton 1951; Euler 1970.
101:30 Culler 1955, 123–30.
102:4   The most striking instance of this in nineteenth-century England was, of course, the Athanasian Creed. See Kelly 1964, 124–27.
102:11 Newman 1848, III, i (Tillotson 1970, 300).
102:13 *Oxford Dictionary of Quotations* 1980, 235.
102:15 Newman 1864, II (Svaglic 1967, 78–88).
102:30 Shuster 1959, 21.
102:33 Culler 1955, 159–60.
103:7   Quoted in J. S. Whitehead 1973, 115–16.
103:16 *Oxford English Dictionary*, IX–2:223.
103:23 A. N. Whitehead 1929, 137–39.
104:7   Hutchins 1963, 19.
104:14 Lindroth 1976, 260.
104:18 Flexner 1910.
104:27 Muller 1984, Ebert and Ginzberg 1988.
104:29 For a valuable bibliography, see Schroeder, Zones, and Showstack 1989, 811–13.
104:34 Fox 1980.
105:13 See the recent historical studies of the development of biochemistry inside and outside schools of medicine by Joseph Fruton 1982 and 1985.
105:14 Ellsworth 1977, 48–73.
105:23 Vergottini 1956, with bibliography.
105:38 Levi 1969, 38–39.
106:11 Levi 1969, 121.
106:15 Niebuhr, Williams, and Gustafson 1957.
106:39 Newman 1864, I (Svaglic 1967, 57), referring to what he thought "in 1832–3."

107:5   Jedin 1963.
107:16   Brown 1934.
107:34   Pelikan 1983, 50.
108:15   Hutchins 1964.
108:16   Grudin 1990, 170–72.
108:25   Stevens 1970, 41.
108:34   Fruton 1951 was an early recognition of the problem.
109:17   Stevens 1970, 41.
109:18   Flexner 1910.

Chapter 11: The Embalming of Dead Genius?

110:11   Newman 1856, VI (Harrold 1948, 328); italics added.
110:14   Eliot 1871–72, II.20 (Hornback 1977, 136–37).
110:21   Culler 1955, 17, 83.
111:11   Newman 1864, III (Svaglic 1967, 108).
111:15   Cross 1945, 10.
111:24   Culler 1955, 160.
111:38   Huxley 1900, 2:226.
112:3   Huxley 1900, 2:328.
112:15   Congar 1967, 211.
112:26   Boyer and Levine 1981, 5–16.
112:31   Carlyle 1841, V (Parr 1920, 147).
112:39   Brough 1953.
113:7   See the essays collected in Lathem 1978.
113:23   Hamlin 1981.
113:33   Gibbon 1796 (Saunders 1961, 68).
114:7   Gibbon 1776–88, 68 (Bury 1896–1900, 7:197–98); italics added.
114:19   Beyerchen 1977, Ericksen 1985.
114:24   Braden 1970.
115:30   Bentinck-Smith 1976 is a useful instance of that evolution.
115:37   Gay 1966, 423–552, and Gay 1969, 571–705, are the very models of
           the genre.
116:39   George Crabbe, *The Library* (1781).
117:16   ACRL 1975 is an examination of these issues and questions.
117:33   McCaughey 1984.
118:2   Wright 1988, 71.
118:14   See Yenawine 1955 for a specific description of this pattern.
118:16   There are helpful comparisons in Danton 1963.
118:32   Vosper 1971.
118:39   H. Bloom 1975.
119:7   John Keats, "On First Looking into Chapman's Homer."
119:33   Weisheipl 1959.
119:38   Holmes 1986.
120:3   Holmes 1990, 349–66, with very useful bibliographical notes.
120:34   Newman 1856, VI (Harrold 1948, 328).

Chapter 12: The Diffusion of Knowledge through Publishing

121:17 Quoted from the manuscript in Culler 1955, 311.

121:22 Day 1914, 8.

122:10 Pusey 1964, 144–45.

122:16 Aristotle, *Nicomachean Ethics* X.7.1177a.

122:20 Boethius, *Consolation of Philosophy* I.1.

122:30 Plutarch, *Parallel Lives,* "Alexander."

122:33 Luke 10:38–42.

122:34 Karl Marx, in Tucker 1978, 145.

123:1 Aristotle, *Rhetoric* I.5.1361a.

123:12 Thomas Aquinas, *Summa Theologica* II–a II–ae, q. 188, art. 6.

123:15 Weisheipl 1974, 25.

124:18 Gould 1989, 16.

124:21 Day 1915, 29.

124:24 Day 1914, 5.

124:32 Power 1942.

126:9 See Holmes 1989 and especially Fruton 1990, on which my analysis has largely been based.

126:21 Fruton 1985.

126:28 Kimball 1990, 106–11.

126:33 Adolf Harnack, as quoted in Von Zahn-Harnack 1951, 48.

126:39 See the illuminating history of Ross 1991.

127:5 For a methodology in political science that does not follow the quantitative trend or the trend of "modeling," but that does illustrate genealogy, compare Strauss 1975 (published posthumously) with Pangle 1980, xiii–xiv.

127:12 See the essays in Fellner 1967, especially the introductory one by John Perry Miller.

127:14 For a general discussion of the issues involved, see Katouzian 1980.

127:30 Plato, *Theaetetus* 149–51.

127:34 The literary, moral, and theological implications of the metaphor are analyzed in Greve 1990.

128:10 Fruton 1990, 158, 139.

128:26 See the studies collected in Levine and Knoepflmacher 1979.

129:22 Quoted in Kaufmann 1982, 7.

129:33 Vogel 1984.

129:40 *Encyclopaedia Britannica,* 11th/12th ed., 23:368–69.

130:16 Pelikan 1984, 80–81.

130:17 Medawar 1969, 58.

130:24 Kerr 1949 stands as a landmark in the field.

130:28 See Sutcliffe 1978 and Black 1984.

130:32 Quoted in Storr 1966, 207.

130:34 Laing 1941, preface.

130:40 Day 1914, 5.

131:5 Newman 1856, VI (Harrold 1948, 328).

131:15 Acton 1961, 40.

131:20   Arnold 1865 (1903, viii, xi–xii).
131:24   Day 1920, 9.
133:9   See Murphy and Bruckner 1976, 383–91.

Chapter 13: Duties to Society

138:3   McGrath 1951.
138:11   Quoted in Culler 1955, 169–70; see the full text in chapter 14 below.
138:20   Bernhard, Crawford, and Sörbom 1982.
138:27   Horwitt 1989, 11.
138:35   Taft 1976; but see Hersey 1970.
139:6   Levi 1969, 148.
139:8   Brubacher 1958 is a history of colleges and universities within the context of American social and political history.
139:10   Bok 1990 is a series of reflections on these and related issues.
139:19   Burke 1790 (O'Brien 1969, 194–95).
139:26   Burke 1790 (O'Brien 1969, 135).
139:34   Andrej Sheptycky, quoted in Pelikan 1990, 81–83.
140:1   Ravitch 1985 is a good example of how this can be done.
140:6   Baron 1966, 189, 271.
140:10   Dahl 1961.
140:21   Boalt 1970.
140:28   Wellek 1955–, 1:191–92.
140:34   Jaeger 1947, 6–7.
141:11   Kernan 1990, 32.
141:16   Wellek 1970, 1–54.
141:22   Lederman 1991.
141:23   See Bonner 1963.
141:40   Barzun 1959, 126.
142:21   The issues are examined for Europe in Raiser 1966 (with interesting comparative judgments about the United States), and for the United States in Feller 1986.
142:26   Katznelson and Weir 1985.
142:34   Rosovsky 1990, 67.
143:1   Comer 1980 is the account of such an "intervention project."
143:4   Morris 1983; Durso 1975.
143:13   Coombs 1964.
143:19   Pross 1955; Fermi 1968; Fleming and Bailyn 1969.
143:21   Klineberg 1966.
144:1   Culler 1955, 159–60; Shuster 1959, 21.
144:11   Humphrey 1967.
144:25   The question has been considered specifically for medical education, but in a way that applies to all professional education, in Schroeder, Jones, Showstack 1989, 809.
144:35   Hamlin 1981, 182–96.
144:39   The worldwide situation is graphically portrayed in Yamaguchi 1981.

145:16   Goodwin and Nacht 1991.
145:22   Hill 1978, based on the study of Sub-Saharan Africa, raises fundamental questions of methodology about area studies.
145:24   McCaughey 1984.

Chapter 14: The University as Ground of Promise in the Future

147:8   Quoted in Culler 1955, 169–70. In comment on Newman's prophecy about "the ease and rapidity of a locomotion not yet discovered," Culler notes that "people might have remarked upon his acumen in predicting the Shannon airport."
147:32   Pelikan 1990, 81–83, 133–45.
147:39   Craig 1984.
148:5   Newman 1856, VI (Harrold 1948, 328).
148:13   Oren 1986 is a fascinating (and humbling) example of the process.
148:21   Egypt [1990], 16.
148:25   Natal 1990, 5.
148:33   Athens 1989, 5.
148:36   Philippines [1990].
149:5   Egypt [1990], 16.
149:8   MEDUNSA 2:91.
149:12   Athens 1989, 5.
149:17   Philippines [1990].
150:10   India 1986, 14, 20–21.
150:20   Natal 1990, 5.
150:23   On the problems associated with such terminology, see D. Green 1987; also Dworkin 1985, 205–13.
150:30   J. H. Franklin 1976, 12–20; DeVane 1957, 48–49.
150:33   Davis 1990 is a thoughtful examination of this drive.
151:10   Culler 1955, 189–90, 238–43.
151:24   Katznelson and Weir 1985.
151:40   Tocqueville 1835, II, iii, 21 (Mayer and Lerner 1966, 616).
152:8   Tocqueville 1835, II, i, 10 (Mayer and Lerner 1966, 427).
152:15   Tocqueville 1835, I, i, 2, 3 (Mayer and Lerner 1966, 38, 48).
152:27   For an earlier statement with continuing force and relevance, see Ramaley 1978.
153:31   Burke 1790 (O'Brien 1969, 194–95).
154:9   Bowen and Sosa 1989.
154:13   See, e.g., the statistics in Shapley 1978–79.
154:25   Athens 1989, 5.
154:27   Natal 1990, 5.
154:31   Gerard Manley Hopkins, "Morning Midday and Evening Sacrifice."
154:38   Grudin 1990, 170.
155:18   Hutchins 1963, 22.
155:32   Grant and Riesman 1978.
156:1   Comer 1980.

156:23   Riesman 1980.
156:28   Sykes 1988.
156:29   A. Bloom 1987.

Chapter 15: The University and the Spread of Revolutionary Doctrines

157:15   Quoted in Tucker 1978, 145; italics in original.
158:34   Horwitt 1989, 11, 408–14.
158:35   Freedman 1990, 344–48.
159:9   Arendt 1965, 279–84; italics in original.
159:21   Palmer 1969, v, 16–17.
160:2   Gibbon 1776, preface (Bury 1896–1900, 1:v).
160:17   A process described historically by Ross 1991.
160:22   Ashby and Anderson 1966 is a comparative study.
160:34   Katznelson and Weir 1985.
161:2   Brennan and Yarborough 1987.
161:8   Burchardt 1975.
161:18   Griswold 1959, 101–13.
161:27   Jarausch 1982 examines student activity in the context of German so-
         ciety before the First World War.
161:29   Dongerkery 1950 is an examination from the point of view of India.
162:5   Arendt 1965, 55.
162:31   Schelling et al. 1956.
163:3   D. Green 1987.
163:19   Burke 1790 (O'Brien 1969, 112).
163:28   Burke 1790 (O'Brien 1969, 172).
163:34   Humphrey 1967.
163:39   Imhof 1981.
164:5   Harbage 1941, 138–57.
164:15   Ellsworth 1977, 92–110.
164:22   Bork 1990, 187–240.
164:26   Hopkins 1940 is the standard history of this process.
164:31   Quoted in Murphy and Bruckner 1976, 362.
164:40   J. E. Smith 1963, 115–60.
165:7   Hegener and Clarke 1976 present an overview of these trends.
165:19   Levi 1969, 38–39.
165:28   Compare Von Zahn-Harnack 1951, 115–27.
166:1   Cruikshank 1987 is a careful and self-critical account of the "delicate
         experiment."
166:35   See the discussion, from the experience of Yugoslavia, in Pečujlić 1987,
         95–105: "The University, Science, and the Development of Society."

Chapter 16: The Task of Initiating a Work of Self-Reformation

168:16   Kreis Hofgeismar 1956.
169:11   Murphy and Bruckner 1976, 77.
169:28   Friday and Hesburgh 1991, 3, 25.

169:34　McGrath 1951.

170:10　Arendt 1958 (1961, 174).

170:13　For example, National Commission on Excellence in Education 1983.

170:27　Freedman 1990, 17–43.

171:16　Freedman 1990, 46–47.

171:28　Freedman 1990, 422.

171:35　Freedman 1990, 48, 271.

171:39　Freedman 1990, 42, 310.

172:8　William T. Grant Foundation [1990].

172:23　Boyer 1983, 120.

172:25　Boyer 1983, 268–80.

173:8　The chapter "The College Connection," in Boyer 1983, 251–67, combines practical information with educational wisdom.

173:22　Freedman 1990, 53.

173:24　Freedman 1990, 345.

173:27　Freedman 1990, 344–48.

175:39　Freedman 1990, 179–80; italics added.

176:7　Hutchins 1952, 3.

176:12　Stabler 1962, 20.

176:15　Powell 1980, 248–52.

176:32　Boyer 1983, 174–78.

176:37　Gifford 1984.

177:7　Weaver 1987 is an analysis of some of these issues.

177:12　A. N. Whitehead 1929, 24–44.

177:17　For this paragraph I have drawn upon the bulletins and reports of two such programs of cooperation: the Ernest O. Lawrence Hall of Science at the University of California in Berkeley, and the Yale–New Haven Teachers Institute.

177:22　See, e.g., Maeroff 1983, 47.

178:1　FitzGerald 1979.

178:18　Cheney 1990.

178:24　On reform of secondary education in France, see Fraser 1971.

179:9　Capretz 1987. Because of my concentration on the university, I am not dealing here with the textbooks, tapes, and cassettes (all part of the package of "the Capretz Method") but with some of the fundamental principles underlying the system of language instruction.

179:19　William T. Grant Foundation [1990].

Chapter 17: Alma Mater

180:22　Newman 1864, IV (Svaglic 1967, 213).

180:25　Newman 1864, IV (Svaglic 334).

180:28　Ker 1976, xi, quoting from Tristram 1957, 63.

181:3　Newman 1848, III, iii (Tillotson 1970, 307–8).

181:8　Culler 1955, 119.

181:11　Arnold 1865 (1903, viii, xi–xii).

181:19　Gibbon 1796 (Saunders 1961, 72).

182:18   Imhof 1981; Pieper 1964.

183:27   Muller 1984, 27.

184:6   For two recent contrasting views (originating from the same law school), see Bork 1990, 133–269, and Wellington 1990, 43–60.

184:14   Schroeder, Zones, and Showstack 1989, 805.

184:27   A. N. Whitehead 1929, 140–41.

186:15   FitzGerald 1979.

186:40   Boyer 1983, 186–201.

188:16   Juvenal, *Satires* X.80.

189:22   Hutchins 1942, 22–23.

WORKS CITED
AND CONSULTED

Acton, Lord. *Lectures on Modern History*. Introduction by Hugh Trevor-Roper. New York: Meridian Books, 1961.

Altschuler, Glenn C. *Andrew Dickson White: Educator, Historian, Diplomat*. Ithaca: Cornell University Press, 1979.

Altschull, J. Herbert. "Leuven/Louvain—The World's Oldest Catholic University Is a House Divided." *Change* (January–February 1981): 42–44.

Andrae, Carl Göran, ed. *Faculty of Arts at Uppsala University*. Stockholm: Almqvist and Wiksell, 1976.

Andrews, F. M., ed. *Scientific Productivity: The Effectiveness of Research Groups in Six Countries*. Cambridge: Cambridge University Press, 1979.

Annarelli, James John. *Academic Freedom and Catholic Higher Education*. New York: Greenwood, 1987.

Arendt, Hannah. "The Crisis in Education." 1958. *Between Past and Future: Six Exercises in Political Thought*, 173–96. New York: Viking, 1961.

———. *On Revolution*. Compass Books ed. New York: Viking, 1965.

Arnold, Matthew. *Essays in Criticism*. 1st ser. 1865. Vol. 3 of *The Collected Works of Matthew Arnold in Fifteen Volumes*. London: Macmillan, 1903.

Ashby, Eric, and Mary Anderson. *Universities: British, Indian, African. A Study in the Ecology of Higher Education*. Cambridge: Harvard University Press, 1966.

Ashmore, Harry S. *Unseasonable Truths: The Life of Robert Maynard Hutchins*. Boston: Little, Brown, 1989.

Association of College and Research Libraries (ACRL). *Faculty Status for Academic Librarians: A History and Policy Statements*. Chicago: American Library Association, 1975.

Athens, National and Capodistrian University of. *Bulletin 1989*.

Bainton, Roland H. *Yale and the Ministry: A History of Education for the Christian Ministry at Yale from the Founding in 1701*. New York: Harper and Brothers, 1957.

Ballough, Vern L. *The Development of Medicine as a Profession: The Contribution of the Medieval University to Modern Medicine*. New York: Hafner, 1966.

Barber, W. J., ed. *Breaking the Academic Mould*. Middletown, Conn.: Wesleyan University Press, 1988.

Baron, Hans. *The Crisis of the Early Italian Renaissance*. Princeton: Princeton University Press, 1966.

Barzun, Jacques. *Teacher in America*. Garden City, N.Y.: Image Books, 1959.

———. *The American University: How It Runs; Where It Is Going*. New York: Harper and Row, 1968.

Bell, R. E., ed. *Present and Future in Higher Education*. London: Tavistock, 1970.

Bennett, William J. *To Reclaim a Legacy: A Report on the Humanities in Higher Education*. Washington, D.C.: National Endowment for the Humanities, 1984.

Bentinck-Smith, William. *Building a Great Library: The Coolidge Years at Harvard*. Cambridge: Harvard University Press, 1976.

Berlin, Isaiah. *The Crooked Timber of Humanity: Chapters in the History of Ideas*. Edited by Henry Hardy. New York: Alfred A. Knopf, 1991.

Bernhard, C. G., E. Crawford, and P. Sörbom, eds. *Science, Technology, and Society in the Time of Alfred Nobel*. Oxford: Pergamon, 1982.

Beyerchen, Alan D. *Scientists under Hitler: Politics and the Physics Community in the Third Reich*. New Haven: Yale University Press, 1977.

Bickel, Alexander M. *The Morality of Consent*. New Haven: Yale University Press, 1975.

Black, Michael. *Cambridge University Press, 1584–1984*. Cambridge: Cambridge University Press, 1984.

Blackwell, Richard J. *Galileo, Bellarmine, and the Bible*. Notre Dame, Ind.: University of Notre Dame Press, 1991.

Bloom, Allan. *The Closing of the American Mind: How Higher Education Has Failed Democracy and Impoverished the Souls of Today's Students*. New York: Simon and Schuster, 1987.

Bloom, Harold. *The Anxiety of Influence: A Theory of Poetry*. New York: Oxford University Press, 1975.

Blum, John Morton. *V Was for Victory*. New York: Harcourt Brace Jovanovich, 1976.

Boalt, Gunnar. *Universities and Research: Observations on the United States and Sweden*. Stockholm: Almqvist and Wiksell, 1970.

Bock, K. D. *Strukturgeschichte der Assistentur*. Düsseldorf: Bertelsmann, 1972.

Bok, Derek. *Beyond the Ivory Tower*. Cambridge: Harvard University Press, 1982.

———. *Universities and the Future of America*. Durham, N.C.: Duke University Press, 1990.

Bonner, T. N. *American Doctors and German Universities*. Lincoln: University of Nebraska Press, 1963.

Bork, Robert H. *The Tempting of America: The Political Seduction of the Law*. New York: Free Press, 1990.

Bouyer, Louis. *Newman: His Life and Spirituality*. Translated by J. Lewis May. Reprint edition. New York: Meridian Books, 1960.

Bowen, William G., and Julie Ann Sosa. *Prospects for Faculty in the Arts and Sciences*. Princeton: Princeton University Press, 1989.

Bowles, Samuel, and Herbert Gintis. *Schooling in Capitalist America*. New York: Basic Books, 1976.

Boyer, Ernest L. *High School: A Report on Secondary Education in America.* New York: Harper and Row, 1983.

———. *College: The Undergraduate Experience in America.* New York: Harper and Row, 1987.

———. *Scholarship Reconsidered: Priorities of the Professoriate.* Princeton: Carnegie Foundation for the Advancement of Teaching, 1990.

Boyer, Ernest L., and Arthur Levine. *A Quest for Common Learning.* Washington, D.C.: Carnegie Foundation for the Advancement of Teaching, 1981.

Braden, I. A. *The Undergraduate Library.* Chicago: American Library Association, 1970.

Breasted, Charles. *Pioneer to the Past: The Story of James Henry Breasted.* Chicago: University of Chicago Press, 1977.

Brennan, S., and S. Yarborough. *Irving Babbitt.* Boston: Hall, 1987.

Broad, W. J. "Fraud and the Structure of Science." *Science* 212 (1981): 137–41.

Brooks, Peter. "Out of the Blue: Perilous Authority?" *Yale Alumni Magazine* 54 (Summer 1991): 24–25.

Brough, Kenneth J. *Scholar's Workshop: Evolving Conceptions of Library Service.* Urbana: University of Illinois Press, 1953.

Brown, William Adams, ed. *The Education of American Ministers.* 4 vols. New York: Institute of Social and Religious Research, 1934.

Browne, C. A. "The History of Chemical Education in America between the Years 1820 and 1870." *Journal of Chemical Education* 9 (1932): 696–728.

Brubacher, John S., and Willis Rudy. *Higher Education in Transition: An American History, 1636–1956.* New York: Harper, 1958.

Burchardt, L. *Wissenschaftspolitik im Wilhelminischen Deutschland.* Göttingen: Vandenhoeck und Ruprecht, 1975.

Burke, Edmund. *Reflections on the Revolution in France.* 1790. Edited by Conor Cruise O'Brien. Harmondsworth: Penguin, 1969.

Busch, A. *Die Geschichte der Privatdozenten.* Stuttgart: Enke, 1959.

———. "The Vicissitudes of the *Privatdozent:* Breakdown and Adaptation in the Recruitment of the German University Teacher." *Minerva* 1 (1963): 319–41.

Butterfield, Herbert. *The Universities and Education Today.* London: Routledge and Kegan Paul, 1962.

Cameron, J. M. *John Henry Newman.* London: Longmans, Green, 1956.

Capretz, Pierre J. *French in Action: A Beginning Course in Language and Culture. The Capretz Method.* Instructor's Guide. 2 parts. New Haven: Yale University Press, 1987.

Carlyle, Thomas. *Lectures on Heroes, Hero-Worship, and the Heroic in History.* 1841. Edited by P. C. Parr. Oxford: Clarendon, 1920.

Carnegie Foundation for the Advancement of Teaching. *The Control of the Campus: A Report on the Governance of Higher Education.* Washington, D.C.: Carnegie Foundation for the Advancement of Teaching, 1982.

Chadwick, Owen. *From Bossuet to Newman: The Idea of Doctrinal Development.* Cambridge: Cambridge University Press, 1957.

Cheney, Lynne V. *Tyrannical Machines: A Report on Educational Practices Gone*

Wrong and Our Best Hopes for Setting Them Right. Washington, D.C.: National Endowment for the Humanities, 1990.

Chickering, Arthur W. *Commuting versus Resident Students: Overcoming the Educational Inequities of Living Off Campus.* San Francisco: Jossey-Bass, 1974.

China, People's Republic of. *Education in China, 1978–1988.* Beijing: State Education Commission, [1988].

Chubb, John E., and Terry Moe. *Politics, Markets, and America's Schools.* Washington, D.C.: Brookings Institution, 1990.

Comer, James P. *School Power: Implications of an Intervention Project.* New York: Free Press, 1980.

Cole, S., and J. R. Cole. "Scientific Output and Recognition: A Study on the Reward System in Science." *American Sociological Review* 32 (1967): 377–90.

Conant, James Bryant. *The Citadel of Learning.* New Haven: Yale University Press, 1956.

Congar, Yves M.-J. *Tradition and Traditions: An Historical and a Theological Essay.* Translated by Michael Naseby and Thomas Rainborough. New York: Macmillan, 1967.

Coombs, Philip Hall. *The Fourth Dimension of Foreign Policy: Educational and Cultural Affairs.* New York: Harper and Row, 1964.

Corner, G. W. *A History of the Rockefeller Institute, 1901–1953.* New York: Rockefeller University Press, 1964.

Cornford, Francis MacDonald. *Microcosmographia Academica.* 5th ed. Cambridge: Bowes and Bowes, 1954.

Cousins, Norman. *Anatomy of an Illness as Perceived by the Patient.* New York: W. W. Norton, 1979.

Craig, J. E. *Scholarship and Nation Building: The University of Strasbourg and Alsatian Society, 1870–1939.* Chicago: University of Chicago Press, 1984.

Cremin, Lawrence A. *American Education: The Metropolitan Experience, 1876–1980.* New York: Harper and Row, 1988.

Cruikshank, Jeffrey L. *A Delicate Experiment: The Harvard Business School, 1908–1945.* Boston: Harvard Business School Press, 1987.

Culler, Dwight. *The Imperial Intellect: A Study of Newman's Educational Ideal.* New Haven: Yale University Press, 1955.

Dahl, Robert. *Who Governs?* New Haven: Yale University Press, 1961.

Daly, Lowrie J. *The Medieval University, 1200–1400.* New York: Sheed and Ward, 1961.

Danton, J. P. *Book Selection and Collections: A Comparison of German and American University Libraries.* New York: Columbia University Press, 1963.

Davis, David Brion. *Revolutions: Reflections on American Equality and Foreign Liberations.* Cambridge: Harvard University Press, 1990.

Day, George Parmly. *The New Era of Publishing at Yale.* New Haven: Yale University Press, 1914.

———. *The Function and Organization of University Presses.* New Haven: Yale University Press, 1915.

———. *The Yale University Press.* New Haven: Yale University Press, 1920.

Dealy, Francis X., Jr. *Winning at Any Cost*. New York: Birch Lane Press, 1990.

DePalma, Anthony. "Higher Education Feels the Heat." *New York Times*, 2 June 1991.

Dessain, C. D. *John Henry Newman*. London: Thomas Nelson and Sons, 1966.

DeVane, William Clyde. "American Education after the War." *Yale Review*, September 1943.

——. *The American University in the Twentieth Century*. Baton Rouge: Louisiana University Press, 1957.

——. *Higher Education in Twentieth-Century America*. Cambridge: Harvard University Press, 1965.

Dilthey, Wilhelm. *Der Aufbau der geschichtlichen Welt in den Geisteswissenschaften*. Leipzig: B. G. Teubner, 1927.

Dogramaci, Ihsan. *A Brief Review of Higher Education in Turkey Past and Present*. Washington, D.C.: American Friends of Turkey, 1989.

Dongerkery, Sunderrao Ramrao. *Universities and National Life*. Bombay: Hind Kitabs, 1950.

D'Souza, Dinesh. *Illiberal Education: The Politics of Race and Sex on Campus*. New York: Free Press, 1991.

Durso, Joseph. *The Sports Factory: An Investigation into College Sports*. New York: Quadrangle, 1975.

Dworkin, Ronald. *A Matter of Principle*. Cambridge: Harvard University Press, 1985.

Ebert, Robert H., and Eli Ginzberg. "The Reform of Medical Education." *Health Affairs*, suppl. (1988): 5–38.

Egypt, Arab Republic of. *Egyptian Education and Development*. Cairo: Ministry of Education, [1990].

Elbow, P. *Embracing Contraries*. New York: Oxford University Press, 1986.

Eliot, George. *Middlemarch*. 1871–72. Edited by Bert G. Hornback. New York: Norton Critical Editions, 1977.

Ellmann, Richard. *Golden Codgers: Biographical Speculations*. New York: Oxford University Press, 1973.

Ellsworth, Frank L. *Law on the Midway: The Founding of the University of Chicago Law School*. Chicago: Law School of the University of Chicago, 1977.

Emerson, Ralph Waldo. *Collected Works*. Volume 1. Edited by Robert E. Spiller. Cambridge: Harvard University Press, 1971.

Engelhardt, W. von, and H. Decker-Hauff. *Quellen zur Gründungsgeschichte der naturwissenschaftlichen Fakultät in Tübingen, 1859–1863*. Tübingen: J. C. B. Mohr (Paul Siebeck), 1963.

Ericksen, Robert P. *Theologians under Hitler: Gerhard Kittel, Paul Althaus, and Emanuel Hirsch*. New Haven: Yale University Press, 1985.

Euler, H. H. *Die Entwicklung der medizinischen Spezialfächer an den Universitäten des deutschen Sprachgebietes*. Stuttgart: Enke, 1970.

Feller, Irwin. *Universities and State Governments: A Study in Policy Analysis*. New York: Praeger, 1986.

Fellner, William, ed. *Ten Economic Studies in the Tradition of Irving Fisher*. New York: Wiley, 1967.

Ferber, C. von. *Die Entwicklung des Lehrkörpers der deutschen Universitäten und Hochschulen*. Göttingen: Vandenhoeck und Ruprecht, 1956.

Fermi, Laura. *Illustrious Immigrants*. Chicago: University of Chicago Press, 1968.

Fischer. Fritz. *Germany's Aims in the First World War*. New York: W. W. Norton, 1967.

Fischer, John H. "Is There a Teacher on the Faculty?" *Harper's*, February 1965, 18–28.

FitzGerald, Frances. *America Revised: History Schoolbooks in the Twentieth Century*. Boston: Little, Brown, 1979.

Fleming, Donald, and Bernard Bailyn, eds. *The Intellectual Migration: Europe and America, 1930–1960*. Cambridge: Harvard University Press, 1969.

Flexner, Abraham. *Medical Education in the United States and Canada*. New York: Carnegie Foundation for the Advancement of Teaching, 1910.

———. *Universities, American, English, German*. New York: Oxford University Press, 1930.

Fox, Daniel M. "Abraham Flexner's Unpublished Report: Foundations and Medical Education, 1909–1928." *Bulletin of the History of Medicine* 54 (1980): 475–96.

Frankena, W., ed. *The Philosophy and Future of Graduate Education*. Ann Arbor: University of Michigan Press, 1978.

Franklin, Fabian. *The Life of Daniel Coit Gilman*. New York: Dodd, Mead, 1910.

Franklin, John Hope. *Racial Equality in America*. The Jefferson Lecture for 1976. Chicago: University of Chicago Press, 1976.

Fraser, W. R. *Reforms and Restraints in Modern French Education*. London: Routledge and Kegan Paul, 1971.

Freedman, Samuel G. *Small Victories: The Real World of a Teacher, Her Students, and Their High School*. New York: Harper and Row, 1990.

Friday, William C., and Theodore M. Hesburgh, eds. *Keeping Faith with the Student-Athlete: A New Model for Intercollegiate Athletics*. Charlotte, N.C.: Knight Foundation, 1991.

Fruton, Joseph S. "The Place of Biochemistry in the University." *Yale Journal of Biology and Medicine* 23 (1951): 305–10.

———. *A Bio-bibliography for the History of the Biochemical Sciences since 1800*. Philadelphia: American Philosophical Society, 1982; *A Supplement to a Bio-bibliography for the History of the Biochemical Sciences since 1800*. Philadelphia: American Philosophical Society, 1985.

———. "Contrasts in Scientific Style. Emil Fischer and Franz Hofmeister: Their Research Groups and Their Theory of Protein Structure." *Proceedings of the American Philosophical Society* 129 (1985): 313–70.

———. *Contrasts in Scientific Style: Research Groups in the Chemical and Biochemical Sciences*. Philadelphia: American Philosophical Society, 1990.

Fuller, Edmund, ed. *The Christian Idea of Education*. New Haven: Yale University Press, 1957.

Furner, M. *Advocacy and Objectivity: A Crisis in the Professionalization of American Social Science, 1865–1905*. Lexington: University Press of Kentucky, 1975.

Furniss, Edgar S. *The Graduate School of Yale: A Brief History*. New Haven: Yale Graduate School, 1965.

Gardner, John W. *On Leadership*. New York: Free Press, 1990.

Gay, Peter. *The Enlightenment: An Interpretation*. 2 vols. New York: Alfred A. Knopf, 1966, 1969.

———. *Freud: A Life for Our Time*. New York: W. W. Norton, 1988.

Gay, Peter, ed. *The Freud Reader*. New York: W. W. Norton, 1989.

Geison, G. L. *Michael Foster and the Cambridge School of Physiology: The Scientific Enterprise in Late Victorian Society*. Princeton: Princeton University Press, 1978.

Gerhard, Dietrich. *Gesammelte Aufsätze*. Göttingen: Vandenhoeck und Ruprecht, 1977.

Giamatti, A. Bartlett. *The University and the Public Interest*. New York: Atheneum, 1981.

———. *A Free and Ordered Space: The Real World of the University*. New York: W. W. Norton, 1988.

Gibbon, Edward. *Autobiography*. 1796. Edited by Dero A. Saunders. New York: Meridian Books, 1961.

———. *The History of the Decline and Fall of the Roman Empire*. 1776–88. Edited by J. B. Bury. 7 vols. London: Methuen, 1896–1900.

Gifford, Bernard R. *The Good School of Education: Linking Knowledge, Teaching, and Learning*. Berkeley: Graduate School of Education, University of California, 1984.

Giles, James E. "Gripes of Academe: A Critical Review." *Cross Currents* 41 (Spring 1991): 116–23.

Gilson, Etienne. "Introduction" to John Henry Newman. *An Essay in Aid of a Grammar of Assent*. Image Books edition. New York: Doubleday, 1955.

Goodwin, Crawford D., and Michael Nacht. *Missing the Boat: The Failure to Internationalize American Higher Education*. New York: Cambridge University Press, 1991.

Gordon, Lynn D. *Gender and Higher Education in the Progressive Era*. New Haven: Yale University Press, 1990.

Gould, Stephen Jay. *Wonderful Life: The Burgess Shale and the Nature of History*. New York: W. W. Norton, 1989.

Grant, Gerald, and David Riesman. *The Perpetual Dream: Reform and Experiment in the American College*. Chicago: University of Chicago Press, 1978.

Green, David. *Shaping Political Consciousness*. Ithaca: Cornell University Press, 1987.

Green, Vivian Hubert Howard. *The Universities*. Harmondsworth: Penguin, 1969.

Greve, Wilfried. *Kierkegaards maieutische Ethik*. Frankfurt: Suhrkamp, 1990.

Griswold, A. Whitney. *Liberal Education and the Democratic Ideal*. New Haven: Yale University Press, 1959.

Grubel, Herbert G. *The Brain Drain: Determinants, Measurement, and Welfare Effects*. Waterloo, Ont.: Wilfrid Laurier University Press, 1977.

Grudin, Robert. *The Grace of Great Things: Creativity and Innovation.* New York: Ticknor and Fields, 1990.

Haight, Gordon Sherman. *George Eliot: A Biography.* New York: Oxford University Press, 1968.

Haight, Gordon Sherman, ed. *The George Eliot Letters.* 9 vols. New Haven: Yale University Press, 1954–78.

Hall, Max. *Harvard University Press: A History.* Cambridge: Harvard University Press, 1986.

Hamlin, Arthur T. *The University Library in the United States: Its Origins and Development.* Philadelphia: University of Pennsylvania Press, 1981.

Harbage, Alfred. *Shakespeare's Audience.* New York: Columbia University Press, 1941.

Harnack, Adolf von. *Aus der Werkstatt des Vollendeten.* Giessen: Alfred Töpelmann, 1930.

Hasselberg, Göran, ed. *Juridiska Fakulteten vid Uppsala Universitet.* Stockholm: Almqvist and Wiksell, 1976.

Hawkins, Hugh. *Pioneer: A History of the Johns Hopkins University, 1874–1889.* Ithaca: Cornell University Press, 1960.

Hegener, Karen Collier, and David Clarke, eds. *Architecture Schools in North America.* Princeton: Peterson's Guides, 1976.

Hersey, John. *Letter to the Alumni.* New York: Alfred A. Knopf, 1970.

Hesburgh, Theodore M. *God, Country, and Notre Dame.* New York: Doubleday, 1990.

Hill, Kim Quaile, and Fred R. von der Mehden, eds. *Data Reliability in Cross-National Research.* Houston: Rice University, 1978.

Hirsch, Eric Donald, Jr. *Cultural Literacy: What Every American Needs to Know.* Boston: Houghton Mifflin, 1987.

Holmes, Frederick L. "Patterns of Scientific Creativity." *Bulletin of the History of Medicine* 60 (1986): 19–35.

———. "The Complementarity of Teaching and Research in Liebig's Laboratory." *Osiris,* 2d ser., 5 (1989): 121–64.

———. "Laboratory Notebooks: Can the Daily Record Illumine the Broader Picture?" *Proceedings of the American Philosophical Society* 134 (1990): 349–66.

Hopkins, Charles Howard. *The Rise of the Social Gospel in American Protestantism.* New Haven: Yale University Press, 1940.

Horwitt, Sanford D. *Let Them Call Me Rebel: Saul Alinsky—His Life and Legacy.* New York: Alfred A. Knopf, 1989.

Huber, Victor-Aimé. *The English Universities.* Translated by Francis W. Newman. 2 vols. London: W. Pickering, 1843.

Humphrey, Richard Atherton, ed. *Universities . . . and Development Assistance Abroad.* Washington, D.C.: American Council on Education, 1967.

Hutchins, Robert Maynard. *The Great Conversation.* Chicago: Encyclopaedia Britannica, 1952.

———. *Education for Freedom.* New York: Grove, 1963.

————. *The University of Utopia*. Phoenix ed. Chicago: University of Chicago Press, 1964.

Hutchinson, G. Evelyn. *The Kindly Fruits of the Earth: Recollections of an Embryo Ecologist*. New Haven: Yale University Press, 1979.

Huxley, Leonard. *Life and Letters of Thomas Henry Huxley*. 2 vols. London: Macmillan, 1900.

Imhof, Arthur Erwin. *Die gewonnenen Jahre: Von der Zunahme unserer Lebensspanne seit dreihundert Jahren: Ein historischer Essay*. Munich: C. H. Beck, 1981.

India, Government of. *National Policy on Education—1986*. New Delhi: Ministry of Education, 1986.

Jaeger, Werner. *Paideia: The Ideals of Greek Culture*. Translated by Gilbert Highet. 3 vols. New York: Oxford University Press, 1943–45.

————. *The Theology of the Early Greek Philosophers: The Gifford Lectures, 1936*. Oxford: Clarendon, 1947.

————. *Aristotle: Fundamentals of the History of His Development*. Translated by Richard Robinson. 2d ed. Oxford: Clarendon, 1948.

James, William. "The Ph.D. Octopus." *Harvard Monthly* 36 (1903): 1–9.

Jarausch, K. H. *Students, Society, and Politics in Imperial Germany*. Princeton: Princeton University Press, 1982.

Jaspers, Karl. *The Idea of the University*. Translated by H. A. T. Reiche and H. F. Vanderschmidt. Boston: Beacon, 1959.

Jedin, Hubert. "L'importanza del decreto tridentino sui seminari." *Seminarium* 15 (1963): 396–412.

Jencks, Christopher, and David Riesman. *The Academic Revolution*. Garden City, N.Y.: Doubleday, 1968.

Kagan, Donald. "An Address to the Class of 1994." *Commentary* 91 (January 1991).

Kant, Immanuel. *Werke*. Edited by Ernst Cassirer et al. 11 vols. Berlin: Bruno Cassirer, 1921–23.

Karim, M. Bazlul, ed. *The Green Revolution: An International Bibliography*. New York: Greenwood, 1986.

Katouzian, H. *Ideology and Method in Economics*. London: Macmillan, 1980.

Katz, Jay. *Experimentation with Human Beings*. New York: Russell Sage Foundation, 1973.

Katznelson, Ira, and Margaret Weir. *Schooling for All: Class, Race, and the Decline of the Democratic Ideal*. New York: Basic Books, 1985.

Kaufmann, Walter, ed. *The Portable Nietzsche*. New York: Penguin Books, 1982.

Kellermann, H. *Der Krieg der Geister*. Weimar: Duncker, 1915.

Kelly, J. N. D. *The Athanasian Creed*. New York: Harper and Row, 1964.

Kenney, Martin. *Biotechnology: The University-Industrial Complex*. New Haven: Yale University Press, 1986.

Ker, Ian Turnbull. *John Henry Newman: A Biography*. Oxford: Clarendon Press, 1988.

Kernan, Alvin. *The Death of Literature*. New Haven: Yale University Press, 1990.

Kerr, Chester. *A Report on American University Presses*. Chapel Hill, N.C.: Association of American University Presses, 1949.

Kerr, Clark. *The Uses of the University*. Cambridge: Harvard University Press, 1963.

Kerr, Clark, ed. *Twelve Systems of Higher Education: Six Decisive Issues*. New York: International Council for Educational Development, 1978.

Kimball, Roger. *Tenured Radicals: How Politics Has Corrupted Our Higher Education*. New York: Harper and Row, 1990.

Klineberg, Otto. *International Exchanges in Education, Science and Culture: Suggestions for Research*. Paris: Mouton, 1966.

Kockelmans, J., ed. *Interdisciplinarity and Higher Education*. University Park: Pennsylvania State University Press, 1979.

Kreis Hofgeismar. *Gedanken zur Hochschulreform*. Göttingen: Verlag der Deutschen Universitäten, 1956.

Kuhn, Thomas S. "The Essential Tension: Tradition and Innovation in Scientific Research." In *Scientific Creativity: Its Recognition and Development*, 341–54. Edited by C. W. Taylor and F. Barron. New York: Wiley, 1963.

Laing, Gordon J. *The University of Chicago Press, 1891–1941*. Chicago: University of Chicago Press, 1941.

Lathem, Edward C., ed. *American Libraries as Centers of Scholarship*. Hanover, N.H.: Dartmouth College, 1978.

Lederman, Leon. *Science: The End of the Frontier?* Washington, D.C.: American Association for the Advancement of Science, 1991.

Lenz, Max. *Geschichte der königlichen Friedrich-Wilhelms-Universität zu Berlin*. 4 vols. Halle: Buchhandlung des Waisenhauses, 1910.

Levi, Edward H. *Point of View: Talks on Education*. Chicago: University of Chicago Press, 1969.

Levine, George, and E. C. Knoepflmacher, eds. *The Endurance of "Frankenstein": Essays on Mary Shelley's Novel*. Berkeley: University of California Press, 1979.

Leslie, William Bruce. "A Comparative Study of Four Middle Atlantic Colleges." Ph.D. diss., Johns Hopkins University, 1971.

Lindroth, Sten. *A History of Uppsala University, 1477–1977*. Stockholm: Almqvist and Wiksell, 1976.

Linehan, P. A. "The Making of the *Cambridge Medieval History*." *Speculum* 57 (1982): 463–94.

McCaughey, Robert A. *International Studies and Academic Enterprise: A Chapter in the Enclosure of American Learning*. New York: Columbia University Press, 1984.

McGrath, Fergal. *Newman's University: Idea and Reality*. London: Longmans, 1951.

McNeill, William H. *Hutchins' University: A Memoir of the University of Chicago, 1929–1950*. Chicago: University of Chicago Press, 1991.

Maeroff, Gene I. *School and College: Partnerships in Education*. Princeton: Carnegie Foundation for the Advancement of Teaching, 1983.

Malik, Charles Habib. *A Christian Critique of the University*. Downers Grove, Ill.: InterVarsity Press, 1982.

Mann, Thomas. "The Sorrows and Grandeur of Richard Wagner." 1933. *Pro and Contra Wagner*, 91–148. Translated by Allan Blunden. Chicago: University of Chicago Press, 1985.

Maritain, Jacques. *Education at the Crossroads*. 1943. Paperbound ed. New Haven: Yale University Press, 1960.

Matthews, Fred. "The Attack on 'Historicism': Allan Bloom's Indictment of Contemporary American Historical Scholarship." *American Historical Review* 95 (1990): 429–47.

Medawar, Peter Brian. *Induction and Intuition in Scientific Thought*. Philadelphia: American Philosophical Society, 1969.

MEDUNSA: Medical University of South Africa, *Leadership Publication*, n.d.

Menacker, Julius. *From School to College: Articulation and Transfer*. Washington, D.C.: American Council on Education, 1975.

Merritt, R. L., E. P. Flerlage, and A. J. Merritt. "Political Man in Postwar German Education." *Comparative Education Review* 15 (October 1971).

Merton, Robert K. *On the Shoulders of Giants*. New York: Free Press, 1965.

———. *The Sociology of Science*. Chicago: University of Chicago Press, 1973.

Mexico, Government of. *Programa integral para el desarrollo de la educación superior*. Mexico City: Asociación nacional de universidades e institutos de enseñanza superior, 1987.

Miller, John Perry. *Creating Academic Settings, High Craft and Low Cunning: Memoirs*. New Haven: J. Simeon Press, 1991.

Moberly, Walter Hamilton. *The Universities and Cultural Leadership*. London: Oxford University Press, 1951.

Moore, Burness E., and Bernard D. Fine, eds. *Psychoanalytic Terms and Concepts*. New Haven: Yale University Press, 1990.

Morris, Willie. *The Courting of Marcus Dupree*. Garden City, N.Y.: Doubleday, 1983.

Muller, Steven, et al. "Physicians for the Twenty-First Century." *Journal of Medical Education* 11 (November 1984): 1–31.

Murphy, William Michael, and D. J. R. Bruckner. *The Idea of the University of Chicago: Selections from the Papers of the First Eight Chief Executives of the University of Chicago from 1891 to 1975*. Chicago: University of Chicago Press, 1976.

Murray, John Courtney. *We Hold These Truths: Catholic Reflections on the American Proposition*. New York: Sheed and Ward, 1960.

Murray, K. M. Elisabeth. *Caught in the Web of Words: James Murray and the "Oxford English Dictionary."* New Haven: Yale University Press, 1977.

Natal, South Africa, University of. *Calendar* 1990.

National Commission on Excellence in Education. *A Nation at Risk*. Washington, D.C.: Government Printing Office, 1983.

National Policy on Education—1986. New Delhi: Ministry of Human Resource Development, 1986.

Neuhaus, Rolf, ed. *Dokumente zur Hochschulreform, 1945–59*. Wiesbaden: F. Steiner, 1961.

Newman, John Henry. *An Essay on the Development of Christian Doctrine*. 1845. Image Books ed. Garden City, N.Y.: Doubleday, 1960.

———. *Loss and Gain*. 1848. In *Newman: Prose and Poetry*, 111–352. Edited by Geoffrey Tillotson. Cambridge: Harvard University Press, 1970.

———. *The Idea of a University Defined and Illustrated*: I. In Nine Discourses Delivered to the Catholics of Dublin [1852]; II. In Occasional Lectures and Essays Addressed to the Members of the Catholic University [1858]. Edited with introduction and notes by I. T. Ker. Oxford: Clarendon, 1976.

———. *Rise and Progress of Universities*. 1856. In *Essays and Sketches*, 2:273–359. Edited by Charles Frederick Harrold. New York: Longmans, Green, 1948.

———. *Apologia pro Vita Sua: Being a History of His Religious Opinions*. 1864. Edited by Martin J. Svaglic. Oxford: Clarendon, 1967.

———. *An Essay in Aid of a Grammar of Assent*. 1870. Edited with introduction and notes by I. T. Ker. Oxford: Clarendon, 1985.

Niebuhr, H. Richard, Daniel Day Williams, and James M. Gustafson. *The Advancement of Theological Education*. New York: Harper and Brothers, 1957.

Nore, Ellen. *Charles A. Beard: An Intellectual Biography*. Carbondale: Southern Illinois University Press, 1983.

Oakley, Francis. "Against Nostalgia: Reflections on Our Present Discontents in Higher Education." *National Humanities Center Newsletter* 12 (1991): 1–14.

Oren, Dan A. *Joining the Club: A History of Jews and Yale*. New Haven: Yale University Press, 1986.

The Oxford Dictionary of Quotations. 3d ed. Oxford: Oxford University Press, 1980.

Palmer, Robert R. *Twelve Who Ruled*. Princeton: Princeton University Press, 1969.

Pangle, Thomas L. *The "Laws" of Plato*. New York: Basic Books, 1980.

Partisan Review. "The Changing Culture of the University." Special Issue, 1991.

Pater, Walter. *Appreciations; with an Essay on Style*. London: Macmillan, 1913.

Pečujlić, Miroslav. *The University of the Future: The Yugoslav Experience*. Translated and edited by Tanja Lorković. New York: Greenwood, 1987.

Pelikan, Jaroslav. *Luther the Expositor: Introduction to the Reformer's Exegetical Writings*. Saint Louis: Concordia, 1959.

———. *Obedient Rebels: Catholic Substance and Protestant Principle in Luther's Reformation*. New York: Harper and Row, 1964.

———. *Scholarship and Its Survival: Questions on the Idea of Graduate Education*. Princeton: Carnegie Foundation for the Advancement of Teaching, 1983.

———. *The Vindication of Tradition: The Jefferson Lecture for 1983*. New Haven: Yale University Press, 1984.

———. *Confessor between East and West: A Portrait of Ukrainian Cardinal Josyf Slipyj*. Grand Rapids, Mich.: Eerdmans, 1990.

Philippines, University of the. *Bulletin*, Office of Research Coordination. Quezon City: Diliman, [1990].

Phillips, Kevin. *The Politics of Rich and Poor*. New York: Random House, 1990.

Pieper, Josef. *Leisure, the Basis of Culture*. Translated by Alexander Dru, introduction by T. S. Eliot. New York: Pantheon, 1964.

Powell, Arthur. *The Uncertain Profession: Harvard and the Search for Educational Authority*. Cambridge: Harvard University Press, 1980.

Power, Eugene B. "Microfilm and the Publication of Doctoral Dissertations." *Journal of Documentary Reproduction* 5 (1942): 37–44.

Prévot, Jacques. *L'Utopie éducative: Coménius*. Paris: Belin, 1981.

Pross, Helge. *Die deutsche akademische Emigration nach den Vereinigten Staaten, 1933–1941*. Berlin: Duncker und Humblot, 1955.

Pusey, Nathan M. *The Age of the Scholar: Observations on Education in a Troubled Decade*. Torchbook ed. New York: Harper and Row, 1964.

Raiser, Ludwig. *Deutsche Hochschulprobleme im Lichte amerikanischer Erfahrungen*. Kiel: Hirt, 1966.

Ramaley, Judith A. *Covert Discrimination and Women in the Sciences*. Boulder, Colo.: Westview Press for the American Association for the Advancement of Science, 1978.

Rashdall, H. *The Universities of Europe in the Middle Ages*. Edited by F. M. Powicke and A. B. Emden. 3 vols. 2d ed. Oxford: Clarendon, 1936.

Ravitch, Diane. *The Schools We Deserve: Reflections on the Educational Crisis of Our Times*. New York: Basic Books, 1985.

Riesman, David. *Constraint and Variety in American Education*. Lincoln: University of Nebraska Press, 1956.

———. *On Higher Education: The Academic Enterprise in an Era of Rising Student Consumerism*. San Francisco: Jossey-Bass, 1980.

Riesman, David, and Verne A. Stadtman, eds. *Academic Transformation: Seventeen Institutions under Pressure*. New York: McGraw-Hill, 1973.

Ringren, Helmer, ed. *Faculty of Theology at Uppsala University*. Translated by Neil Tomkinson. Stockholm: Almqvist and Wiksell, 1976.

Rosovsky, Henry. *The University: An Owner's Manual*. New York: W. W. Norton, 1990.

Ross, Dorothy. *The Origins of American Social Science*. New York: Cambridge University Press, 1991.

Sanderson, Michael. *The Universities and British Industry, 1850–1970*. London: Routledge and Kegan Paul, 1972.

Sarason, Seymour B. *The Culture of the School and the Problem of Change*. 2d ed. Boston: Allyn and Bacon, 1982.

Saudi Arabia, Kingdom of, Ministry of Higher Education. *Catalogue of King Faisal University, 1402/1982*. Al-Hasa and Dammam: King Faisal University, 1982.

Savage, Howard James. *Games and Sports in British Universities*. New York: Carnegie Foundation for the Advancement of Teaching, 1927.

———. *American College Athletics*. New York: Carnegie Foundation for the Advancement of Teaching, 1929.

Savage, Howard James, John T. McGovern, and Harold W. Bentley. *Current Developments in American College Sports*. New York: Carnegie Foundation for the Advancement of Teaching, 1931.

Sayers, Dorothy L. *Gaudy Night.* 1935. London: Victor Gollancz, 1958.

Scanlon, David G., ed. *International Education: A Documentary History.* New York: Teachers College of Columbia University, 1960.

Scanlon, David G., and James J. Shields. *Problems and Prospects in International Education.* New York: Teachers College of Columbia University, 1968.

Schelling, Friedrich Wilhelm, Johann Gottlieb Fichte, Friedrich Schleiermacher, Henrik Steffens, and Wilhelm von Humboldt. *Die Idee der deutschen Universität: Die fünf Grundschriften aus der Zeit ihrer Neubegründung durch klassischen Idealismus und romantischen Realismus.* Darmstadt: H. Gentner, 1956.

Schmitz, R. *Die Naturwissenschaften an der Phillips-Universität Marburg, 1527–1977.* Marburg: Elwert, 1978.

Schroeder, Steven A., Jane S. Zones, and Jonathan A. Showstack. "Academic Medicine as a Public Trust." *Journal of the American Medical Association,* 11 August 1989, 803–12.

Schwabe, K. *Wissenschaft und Kriegsmoral.* Göttingen: Musterschmidt, 1969.

Seabury, P., ed. *Universities in the Western World.* New York: Free Press, 1975.

Segert, Stanislav, and Karel Beránek. *Orientalistik an der Prager Universität.* Prague: Charles University, 1967.

Shapley, Willis H., ed. *Research and Development.* Washington, D.C.: American Association for the Advancement of Science, 1978–79.

Shepherd, Gordon M. *Neurobiology.* New York: Oxford University Press, 1983.

Showalter, Elaine. *Sexual Anarchy: Gender and Culture at the Fin de Siècle.* New York: Viking, 1990.

Shuster, George N. "Introduction" to John Henry Newman, *The Idea of a University.* Image Books ed. Garden City, N.Y.: Doubleday, 1959.

Simon, Brian. *The Politics of Educational Reform, 1920–1940.* London: Lawrence and Wishart, 1974.

Smith, John E. *The Spirit of American Philosophy.* New York: Oxford University Press, 1963.

Smith, Page. *Killing the Spirit: Higher Education in America.* Penguin ed. New York: Penguin, 1991.

Speakman, Cummins E. *International Exchange in Education.* New York: Center for Applied Research in Education, 1966.

Sperber, Murray. *College Sports, Inc.: The Athletic Department vs. the University.* New York: Henry Holt, 1990.

Stabler, Ernest, ed. *Education of the Secondary School Teacher.* Middletown, Conn.: Wesleyan University Press, 1962.

Steel, Ronald. *Walter Lippmann and the American Century.* Boston: Little, Brown, 1980.

Steiner, George. *In Bluebeard's Castle: Some Notes towards the Redefinition of Culture.* New Haven: Yale University Press, 1971.

Stevens, Robert. "Aging Mistress: The Law School in America." *Change* 2:1 (1970).

Stoff, Michael, ed. *The Manhattan Project: A Documentary Introduction to the Atomic Age.* New York: McGraw-Hill, 1991.

Stone, James. *Breakthrough in Teacher Education*. San Francisco: Jossey-Bass, 1968.

Storr, Richard J. *Harper's University: The Beginnings*. Chicago: University of Chicago Press, 1966.

Strauss, Leo. *The Argument and the Action of Plato's "Laws."* Chicago: University of Chicago Press, 1975.

Ström, Gunnar, and Ulf Söderberg, eds. *Faculty of Medicine at Uppsala University*. Stockholm: Almqvist and Wiksell, 1976.

Strömholm, Stig, and Torgny Nevéus. *Universitet i Utveckling: Uppsala Universitet under Torgny Segerstedts rektorat, 1955–1978*. Stockholm: Almqvist and Wiksell, 1978.

Stybe, Svend Erik. *Copenhagen University: Five Hundred Years of Science and Scholarship*. Translated by Reginald Spink. Copenhagen: Royal Danish Ministry of Foreign Affairs, 1979.

Sutcliffe, Peter. *The Oxford University Press: An Informal History*. Oxford: Oxford University Press, 1978.

Sutherland, James, ed. *The Oxford Book of Literary Anecdotes*. London: Oxford University Press, 1975.

Svaglic, Martin J. "Introduction" to John Henry Newman, *The Idea of A University*. Notre Dame: University of Notre Dame Press, 1960.

Svaglic, Martin J., ed. John Henry Newman. *Apologia pro Vita Sua: Being a History of His Religious Opinions*. 1864. Oxford: Clarendon, 1967.

Sykes, Charles J. *Profscam: Professors and the Demise of Higher Education*. Washington, D.C.: Regnery Gateway, 1988.

Taft, John. *May Day at Yale: A Case Study in Student Radicalism*. Boulder, Colo.: Westview, 1976.

Taylor, A. E. *Socrates*. 1933. Reprint ed. Westport, Conn.: Greenwood, 1975.

Thorndike, Lynn. *University Records and Life in the Middle Ages*. New York: Columbia University Press, 1944.

Tocqueville, Alexis de. *Democracy in America*. 1835. Edited by J. P. Mayer and Max Lerner. Translated by George Lawrence. New York: Harper and Row, 1966.

Torrance, Thomas F. "The University within a Christian Culture." In *The Christian Frame of Mind*, 49–62. Edinburgh: Handsel Press, 1985.

Tristram, Henry, ed. *John Henry Newman: Autobiographical Writings*. New York: Sheed and Ward, 1957.

Tuchman, Barbara. *The Guns of August*. New York: Dell, 1963.

Tucker, Robert C., ed. *The Marx-Engels Reader*. 2d ed. New York: W. W. Norton, 1978.

Universities and Museums: Report on the Universities in Relation to Their Own and Other Museums. London: H.M.S.O., 1968.

Veblen, Thorstein. *The Higher Learning in America: A Memorandum on the Conduct of Universities*. New York: B. W. Huebsch, 1918.

Verba, Sidney, and Gary R. Orren. *Quality in America*. Cambridge: Harvard University Press, 1985.

Vergottini, G. de. *Lo studio di Bologna, l'impero, il papato.* Bologna: Studi e memorie per la storia dell'Università di Bologna, 1956.

Veysey, L. R. *The Emergence of the American University.* Chicago: University of Chicago Press, 1974.

Vogel, Martin. *Nietzsche und Wagner: Ein deutsches Lesebuch.* Bonn: Verlag für systematische Musikwissenschaft, 1984.

Vosper, Robert G. "Collection Building and Rare Books." In *Research Librarianship: Essays in Honor of Robert B. Downs,* ed. Jerrold Orne, 91–111. New York: Bowker, 1971.

Walgrave, J.-H. *Newman the Theologian: The Nature of Belief and Doctrine as Exemplified in His Life and Works.* Translated by A. V. Littledale. New York: Sheed and Ward, 1960.

Wallace, William A., ed. *Reinterpreting Galileo.* Washington, D.C.: Catholic University of America Press, 1986.

Warch, Richard. *Schools of the Prophets: Yale College, 1701–1740.* New Haven: Yale University Press, 1973.

Ward, Maisie. *Young Mr. Newman.* New York: Sheed and Ward, 1948.

Weaver, Timothy. *America's Teacher Quality Problem: Alternatives for Reform.* New York: Praeger, 1987.

Webster's New Dictionary of Synonyms. Springfield, Mass.: Merriam Webster, 1968.

Weisheipl, James A. *The Development of Physical Theory in the Middle Ages.* New York: Sheed and Ward, 1959.

———. *Friar Thomas D'Aquino: His Life, Thought, and Work.* Garden City, N.Y.: Doubleday, 1974.

Wellek, René. *A History of Modern Criticism.* New Haven: Yale University Press, 1955–. 7 volumes to date.

———. *Discriminations: Further Concepts of Criticism.* New Haven: Yale University Press, 1970.

Wellington, Harry H. *Interpreting the Constitution: The Supreme Court and the Process of Adjudication.* New Haven: Yale University Press, 1990.

Whitehead, Alfred North. *The Aims of Education and Other Essays.* New York: Macmillan, 1929.

———. *Adventures of Ideas.* Harmondsworth: Penguin, 1942.

———. *Science and the Modern World.* New York: New American Library, 1948.

Whitehead, John S. *The Separation of College and State: Columbia, Dartmouth, Harvard, and Yale.* New Haven: Yale University Press, 1973.

William T. Grant Foundation, Commission on Work, Family and Citizenship. "The Forgotten Half: Non-College Bound Youth in America." New York: Grant Foundation, [1990].

Wilshire, Bruce. *The Moral Collapse of the University.* Albany: State University of New York Press, 1990.

Wilson, Howard A. *Invasion from the East.* Minneapolis: Augsburg, 1978.

Wind, James P. *The Bible and the University: The Messianic Vision of William Rainey Harper.* Atlanta: Scholars Press, 1987.

Wright, Robin. "A Reporter at Large: Teheran Summer." *New Yorker,* 5 September 1988.

Yamaguchi, Tomio, ed. *Color Atlas of Clinical Parasitology.* Philadelphia: Lea and Febiger, 1981.

Yenawine, Wayne S. "The Influence of Scholars on Research Library Development at the University of Illinois." Ph.D. diss., University of Illinois, 1955.

Young-Bruehl, Elisabeth. *Hannah Arendt: For Love of the World.* New Haven: Yale University Press, 1982.

Zahn-Harnack, Agnes von. *Adolf von Harnack.* 2d ed. Berlin: Walter de Gruyter, 1951.

Ziolkowski, Theodore. "*Faust* and the University: Pedagogical Ruminations on a Subversive Classic." In *Texte, Motive, und Gestalten der Goethezeit: Festschrift für Hans Reiss,* 65–79. Edited by John L. Hibberd and H. B. Nisbet. Tübingen: Max Niemeyer Verlag, 1989.

———. "The Ph.D. Squid." *American Scholar* 59 (1990): 177–95.

INDEX